Leading the Digital Workforce

Future information technology (IT) leaders won't be technology leaders, they'll be business leaders who understand technology. *Leading the Digital Workforce* takes a fresh look at technology leadership, exploring how to lead and manage in today's digital workplace where the pace of change is exponential. This book walks you through building personal resiliency and avoiding stress and burnout to creating a strategy, building a high-performance team, and examining how technology will change the workforce of the future. Technology leadership requires a unique set of skills, which is why traditional leadership approaches don't always work. This book provides actionable advice on how to create a culture of innovation while driving successful change initiatives.

Leading the Digital Workforce provides strategies for empowering people, optimizing processes, and inspiring innovation. This book offers insights into managing change, leveraging technology, and building strong relationships within your organization, including how to understand and work with company culture. Finally, it shares strategies for using technology and innovation to create a competitive edge to unlock new opportunities.

Leading the Digital Workforce is essential reading for IT leaders who want to develop their skills, stay ahead of the digital curve, and lead their organizations into the future. No matter if you're a new IT leader, an aspiring one, or a seasoned leader who's been at it for years, there's something in this book that will help you level up your game.

Security, Audit and Leadership Series
Series Editor:
Dan Swanson, Dan Swanson and Associates, Ltd.,
Winnipeg, Manitoba, Canada.

The *Security, Audit and Leadership Series* publishes leading-edge books on critical subjects facing security and audit executives as well as business leaders. Key topics addressed include Leadership, Cybersecurity, Security Leadership, Privacy, Strategic Risk Management, Auditing IT, Audit Management and Leadership

Information System Audit: How to Control the Digital Disruption
Philippe Peret

Agile Audit Transformation and Beyond
Toby DeRoche

Mind the Tech Gap: Addressing the Conflicts between IT and
Security Teams
Nikki Robinson

CyRM^SM: Mastering the Management of Cybersecurity
David X Martin

The Auditor's Guide to Blockchain Technology: Architecture,
Use Cases, Security and Assurance
Shaun Aghili

Artificial Intelligence Perspective for Smart Cities
Vahap Tecim and Sezer Bozkus Kahyaoglu

Teaching Cybersecurity: A Handbook for Teaching the Cybersecurity
Body of Knowledge in a Conventional Classroom
Daniel Shoemaker, Ken Sigler and Tamara Shoemaker

Cognitive Risk
James Bone and Jessie H Lee

Privacy in Practice: Establish and Operationalize a Holistic Data
Privacy Program
Alan Tangsss

Leading the Digital Workforce: IT Leadership Peak Performance and Agility
Jeff Brown

For more information about this series, please visit: https://www.routledge.com/Internal-Audit-and-IT-Audit/book-series/CRCINTAUDITA

Leading the Digital Workforce

IT Leadership Peak Performance and Agility

Jeffrey W. Brown

CRC Press
Taylor & Francis Group
Boca Raton London New York

CRC Press is an imprint of the
Taylor & Francis Group, an **informa** business

First edition published 2023
by CRC Press
6000 Broken Sound Parkway NW, Suite 300, Boca Raton, FL 33487-2742

and by CRC Press
4 Park Square, Milton Park, Abingdon, Oxon, OX14 4RN

Library of Congress Cataloging-in-Publication Data
Names: Brown, Jeffrey W., author.
Title: Leading the digital workforce / Jeffrey W. Brown.
Description: 1 Edition. | Boca Raton : CRC Press, 2023. | Series: Security, audit and leadership | Includes bibliographical references and index.
Identifiers: LCCN 2022059035 (print) | LCCN 2022059036 (ebook) | ISBN 9781032323725 (hardback) | ISBN 9781032323732 (paperback) | ISBN 9781003314707 (ebook)
Subjects: LCSH: Personnel management--Technological innovations. | Management--Technological innovations. | Information technology--Management. | Leadership.
Classification: LCC HF5549.5.T33 B76 2023 (print) | LCC HF5549.5.T33 (ebook) | DDC 658.300285--dc23/eng/20230223
LC record available at https://lccn.loc.gov/2022059035
LC ebook record available at https://lccn.loc.gov/2022059036

ISBN: 978-1-032-32372-5 (hbk)
ISBN: 978-1-032-32373-2 (pbk)
ISBN: 978-1-003-31470-7 (ebk)

DOI: 10.1201/9781003314707

Typeset in Sabon
by KnowledgeWorks Global Ltd.

Dedicated to the memory of Debarghva "Deb" Sengupta.

Contents

Preface

Leadership, like swimming, cannot be learned by reading about it.

Henry Mintzberg

There are many books on leadership, and that's because it's a complex subject. Leadership is about making tough decisions, inspiring others, and getting things done. It's about influencing people and managing change. It's a tough job, but it can also be rewarding. *Technology* leadership comes with its own set of complications, which is why there are fewer books on the subject. It takes experience and knowledge to become an effective technology leader and the things that work in the textbooks have a habit of not working out so well in the real world. Textbooks have simple scenarios with happy endings and all the problems solved with straightforward solutions. But life isn't like that. Sometimes our problems aren't fully resolved and tensions remain uneasy. Some problems come back to haunt us and we must come back again tomorrow and try harder.

Leadership development is a global industry estimated to be worth more than $50 billion. Unfortunately, most of services, books, articles, and conferences purporting to have the answers are delivering disappointing results. There is no "silver bullet" that will singlehandedly make the difference between leadership success and failure. This book, by itself, will not make you a better technology leader and no book can.

This is a book about the *process* of becoming a great technology leader. I believe that the answers to tough leadership problems are already inside you. That's because the right answers are going to be specific to your circumstances and draw from your own unique experience. You are the one who needs to make the journey. No matter if you're a new IT leader, an aspiring one, or a seasoned leader who's been at it for years, there's something in this book that will help you level up your game. I'll warn you now though, the path never ends and I'm still walking it myself after almost 30 years in technology.

The book is divided into two sections: Foundations and Leadership in Action. Even if you're an experienced leader, I encourage you not to skip over the foundations section. No matter where you're starting from, there's benefit in making sure that your foundation is strong. Michael Jordan once said:

"*Winners don't just learn the fundamentals, they master them. You have to monitor your fundamentals constantly because the only thing that changes will be your attention to them.*" In other words, over time even seasoned leaders lose track of fundamentals and fall back on old habits. Your mastery of the fundamentals makes everything that comes later in your leadership journey easier.

Writing a book about technology leadership takes a bit of nerve if you're not Tim Cook or Elon Musk. But with all due respect to these industry giants, most of us probably wouldn't benefit from their leadership perspectives. When you're the CEO of a large company, everyone is obliged to follow your orders regardless of how good or bad you are at leadership. In fact, many of these superstar leaders are perceived as out of touch with their frontline workers. In 2020, CEOs from the top 350 firms in the United States made an average of $24.2 million, a stunning 351 times more than a typical worker. And while most technical workers are well-compensated, with the majority earning a six-figure salary, it's clear that emulating the playbooks of billionaire CEOs will probably not help you that much with your day job.

When I was approached to write a book on IT leadership, I was skeptical it was necessary. There are plenty of books about leadership, most as I said won't make you a better leader. Many books and courses are produced by people who have never held a leadership position. Others are ghost-written biographies of superhero leaders looking back in time at their success instead of forward toward an uncertain future. From this perspective, many leadership books serve as either entertainment or as an academic treatment of the subject. They are the theory of, but not the practice, of leadership. Leadership is a personal journey and you should be rightfully skeptical about professional authors, bloggers, and influencers who have never held a leadership position telling you how easy it will all be if you subscribe to their YouTube Channel or podcast.

As I write this, I am holding down a demanding day job as the first Chief Information Security Officer (CISO) for the State of Connecticut. Being a first CISO anywhere brings a lot of challenges from getting funding for the program to getting the right people and skills in place and making sure everyone buys into your vision. The State is also centralizing their IT employees who are now going through more change than they have in the last 20 years. They're being pulled out of their agencies and centralized in a new team with new managers. Most are also now working remotely for the first time ever in their career and it's likely to stay that way.

I'm also in charge of a second team that's suffering from a sudden void in leadership after the death of a much-loved and respected leader. Both teams depend on me to remove their obstacles, support their career growth, set a good example, and have their best interests in mind. Handling tough challenges in the real-world levels up your leadership skills, not reading case studies. What makes you a better leader doing your best, learning from your mistakes and then doing a better job tomorrow than you did today. This is the process of becoming a great leader, which is the central theme of this book.

WHAT MAKES TECHNOLOGY LEADERSHIP DIFFERENT?

Technology leaders require a unique set of skills and abilities. They need to understand complex technical concepts and communicate them in a way that our businesses can understand. They need to think strategically and anticipate future needs and technology trends. They need to manage and motivate teams of engineers, many of whom are quirky, introverted, and sometimes lost in the details. This is the environment where a technology leader is expected to foster a culture of innovation and creativity and encourage collaboration. Technology leaders also play a vital role in the success of any organization that relies on technology, which is now every organization. The demands and pressure to go faster and do more have never been higher.

When technology succeeds, the company succeeds. During the COVID-19 pandemic, many businesses thrived while others shut their doors forever. Some businesses were forced to pivot to online sales just to survive. These companies saw massive increase in their online offerings while portions of their brick-and-mortar businesses were temporarily or permanently shuttered. The move toward digitization that was well under way at most firms became an accelerated push to maximize digital product delivery, automate existing business processes, and start new ones such as curb-side pickup. Companies with established online commerce strategies increased their offerings and changed the way that they thought about doing business. Others were simply left behind.

The emphasis on technology and the need for technologists is greater now than ever. Zoom and Shopify became pandemic poster children, reaching lofty stock market valuations that have now come back to earth. Even some traditional in-person businesses like gyms were able to pivot to online classes serving a much wider audience than would have been possible in a brick-and-mortar model. Technology has enabled businesses to grow and innovate and thrive at levels that simply weren't possible before, serving a global customer base.

Many legacy brick-and-mortar businesses have now declared themselves digital businesses, regardless of whether the facts really support this statement. Banks, insurers, and other many other industries are hobbled by years of legacy processes and systems. They spend billions of dollars on digital transformation efforts that either fail or wither away and die on the vine. They struggle to attract and retain the technical talent needed to truly transform the business.

There are also many new businesses have been born and raised in the cloud. They are fully remote with no office space at all and are completely dependent on technology to survive or even just exist. Technology allows single-person companies to run million-dollar businesses from their homes. These "solopreneurs" start businesses on a shoe-string budget and pivot quickly if the market changes. They are true digital businesses. The difference between these two types of companies is not just a matter of degrees, but a matter of thinking differently about what a business is and does. One model tries to shoehorn old-fashioned business practices into a digital world, while the other leverages digital tools to create a new business with the power to transform an industry the way that Amazon transformed how we do online shopping. No matter which type of company you work for, technology is going to be critical for survival.

Chief Information Officers (CIOs), Chief Technology Officers (CTOs), and even Chief Executive Officers (CEOs) have contributed to the views expressed in this book. But I've also spent close to a quarter of a century leading teams of my own ranging from a few people to over 100. I've had many challenges thrown at me over my career and I also draw on that experience in this book. But this book isn't about me, it's about you and your own leadership journey. I hope you will take what you learn from this book and refine what works for you and make it your own. The process of great leadership is about doing things better than you did yesterday and the day before that. This is something that I call the algorithm of IT leadership.

THE ALGORITHM OF IT LEADERSHIP

Anyone who isn't embarrassed of who they were last year probably isn't learning enough.

Alain de Botton

We are all creatures of habit. We like routines and rituals, from our morning coffee to the way we wind down in the evenings. Sometimes our routines don't serve us though. Watching TV may seem like a good way to recover from a long day, but mindless binge-watching night after night doesn't make you any better at what you do. Nor does it set you up for an easier day tomorrow or for your future growth. Great leadership is a process, not an outcome. Too many companies treat leadership development as a class, course, or other one-time event. But you don't wake up one day having "made it." You're never done learning, growing, or getting better. The world changes. Technology changes. You need to change with it and be open to new ways of thinking and acting regardless of where you are in your career.

Throughout this book, I highlight actions you should take to help you think about your own leadership journey. Don't skip these exercises. Instead, think about your answers carefully and write them down. When you read something, you take information in secondhand. If you think about your answer to a question without writing it down, the answer may still not entirely be your own. Writing something down forces you to slow down and really think about what you absorbed. When you write your answers down, you are also engaging in a process called metacognition. Metacognition is just a fancy word that means "thinking about thinking." When we engage in metacognition, we are more likely to understand and remember information and are also more likely to be able to apply the information for our growth and development. Success has a bias toward those who act. A large percentage of people who get this book probably won't get around to reading it. Others may read it and feel like there are some good ideas, which they'll forget when the demands of our jobs take our attention. But those who act will develop faster and go farther than everyone else. And those who act *consistently* will do great things in their career. The more consistently you act, the more your success becomes inevitable.

Writing is a great way to engage in metacognition, but it's not the only way. You can also talk to someone about what you are learning. Explain the concept to them in your own words and see if they can explain it back to you. If they can, then you know that you understand the concept. Learning is an active process and we learn best when we are engaged with the material.

This is not a traditional academic treatment of leadership, so it would be beneficial at this point to review some high-level values and principles for his book including:

- **Valuing skills over knowledge.** Knowledge is something that you know. A skill is something you can do. Knowledge is an important part of the learning process but taking knowledge and turning it into a usable skill is much more powerful. Theoretical knowledge is important, but it's only useful if you can apply it to real-world situations.
- **Principles not playbooks.** Applying a simple principle to many different situations is better than building a playbook that covers every possible situation. Principles are what make us who we are. Our principles guide us through uncertainty. Canned answers don't work for unique situations.
- **Process over perfection.** The goal isn't to be perfect, but to learn and grow and iterate. Make mistakes, learn from them, and refine your approach. Set yourself up with systems that support your goals. Make small improvements every day and then do it again tomorrow. Again, there is a process to becoming a great leader and there are no shortcuts to that process.
- **Intrinsic motivation not extrinsic motivation.** Intrinsic motivation means being driven by a personal interest or desire to learn. Extrinsic motivation comes from external factors such as rewards and punishments. Intrinsic motivation is sustainable and leads to better long-term results. This is why forcing bad bosses into leadership training never works. The whole world can want you to change, but if you don't want to change, then nothing is going to happen.

- **Developing grit.** Grit is a combination of passion and perseverance. It's the ability and determination to maintain focus and effort over a long period of time. Natural abilities will only take you so far, but grit will get you through the humps and plateaus. You'll go further and do more with grit than with raw talent alone.
- **Using a systems mindset.** A systems-thinking approach is the idea that you can reach your goals by manipulating the systems that support them. When you set a goal and don't have a system to achieve that goal, you are leaving the outcome to chance. When you set a goal and put a system in place to get you there, you're one step closer to making success inevitable. The right systems make it harder to fail and easier to succeed.

My goal is to put you on a path to develop or improve your own technology leadership skills regardless of your starting point. This book doesn't offer an easy fix for the technology leadership problem. But it does provide you with a better understanding of the problem and how we can begin to solve it one leader at a time.

Action: what habits do you want to change that no longer serve you? Make a conscious decision to create some new habits that can help you unlock your potential, such as reading or learning something new.

REFERENCES AND FURTHER READING

Clear, James. *Atomic Habits: Tiny Changes, Remarkable Results: An Easy & Proven Way to Build Good Habits & Break Bad Ones*. CELA, 2021.
Collins, James C. *Good to Great*. Random House Business, 2001.
Fogg, Brian J. *Tiny Habits: The Small Changes That Change Everything*. Mariner Books, 2020.
Hardy, Benjamin. *Be Your Future Self Now: The Science of Intentional Transformation*. Hay House, Inc., 2022.
Hardy, Benjamin. *Personality Isn't Permanent*. Portfolio, 2020.

Acknowledgments

Writing a book is never easy. Getting the words on paper is only one small part of the process. Writing a book about leadership can take a lifetime. With that perspective in mind, I'd like to thank the following people who helped me get here.

- Every team I've managed. Leadership is a continuous learning process for me and for all of us. Thank you for the opportunity to work together and thank you to the many who have kept in touch well after our paths diverged.
- CRC Press and the folks at Routledge. I worked at a publishing house on the other side of the table earlier in my career and I appreciate all that you do.
- Dan Swanson for being a great sounding board.
- My own leaders and mentors: Phil Venables, Brian Redler, Oscar Gonzalez, and William Kolbert. Thank you for your many lessons and for casting very long shadows.
- My Wife, Zsuzsa, for getting me through another book. And our Springer Spaniel, Gracie, for giving us laughs, early dinner reminders, and endless belly rubs.

About the author

Jeffrey W. Brown, CISSP-ISSMP, CRISC, CISM, PMP, is the first Chief Information Security Officer (CISO) for the State of Connecticut. The Center for Digital Government recently gave national recognition to Connecticut for leadership and collaboration by ranking it third in the nation. Jeff is a recognized information security and IT risk expert with a strong track record of over two decades implementing cost-effective controls for global Fortune 500 financial institutions including Merrill Lynch, Goldman Sachs, Citigroup, GE Capital, BNY Mellon, and AIG. He is a two-time winner of CISOs Connect™ Top 100 CISOs (C100).

Jeff worked briefly in the publishing industry as an editor for HarperCollins before pursuing his passion for technology full time. While at HarperCollins, he set up the College division's first web presence and was involved helping plan distance learning programs, a relatively new concept back in 1995. He never strayed far from these roots and has since gone on to co-author the *Web Publisher's Deign Guide for Windows* (Coriolis, 1993) and Mission Critical Internet Security (Syngress, 2000) and is the author of *The Security Leader's Communication Playbook* (CRC Press, 2001).

Jeff is a frequent speaker at events and conferences and is a co-chair of Evanta's New York CISO Executive Summit events. He is a board advisor for Cowbell Cyber, iQ4, and the University of New Haven/Connecticut Institute of Technology. In his free time, he enjoys hiking, writing, playing guitar, and spending time with his wife and English Springer Spaniel, Gracie. He holds multiple industry certifications, a BA in Journalism, and an MS in Publishing from Pace University as well as a certificate in Cybersecurity from Ithaca College, where he serves as an advisor for the program.

Part I

Foundations

Leadership agility is about being able to adapt and respond to changing events quickly, while maintaining a sense of calm and clarity and purpose. Leaders who are agile remain flexible in their thinking, are open to new ideas, and are responsive to the needs of their team. They are also able to make decisions quickly, without overthinking things or getting bogged down in the details. Developing your own leadership agility will help you thrive in any environment.

Organizations need leaders who can make decisions quickly, adapt to new situations, and lead their teams through change. Leaders who are agile are better equipped to handle the challenges of today's business world and build successful, thriving organizations, no matter what the world throws at them. The agile leader is a high-energy individual with the ability to make quick decisions based on limited information. They take risks as necessary and can assess risk quickly.

Part I of this book provides an overview of leadership foundations and peak performance topics that include mastering your mindset, managing emotions, and other foundational skills you will need to show up as a leader. This section establishes the fact that anyone can improve their leadership skills and that great leaders aren't necessarily born that way. It also explains how traditional leadership strategies can backfire or fall short when you're leading technologists.

All too often, people are thrown into leadership positions before they have their own act together and it's hard on both the leader and the team. Many leaders regardless of their tenure don't spend enough time getting their own foundation right. They can barely prioritize their own time, but they expect their team to prioritize theirs. If we can't handle our own stress and burnout, how can we expect our teams to do the same? The foundations section of this book will help you manage yourself better so you can manage your team better. If you want a high-performance team, you must be the change you want to see with your team. Leadership books typically jump right into the weeds of managing a team without addressing all the headwinds that will make your job difficult. Imposter syndrome, burnout, and stress are going to make you a lousy leader and you need to navigate through these challenges before you are going to be effective.

If this all sounds like more work than you want to put into your job, remember that when you build a better personal foundation, you are not just improving performance at work. Leadership skills and a strong personal foundation will make you more resilient in all aspects of your life. I remember when I started my own business. There were so many things I didn't know about running a business. I had to lean on my own foundational skills, which helped me become a business owner rather than someone who just talks about it.

In fact, the connection between leadership and entrepreneurship is strong. Entrepreneurs who try to do everything themselves and do it alone find themselves burnt out, stressed, and often trading a stable job for a nightmarish lifestyle working days, nights, and weekends. They become resentful of their business and it comes out in their company performance. Successful leaders and successful entrepreneurs know they can't be experts in everything. Delegating or outsourcing tasks is a critical skill no matter if you are a team leader, a business owner, or the leader of a Fortune 500 company.

Part II of the book takes your foundational skills back to the office, where knowledge becomes actions that are practiced and refined over time. There is no other shortcut. They say that how you do something is how you'll do everything. People who were great leaders in corporate settings tend to go on to serve on boards of directors, write books, and start new companies well after their financial needs are covered. They continue delivering results because it's what they do and it's who they are. No matter where you are in your career, there's always time to level up your game. It's a process that never ends and it's never too late to improve from wherever you are starting from.

I wrote this book with a broad audience in mind, including anyone in or aspiring to a technology leadership role, C-level technology executives, IT directors, and technical team leaders all the way up to business leaders and human resource departments trying to understand how to attract and retain technical talent better in a hybrid work model. This book covers topics including strategic planning, organizational behavior, strategy, and leadership skills. It also takes a speculative look at what the future of work might bring. This is not a book about leadership theories and the latest management fads. What you will learn is how to communicate more effectively with business leaders, how to influence others to get things done, how to develop and execute a strategy that delivers results, how to build and lead high-performing teams, and how to foster a culture of creativity and innovation. My hope is that this book will become an essential handbook for anyone aspiring to be a better technology regardless of where they currently are on the journey.

Chapter 1

Playing the long game of leadership

THE DIGITAL WORKFORCE

Years ago, the term "digital workforce" described automation technologies, including robotic process automation (RPA). RPA is used to drive efficiencies and automation in the workplace, and I'm a big fan of automation. But if you picked up this book hoping to learn ways of creating a robotic workforce that mindlessly does your bidding, I'm afraid this isn't the book for you. This is a book about leading humans who happen to work in technology. And leading humans isn't easy. Humans are complicated. They get into bad moods. They don't always listen to what you say. They have complex emotions which often overrule reason and logic. No matter if you think the human brain is like a computer or not, that last point makes us fundamentally different from the machines. Technology is relatively straightforward. Computers don't have emotions, intentions, or hidden agendas. Technology does exactly what it was programmed to do and when it fails, there's often a human error in there somewhere.

Technical employees tend to be analytical. They are often introverted and often less interested in social interactions. This may make them seem aloof or arrogant sometimes. They like to be precise and they want you to do the same if you're contributing to the conversation. Technologists enjoy a level of independence in solving problems, but they can also get lost in the details and sometimes miss the big picture. I know this because I still carry a lot of these quirks around with me today.

WHAT MAKES TECHNICAL WORK SO CHALLENGING?

Technical work, like most knowledge work, is deceptively difficult. There's an element of complexity and puzzle solving involved and the work doesn't always fit into well-defined predictable patterns. It's not as easy to estimate how long it takes to create a breakthrough software product as it is to build a house. Technical problem-solving isn't always predictable and repeatable. While there are frameworks that can assist with both creativity

DOI: 10.1201/9781003314707-2

and problem-solving, there are many variables that make it hard to predict timely outcomes with a high degree of accuracy. Apple releases a new iPhone year over year at roughly the same time, but what you don't see behind the scenes are all the features that were dropped from the final release. Those items go on a wait list for the next version or get dropped altogether. In other words, Apple changes the work to fit the time. This is very different from building a house, which fits into a predictable timeframe, uses the same general approach for each project, and wouldn't benefit from dropping features like the bathroom to save time on the overall process.

Of course, most companies don't execute anywhere near as well as Apple. In fact, some information technology (IT) projects never finish at all. This is especially true when the work isn't clearly defined, such as with the impossibly vague digital transformation efforts going on at many companies. Consulting firm McKinsey found that 17 percent of IT projects go so badly wrong that they can threaten the very existence of a company. Kmart's massive $1.2B failed IT modernization project is a good example and is one that was seen as a big contributor to their bankruptcy.

IT projects are growing in importance across all industries, affecting more areas of the organization and posing a greater risk to the business if something goes wrong. And things do go wrong. Large IT projects run the biggest risk of cost and schedule overruns or even outright failure. While some failures can be blamed on bad project management, there is no one else to blame but the leader. Poor project managers can be replaced by good leaders who see the problems and act in time. Failing to act is often worse than taking no action at all. As Joko Willink, author of *Extreme Ownership: How U.S. Navy SEALs Lead and Win*, says: "Leaders must own everything in their world. There is no one else to blame."

As technology advances, businesses are becoming increasingly dependent on technology projects to adapt and survive in a changing world. Technology enables companies to connect with their customers and employees in new and innovative ways. It also enables them to manage operations more efficiently and profitably. The need for strong technology leadership has never been greater and the stakes have never been higher.

Demands on IT professionals are also high, often requiring long hours and sometimes working evenings and weekends. But working harder and longer with technical work produces diminishing returns and decreased productivity. Knowledge work is something you do with your brain, not with your hands. This means that working longer doesn't always help the work get done faster. Trying to muscle your way through complex cognitive work by "thinking harder" is not a sustainable strategy. Neuroscience tells us that what works best for long-term cognitive work is frequent breaks and rest and recovery periods. But companies still build workdays around outdated 9-5 schedules, with some industries like finance, healthcare and technology expecting far longer than a 40-hour workweek.

Silicon Valley itself is notorious for overwork and burnout. Executives like Elon Musk reportedly slept on the floor under his desk in the early days of Tesla rather than going home to recover and recharge and have a personal life. Our leaders set the tone. If your boss values long hours, the perception will be that long hours are what will get you ahead. We live in a world where you're expected to start early, work a minimum number of hours, and then do it all over again tomorrow. The only thing that's changed with this model over the years is if you're lucky enough to work remotely and drop the commute. Although working remotely has its perks, it hasn't helped with employee burnout. For remote employees, the lines between work and home are now blurred, and some people are finding themselves working longer hours than ever before.

To attract and retain top technical talent, some companies have gone as far as providing unlimited paid time off (PTO) days for their employees. Unlimited PTO sounds like a dream come true, but it turns out that employees at these firms are taking fewer vacation days than employees with more traditional PTO policies. Without any formal guardrails around how much time off to take, employees are unsure how many days are "too many" and the norms end up being set by individual managers who are probably not taking enough time off themselves. This system is working so poorly that some firms like Evernote started giving employees a $1,000 bonus to take five consecutive days off.

It is becoming increasingly common for technical workers to quit high six-figure jobs citing long hours and burnout. Some employees take time off to focus on their own side projects or consulting engagements because they find the work at their job unfulfilling. We are still using factory-worker methods in a tired old "punch the clock" model, but the work is no longer happening in an assembly line. The 40-hour workweek concept started back in 1926, when Henry Ford mandated that his workers put in this much time weekly as a benchmark standard. The US government later adopted the 40-hour work week for all hourly workers. But salaried workers have no such boundaries and the work continues to expand, with some workers wearing 60- or 70-hour workweeks as a badge of honor.

The average adult brain consumes about 20 percent of the body's energy. From this perspective, the brain is one of the most energy-demanding organs in the body. Technical work is complex and requires a lot of brain power. You may not be able to influence how many hours your company expects from their employees, but at least take small breaks during the day and encourage your team to do the same. More work doesn't always translate to better results. Taking time off isn't being lazy and forcing people to pile on work before they leave and scramble to catch up once they return is making the workplace worse for everyone.

It is against this backdrop that we look at what it takes to be a successful technology leader. Today's IT leader needs to do more than just write code or manage IT infrastructure. They need to be able to juggle multiple projects and competing demands with ever-changing technologies. Leaders need to have a strategic vision and be able to execute on that vision. They need to be able to inspire and motivate their team. They need to be able to build and nurture relationships with other leaders. And they need to be able to do all of this while maintaining some semblance of a life outside of work. As you'll learn in this book, the key to managing all this isn't working harder, but taking an agile approach and focusing on the things that matter most right now.

Action: what is your company's culture like? Do they glamorize long hours and being busy? Is this translating to better results? Could you give yourself and your team the freedom to take more breaks during the workday to mentally recharge?

SHOULD YOU JUST GET AN MBA?

> Education is the great equalizer of our time. It gives hope to the hopeless and creates chances for those without...
>
> Kofi Annan

Companies value people who understand both business and technology. This means that people who understand both subjects are more likely to progress into senior leadership roles. If you're considering a career in technology leadership, you might be wondering if you should get a Master of Business Administration (MBA). An MBA can potentially propel you up the corporate ladder, but it can also take two additional years of full-time study and cost a lot of money. As someone who went to grad school while holding down a full-time day job, I can vouch that this lifestyle is going to take up evenings and weekends and it will feel like a second job. An accelerated one-year program takes less time than a traditional MBA program but requires even more discipline and the ability to cope with a concentrated academic workload.

While an MBA can help you develop some of the skills required to be a successful leader, it's not the only path and may not even be the preferred path anymore. Emerging IT leaders have more options for career advancement than previous generations ever did, and fewer technologists than ever are pursuing an MBA to get to the top. After all, the average payback period for most MBA programs is close to 5 years, according to the University of Illinois, and the average cost ranges from $55,727 to $161,810, according to MBA Today. That's a lot of money for most people and the immediate return on investment (ROI) isn't going to be there for everyone. In addition, pursuing an MBA from a no-name school is almost always a bad idea. There are simply too many institutions offering MBAs today and the elite nature of the degree has been watered down. But an ivy league MBA, if you can get into the program at all, costs over $200,000.

Experience is a key factor in becoming a successful technology leader and it is far more important than your formal education. It's also rare that an MBA is a job requirement, even at the Chief Information Officer (CIO) level. Curiosity will take you further than any degree or program ever will. The MBA can serve a purpose, but in the fast-moving world of technology, a lifelong learning habit will take you much farther. IT leaders remain relevant not because of their degrees, but because of their continuous education and their hands-on experience.

There is no curriculum, course, or certification that proves you're a good leader. If you're considering pursuing an MBA, ask yourself if it's worth the investment or if you can achieve your goals without one. For most IT leaders, an MBA is unnecessary. It used to be considered the crown jewel in your resume, but employers value the ability to get results and business acumen over degrees and certifications. At the right school, you might find value in making connections and networking. But that's not the only path to growing a personal network.

Before pursuing an MBA, consider investing money on your own focused course of learning that includes both business and technology skills. There has never been a better time in the history of mankind to find classes and courses that you can access online. When you are on a path of continuous learning, you can roll your own degree and create a curriculum that takes you exactly where you want to go both in work and in life.

BORN OR MADE: CAN YOU LEARN LEADERSHIP?

> If you work on your job, you'll make a living. If you work on yourself, you'll make a fortune.
>
> Jim Rohn

Are leaders born or made? The answer isn't black and white. On the surface, leadership seems to be a natural character trait for some people. But it's also clear that we can teach leadership skills and grow leaders. So, are leaders born or made? The answer is both. There are certain traits that come naturally to some people, making them better suited for and more likely to pursue leadership roles. But there are also leadership skills that can be taught and developed over time. Experts believe that while personality plays a role, it's not the most important factor. Instead, they believe that leadership is mostly about learned skills and behaviors. Anyone can learn to be a leader, but some people are inherently more likely to go on the journey than others.

Successful leaders seem to share a few key qualities. Confidence, engagement, good judgment, and the ability to bring people together are some of the most important traits of the best leaders. Other traits, such as introversion or extroversion, play a surprisingly small role. While extroverts may seem like natural leaders due to their confidence and social nature, introverts can be just as effective – if not more so – in complex or unpredictable settings. Introverted leaders tend to build the most meaningful connections with employees and clients, focus better amid distraction, and solve problems thoroughly rather than hastily. Extroverts may work better in leadership positions that require many fast decisions and lots of social interaction with customers or teams. There is no right personality type. Steve Jobs from Apple was extroverted, and Bill Gates was practically the poster child for introverted leaders when he was the CEO of Microsoft.

Don't confuse introversion with being shy. Introversion and extroversion have more to do with the way individuals process information and the type of environment that they prefer. Some introverted leaders are comfortable with public speaking and high-stress situations, but then they prefer more quiet pursuits to unwind afterward such as reading. There's plenty of room for both personality types in the workforce. That said, there seem to be a lot of introverts working in technology. This means it might be useful for you to understand how introverts operate if you happen to be an extrovert. I'm a big introvert myself. My downtime is critical to my mental well-being. It's not unusual for me to be the first one out the door at a social event, if I show up at all.

Introvert or extrovert, the best way to learn leadership is to practice leadership. Even if someone is naturally gifted with some leadership ability, they still need practice to be good at it. Like any skill, you get better at doing something by doing it more. The same is true for swimming, flying, driving, or learning an instrument. New skills result in tangible outcomes, like a musician playing a tune or an athlete making a catch. But many companies simply promote people into management positions without any plan to train the skills that will make better leaders. Aspiring leaders should be given opportunities to lead smaller teams under the careful observation of an experienced leader. Apprenticeships and mentoring are two of the best ways to develop leaders faster, not onetime corporate classes or providing no training at all and hoping for the best.

Action: how does your company support leaders and aspiring leaders? Are there opportunities to pair high-promise individuals with leadership opportunities? Even just leading a small project can provide aspiring leaders with the experience they need to develop.

THERE IS NO FAILURE

I have not failed. I've just found 10,000 ways that won't work.

Thomas Edison

Unless you're not trying or not trying hard enough, you are going to encounter some failures in your career. But the word failure comes with a lot of baggage. People adopt failure as an identity: "I'm a failure." If you want to grow as a leader and as a person, don't think of your mistakes as failures, think of them as lessons. You act and you get results. If those results are not the ones you wanted, you need to try different actions to get different results. From this perspective, failure isn't the opposite of success, it's an integral part of it.

There's a great story from Tom Watson Sr. from IBM. An employee in charge of landing a critical million-dollar deal lost the bid due to a few mistakes. When the employee handed in an envelope with their resignation, Watson asked what had happened. The employee outlined every step of the deal, highlighting where he made mistakes and what he would have done differently. When he finished, the he added "Thank you, Mr. Watson, for giving me a chance to explain. I know we needed this deal. I know what it meant to us." He rose to leave. The story goes that Watson handed the envelope back saying, "why would I accept this when I have just invested one million dollars in your education?"

Hopefully you won't lose any million-dollar sales, but you're going to make some mistakes in your career. If you don't, you're not stretching far enough and challenging yourself. You will encounter situations that aren't in leadership books, and you'll need to figure them out for yourself. Sometimes you'll be right and sometimes you won't. But mistakes will teach you more about yourself and the people you work with than success. That's because when we make a mistake, it's what happens afterward that defines who we really are. If we learn from our mistakes and try not to repeat them, we become better at what we do. If we ignore our mistakes, there won't be any growth. Worse yet if we ignore our mistakes, there's a tendency to repeat them. Would you rather work for someone who has made very few mistakes either by chance or by playing it too safe, or someone who has made mistakes only once and then learned from the experience? Experience, time, and an improvement process are the teachers that will make you a great leader. Reflecting and adapting are better strategies than hoping for constantly favorable circumstances. The best leaders use reflection as a tool for personal growth and development and they learn to adapt to any environment or circumstance.

The improvement cycle (see Image 1.1) starts with trying something new. There is no improvement without first acting. Then we review our results and if it wasn't what we want, we try something new and repeat the cycle. We try, we get results, and we get better over time. This is how we improve. This is the scientific method. And it's how we should approach our personal development and goals. But the problem is that many people never get past the first step. They never even try something new. They stay in their comfort zone and don't take any action. And if you don't take any action, you can't improve. You need to get out of your comfort zone and try something new if you want to improve your life. But it can be scary to try something new. It's easier to stay in our comfort zone where we feel safe. But if we want to improve, we need to push ourselves out of our comfort zone and into the unknown. We need to take risks and try new things. And sometimes, these new things won't land exactly where we were hoping.

Reframing our mistakes as learning opportunities isn't easy. Mistakes happen in the heat of the moment, maybe when you're acting with limited information that will seem obvious later in hindsight. Sometimes mistakes

Improvement Loop

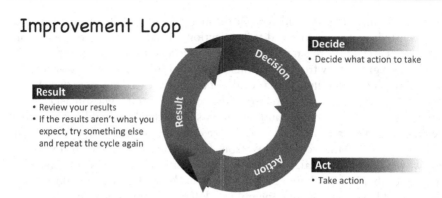

Image 1.1 An improvement loop helps leaders grow by enabling them to evaluate their performance continuously, identify areas for improvement and take action to make meaningful changes.

happen because you didn't give something enough attention, and sometimes they happen because it was the wrong approach right from the start. In either case, it can be hard to handle the aftermath of a mistake. You might face disappointed customers, an angry boss, or a project that's now late with an overrun budget. Owning your mistakes and treating them as lessons lets you move on more quickly and get yourself back on track.

No one likes being wrong, but mistakes can be a valuable tool for self-improvement. When something does go wrong at work, take ownership immediately. Don't try to sweep it under the rug or deny your involvement. Learning from mistakes starts with owning the mistake. The more you're able to learn from your mistakes, the more likely you are to avoid making them again in the future. But if you try to avoid mistakes, you won't learn and grow as a leader. You will avoid taking the risks that can lead to breakthrough products, innovation, and creative solutions. You'll also hold back your team in a safe, but mediocre environment if you don't support this learning process.

Of course, you need to manage your risk taking. In cybersecurity and many other technical disciplines, small mistakes can lead to big problems. But if you're not making mistakes, you're probably not doing anything interesting or challenging enough or you're moving too slowly and carefully. When you're taking risks and trying new things, some of those things are going to fail. It's just part of the process. The key is to learn from your mistakes and avoid making them twice. This starts with admitting that you made a mistake in the first place.

Action: think of a problem or situation you faced in your life that didn't work out as planned. What happened? What went wrong and what worked right? Did luck play a role? How could you do better next time?

Action: do you tolerate mistakes on your team? Punishing honest mistakes is one of the worst things a leader can do. Understand that mistakes are part of the growing and learning process, both for you and for your team.

THE IMPACT OF POOR LEADERSHIP

Bad leaders leave scars all over the workforce. I've worked for several bad leaders in my career. They are typically the people who undermine their employees at every opportunity or take all the credit for anything good that happens. It's not fun working for someone like this. Bad leaders do a lot of damage to a company and to employee morale. Poor leadership has taken down companies like Enron, Toys R Us, and Lehman Brothers. But poor leadership includes leaders who failed to innovate or react to change quickly enough, including Kodak, Xerox, Blockbuster, and Blackberry.

Bad leaders never seem to get better. They keep making the same mistakes and keep using some tired playbook that worked for them in a previous company. This happens even at the most senior levels of technology leadership. Superstar leaders making superstar salaries come in promising to transform technology, but they never hit these lofty objectives. In a few years, they're out, nothing has changed.

You may have had a bad boss or two in your career. They're usually easy to spot, but here are a few characteristics.

- They don't support the team with praise or credit, but they are quick to blame everyone around them.
- They are self-promoters who are difficult to connect with on a personal level.
- They don't learn or improve. If anything, they seem to get worse over time.
- They spend most of their time managing up rather than managing their team and the work at hand.
- They do just enough to make sure no big problems happen on their watch, but not much more.

There may not be much you can do if you report to a bad leader, but at least make sure you're not part of the problem by being one yourself. Bad leaders have a ripple effect including:

- **Bad leaders kill company culture.** Leaders set the tone for the culture of their team that employees tend to imitate. Unfortunately, this is true for both the good and bad examples they set. People mirror the behavior they see, and sometimes they even do it unconsciously. This is especially true for bad leaders who get results through aggressive leadership tactics including intimidation, fear, and punishment. When there are enough bad leaders in an organization, eventually you have a toxic organization.
- **Bad leaders drive away top talent.** There's a saying that people don't quit the company, they quit their boss. Top talent quits right away for a simple reason: because they can. I've done this myself when I realized I

had a bad boss. The best employees have options, and they will exercise those options if they don't feel valued.

- **Bad leaders stifle innovation.** Bad leaders who create a culture of fear stifle innovation. They create environments where people are afraid to make mistakes. This leads to employees being less creative, less productive, and less engaged. It becomes safer for the team to do the bare minimum to not get fired and keep out of trouble.
- **Bad leaders create stress and anxiety for everyone.** Not every bad leader uses aggressive tactics. Some just fail to lead. When these people are in the top jobs, they don't set a direction while everyone else struggles and wonders where their career is going.

Great leaders encourage and motivate their employees to work harder, do more, and go above and beyond what's expected of them. They create an environment where employees feel appreciated and respected. In return, employees are more likely to be productive, innovative, and engaged. They know how to delegate tasks and responsibilities. They trust employees to do their jobs and give them the autonomy to work independently. This fosters a sense of ownership and responsibility among employees and helps them to feel invested in their work. The COVID pandemic and the rise of remote work showed us what many workers really wanted all along: autonomy.

THE LONG-TERM PERSPECTIVE

Your influence as a leader will be felt by your team for years to come, regardless of if you're a good or a bad boss. While I'd just as soon forget my bad bosses, I remember the best leaders I've worked for. These are the ones who made me want to come to work and who made me a better person. One boss who refused to give up the name of a security employee who had accidentally taken down the entire trading floor at one of the world's largest trading firms on Wall Street. When angry executives came looking for the employee who did it, he stood there like Clint Eastwood saying, "the only name you're getting today is mine." That's a leader who has everyone's back. It was also over 25 years ago, but I remember every detail.

They say that people won't remember what you said but will remember how you made them feel. I feel good about my great bosses, and I keep in touch with many of them to this day. What do you want people to remember about you years down the road? I'm disheartened when I hear former employees tell me I was the only great boss they had in their career. We need to do better than this.

What you do every day builds your character and your life. Short-term thinking keeps us from having tough conversations with underperforming employees. Short-term thinking makes us avoid problems because it's easier than dealing with them. Recognizing and addressing the need for a difficult conversation is hard, but it brings compounding results over time. The path of least resistance isn't always the best path to take.

Sooner or later, you will face headwinds and setbacks in your career. You will be discouraged. You won't get that promotion or job offer. Your projects will have problems. Your best efforts will go unnoticed. The best leaders learn from these events and move forward carrying lessons with them. Leaders become great by challenging themselves and their employees. They push themselves and their teams to do better and to be better. No matter where you are right now in your career, there's always time to make a bigger difference.

Action: leadership casts a long shadow. What impact do you think you're having on your team? What impact do you think your management style has on them? Do you think they would voluntarily work for you again in the future if it were a choice? That's a sure sign of a great leader.

SUMMARY

In this chapter, we've learned that great leaders encourage and motivate their employees to work harder, do more, and go above and beyond what's expected of them. Leaders should also delegate tasks and responsibilities and trust employees to do their jobs independently. This fosters a sense of ownership and responsibility among employees and helps them to feel invested in their work. We've also learned:

- Managing technologists calls for a different style of leadership. Technologists are independent, creative people who want to be challenged and given the freedom to do their jobs without a lot of supervision. They are passionate about their work and can be highly opinionated. The best leaders provide a clear vision and direction while still allowing their employees the freedom to be creative and innovative.
- Working with technology is not always a straightforward, repeatable process. The nature and complexity of technical work require a different leadership approach.
- A leader is someone who inspires their team to do better and be better. Your team will remember what it was like to work with you and how you made them feel.
- Don't hold off on decisions that could have compounding benefits and ignore the problems that will drain your team's morale and productivity. Addressing problems may be uncomfortable but it will have compound benefits in the long term.

REFERENCES AND FURTHER READING

Bloch, Michael, Sven Blumberg, and Jürgen Laartz. *Delivering Large-Scale It Projects on Time, on Budget, and on Value.* McKinsey & Company, 2020, https://www.mckinsey.com/business-functions/mckinsey-digital/our-insights/delivering-large-scale-it-projects-on-time-on-budget-and-on-value.

Ethier, Marc. *What It Now Costs to Get an MBA at a Top Business School.* Poets & Quants, 2021, https://poetsandquants.com/2021/11/29/what-it-now-costs-to-get-an-mba-at-a-top-business-school/.

Fournier, Camille. *The Manager's Path: A Guide for Tech Leaders Navigating Growth and Change.* O'Reilly, 2017.

Grenny, Joseph. *Crucial Conversations: Tools for Talking When Stakes are High, Third Edition.* McGraw Hill, 2021.

Chapter 2

The average IT leader
is ... average

If you're going to be a bear, be a grizzly.

Oscar Gonzalez

THE TECHNOLOGY LEADERSHIP CRISIS

There are many technology managers in the world and most of them feel over-worked, overwhelmed, and underappreciated. This is because they are expected to absorb a hefty load of responsibilities and are dealing with increasing complexity (see Image 2.1). Today's companies are also more matrixed and managers need to excel at getting things done from more people, many of whom don't have a reporting relationship. The pace of change has also accelerated. The pace of technology change isn't linear like it is in many other industries. The pace of change in technology is exponential. Self-driving cars, virtual reality, and automation are all coming on strong and are likely to change the technology landscape yet again. This means that our future managers will have an even broader and more complex array of responsibilities than they do today. We'll take a speculative look at this future in Chapter 11.

Companies often promote technical experts into leadership roles because they are perceived as the most competent person for the job. These leaders have technical knowledge and they may be well-respected in the organization. But they don't always have the people skills necessary to lead a team. But just because someone is smart and oversees a team doesn't mean they will make a good leader or even just a good boss. To be an effective leader, you need to be able to motivate and inspire people. You need to be able to manage conflict and build consensus. You need to be able to make difficult decisions and delegate authority. And you need to be able to do all of this while maintaining your sanity and having a life outside of work.

Many technologists end up in leadership roles without learning the new skills they need to succeed. It's hard enough to keep on top of the changing technology landscape. Asking someone to let go of their technical education to start learning management skills is a difficult ask for many technologists.

DOI: 10.1201/9781003314707-3

IT Leaders have many challenges...

Image 2.1 IT leaders align technology with business objectives, manage complex systems and try to keep up with evolving technology trends while still ensuring security and compliance requirements.

After all, it's their technical skills that made them successful in the first place. Making room for new material can create anxiety. But not making room for the new skills that will be needed to manage a team can be a recipe for disaster, or at least a recipe for mediocre results.

If any support is provided for the newly promoted manager, it's usually in the form of some corporate training class that doesn't help much. Many companies don't offer any leadership training at all, or they reserve it for the most senior leaders who have probably been through enough trial and error not to need it anymore. Yet the best way to have junior leaders become senior leaders is to have them to work alongside their boss closely and learn as a form of apprenticeship or mentoring. But many managers are too busy themselves to prioritize the time it takes to develop their staff.

If your company provides leadership training at all, it's almost certainly missing the mark. It's most likely a one-time course or event with no refreshers. Leadership training also rarely factors in the human complexity that helps us bring lessons back from the classroom to the office. Leadership training usually portrays uncomplicated and unrealistic scenarios that have simple, straight-forward answers. Few programs discuss the importance of leading by example. Attendees go through their paces in these classes, but they usually come back with no usable skills or skills that are quickly forgotten. That's because leadership development is not a class, course, or event. Leadership development is a process. It's not just about acquiring knowledge but also about turning knowledge into skills and refining and personalizing what works for you and eliminating what doesn't. It's about double-clicking on your mistakes and changing your approach in the future. The leadership process is about challenging your assumptions and disrupting yourself over and over again.

There are also many "good enough" managers who get by and are not total disasters, but they are also nothing special. They don't grow and they coast along hoping there are no big problems under their watch. But the moment you stop growing is the moment you start losing relevancy. There's always someone out there who is hungrier than you who will take your place. There are always people who are willing to work harder and become smarter than you. If you're not learning and growing as a leader, someone will eventually surpass you and you'll be reporting to them.

There are good and bad leaders, and both are remembered for different reasons. The rest are forgotten. The rest are the people who preserved the status quo and didn't leave any lasting impression. Being average means being about as good as everyone else. But when you look around, maybe this isn't the best benchmark. I also imagine you didn't pick up this book so you could be more average. The good news is that given the state of leadership development in the corporate world, almost anything you do to improve yourself will propel you into the above average category and eventually into leadership excellence. Great leadership starts with showing up every day, paying attention, and being engaged. Great leadership is about challenging everyone's thinking, starting with your own.

WHAT IS LEADERSHIP, ANYWAY?

People usually define leadership with some dull and lifeless definition like "the action of leading a group of people or organization, or the ability to do this." These definitions don't capture the flavor or spirit of what it means to be an accountable information technology (IT) leader. However, defining leadership in a way that everyone agrees with is surprisingly difficult. Even CEOs struggle to provide clear and consistent definitions of leadership. Why is it so hard to define something that seems so simple?

Leadership is not about seniority, a position, or a title in your company. You also don't need a team of direct reports to be a leader. Leaders are found in your neighborhood, your family and your company. Leaders don't even have to be the most charismatic people. In fact, charisma alone doesn't seem to provide any lasting results. Leadership comes from influence rather than from power and hierarchy. Without leadership, there is no direction or purpose in an organization. A simple definition of leadership is that it's your ability to influence people toward a common goal regardless of who's in charge. This means that leadership can come from anywhere in an organization, not just from the top. And it's not about personality traits or seniority. Anyone can be a leader if they can influence others.

You might think that if you're the boss, you can simply tell your team what to do and they will do it. Who needs leadership when you're in charge? But leadership is not about telling people what to do, that's for drill sergeants. Leadership is about inspiring people to do their best work and anticipate problems. Today's technology teams need to collaborate more than ever to get things done. Leaders need to work well with others and build relationships.

One of the most important qualities of a leader is the ability to inspire others. A good leader is someone who can not only articulate their vision but also rally others around them to achieve it. Great leaders are the catalyst that inspires change and helps gets results.

Action: your personal definition of leadership is important and will be one of the principles that helps you make future decisions. Take some time to think about what being a leader means to you. Create your definition of leadership based on your personal values. Are you motivated by a desire to help others or make an impact? Do you want to lead change or inspire those around you? Whatever your motivation, creating a personal definition of leadership will help you stay true to yourself as a leader.

THE MANAGEMENT-LEADERSHIP CONTINUUM

> Managers who don't lead are quite discouraging, but leaders who don't manage don't know what's going on. It's a phony separation that people are making between the two.
>
> Henry Mintzberg

There's an unproductive argument about leadership versus management, usually viewing managers in a negative light and artificially putting leaders on a pedestal. But management is a critical function for any organization. Managers get things done. But leaders challenge the status quo. They help figure out where a company needs to go and helps everyone get there together. Leadership refers to the ability to influence, to be a catalyst for change, to motivate, and to engage others. Leaders set the direction, but they also use management skills to guide their people.

Managers focus on the day-to-day operations of their team or department, while leaders are more focused on the overall direction and vision of the organization (see Image 2.2). Leaders need to have a clear vision for where they want the organization to go and they need to be able to articulate that vision in a way that inspires others to buy into it. And guess what? Leaders usually need to manage a team. If you're in charge of a team, congratulations you're a manager regardless of how good or bad you are at leadership.

Leadership and management are different ends of a continuum and even seasoned leaders probably started out on the manager side of the scale. If you're a manager with no leadership skills, you might be able to keep the trains running on time, but you're not going to be able to think about where your function or company needs to go or how to get there. But a leader who doesn't have any management skills is also not going to be effective. Leaders without management skills are going to be overly focused on big-picture thinking and will have no idea how to execute on their vision.

While leadership is focused on inspiring and motivating others to achieve goals, management is focused on planning and implementing strategies to

Leading versus managing

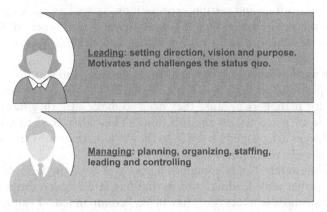

Leading: setting direction, vision and purpose. Motivates and challenges the status quo.

Managing: planning, organizing, staffing, leading and controlling

Image 2.2 Leadership and management both involve directing and guiding people towards achieving organizational goals.

accomplish those goals. Leaders tend to be more strategic, innovative, and creative, while managers are more process-oriented and detail-oriented. Leaders focus on people, while managers focus on systems and process. Your leaders set the tone, but your managers carry the culture in the way they operate. While you can manage people simply because you're the boss, the best leaders do it through persuasion and inspiration. I will use the words "leader," "manager," and "boss" somewhat interchangeably throughout this book because they are ultimately the same thing with the exception that a leader doesn't exclusively depend on having direct reports to get things done.

Let's break down the role of a manager to help understand the relationship between leading and managing a little better. Henri Fayol was one of the first theorists to define the functions of management in his 1916 book *Administration Industrielle et Generale*. There are five commonly accepted functions of managers including planning, organizing, staffing, leading, and controlling.

- **Planning**: planning includes setting objectives and determining a course of action to achieve those objectives. Planning is one of the most fundamental elements of being a manager. Even on an operational team, there's still some planning necessary. Systems upgrades and other changes need to be tested, scheduled, and deployed. New system rollouts may have so many components that a formal project manager is assigned to help. Planning helps determine goals, strategies, and actions. It also involves scheduling meetings, setting agendas, determining budgets, and other administrative tasks.

- **Organizing**: organizing includes creating a structure, assigning tasks to individuals, and setting deadlines. Organizing also includes creating job descriptions and setting expectations, as well as tracking timelines for projects and tasks. Organizing is an important function. Being able to create some order out of complexity and chaos helps everyone to be more effective and efficient.
- **Staffing**: staffing involves recruiting, selecting, and training employees and getting the right resources in place. This is an important function for managers because they need to make sure they have the right people in place to get the job done. They also need to ensure that employees are properly trained so they can do their jobs effectively and that they have the right resources and tools.
- **Leading**: interestingly enough, Henri Fayol used the term "commanding" rather than leading, a term that has largely been dropped since I imagine most workers don't like being "commanded." Leading involves motivating and guiding individuals in the organization. From this perspective, leadership is simply part of being a manager. Of course, leadership is more than simply assigning tasks and hoping that they'll get done. Leading includes setting goals and expectations, providing feedback, and helping employees develop their skills. It's important for managers to be good leaders so they can inspire their team to do their best work.
- **Controlling**: controlling involves monitoring progress and taking corrective action where necessary. This includes tracking metrics, analyzing data, and making decisions based on that data. Managers need to control the resources and budget requirements for their team, as well as make sure that projects are on track through status reporting.

There's one other element that's essential for technology leaders, which is managing change. Technology is always changing and evolving. Companies need to be able to adapt to new trends and technologies to stay competitive. They need to react when the business climate changes or when one company buys another. It's important for technology managers to be able to react to these changes so they can help their team transition smoothly and keep the business running. The bottom line is that the best managers are leaders, and the best leaders are usually pretty good managers too. The two skill sets complement each other and one without the other is not enough.

Action: do you understand the difference between good leadership and good management? How could you be a better leader? Are there places where could you also be a better manager?

Action: think about a process or responsibility in your group that needs improvement. These are all candidates for showing initiative and leadership. Smaller issues might be good starting points for aspiring managers on your team to practice their own leadership skills.

ARE YOU SURE YOU WANT TO LEAD?
TEN QUESTIONS TO ASK

No one aspires to a leadership position thinking how much they will enjoy all the challenges, roadblocks, and problems that lie ahead of them. It's important to be realistic about what you're getting yourself into before making the decision to take a leadership position or when deciding to stay in a leadership position that isn't a good fit. Everyone isn't cut out to be a leader and you should be honest with yourself before taking or retaining a leadership position that isn't right for you. Staying in the wrong position has an impact on you, your team, and everyone they work with.

Fortunately, some businesses have embraced the idea of a senior technical individual contributor job because they understand that not everyone should manage people. Typically, this is referred to as a "technical fellow" or something similar. Although the title sounds a little odd at first, this senior position is meant to elevate and promote the professional development of significant contributors who shouldn't be managers or who don't want to manage people. All too frequently, companies "reward" senior technologists by giving them a team to manage as a perceived promotion. There's no shame if you don't want to manage people. When it comes to leadership, there's no single right path and the technology fellow role provides leadership skills and recognition without all the personality conflicts.

Some IT managers who are promoted into management roles are disappointed when they realize how far away from the technology they need to become to succeed in the role. They miss the hands-on technical work and don't want to leave it behind. Be sure you know what you're getting into if you're going to manage a big team. You might retain a little hands-on work with a smaller team, but the bigger your team, the more your daily work is going to center around communications, management tasks, and building relationships.

Newly promoted managers are also sometimes surprised when they realize they are no longer part of the water cooler talk. They may be even more surprised that they are the subject of the water cooler talk. There's a certain loneliness to leadership. Think about how close you want to be with your own boss and you may begin to understand that sometimes maintaining a professional distance is a good thing. You need to treat everyone fairly on your team and that means close friends who may have been peers should not be treated as favorites when you become their manager. As a leader, you are also going to need to make decisions that might not be popular with your team. Before you begin or stay in a management position that may not be a good fit for you, ask yourself the following questions:

- **Are your technical skills good enough?** I've seen disastrous consequences because a new manager simply didn't know enough about the function they were leading. You probably shouldn't manage the database team if you don't know anything about how databases work or the security team if you don't know the first thing about cybersecurity. Just as a good lawyer wouldn't make a good doctor, the leader needs to be comfortable enough with their subject matter.

- **Are you comfortable not being the smartest person on the team?** Having enough technical knowledge doesn't mean you need to have the *most* technical knowledge. Many managers feel like imposters if they aren't perceived as "experts" in their function. They become paranoid that they will be discovered and they do everything they can to keep the people underneath them who may seem more knowledgeable invisible. This leads underutilizing high performers and stalling career development for everyone. It also leads to answering questions incorrectly just to have an answer. Be comfortable that you may not know everything and you don't have to know everything. This can happen to anyone and isn't just applicable to new managers. Imposter syndrome is a subject I will cover later in the book.
- **Are you comfortable telling people what to do?** I've seen seasoned leaders fall back to doing the work themselves because they think they're the best person to get something done. You will be required to complete more work as a leader than you would as an individual contributor. But your team needs to do most of the work, not you. On a big team, you won't be effective if you're doing hands-on technical work all day. It will pull you away from important functions including developing a strategy, removing obstacles, and communicating up and down the management chain. Lines of code generated, patches deployed, and other typical productivity measures don't work for managers. Your performance will be judged over time and will be more about your effectiveness than about your hands-on contribution.
- **Can you handle not getting involved in every detail?** Control freaks don't scale. Control freaks torture the teams they lead and frustrate smart workers who know better ways of getting things done. Control freaks simply don't make great technology leaders. The command-and-control style of leadership is sometimes necessary when you're responding to a crisis, but you will never keep and retain the best technology workers using this approach all the time. Instead of dictating every step of the process, provide clear outcomes and focus on results. Bonus: you'll free up a bunch of time to work on important leadership tasks like your strategy.
- **Can you deal with criticism?** Leadership comes with a lot of responsibility and sometimes criticism. Criticism can be difficult to deal with, but it's important to remember that it's part of the job. There will always be people who don't like your decisions, no matter how well-meaning or well-thought-out they were. Take criticism constructively and use it to improve your leadership skills where you can. Accept that even when you're trying to reach consensus, there may be people who disagree with you.

- **Can you stay calm under pressure?** Leaders often make decisions under pressure. Decisions may have an impact on people, time, budget, and the company's overall strategy. Stress is a big problem for many leaders, so you'll need to find ways to manage it, which we discuss later in this book. Don't worry too much about getting stressed sometimes, everyone does. But if you're too high strung all the time, people are going to have trouble approaching you and you'll have trouble connecting with your team.
- **Can you maintain your focus when things get chaotic?** Business can be chaotic. Anyone in a professional environment knows that meeting project deadlines, going through mergers, and dealing with unexpected problems and system outages are simply part of the job. Maintaining your focus during these times is essential for success.
- **Do you have good communication and interpersonal skills?** You're going to need to communicate a lot as a leader. You'll need to be able to articulate your ideas and vision clearly and being able to listen carefully what others are saying. Strong communication skills allow you to build trust with your team and get the best results from them. Strong communication is arguably the most important trait of leadership because without it no one will understand your vision and you will have a hard time getting people to understand you, much less follow you.
- **Can you work well with a team?** I've seen people in leadership positions who wouldn't even make a good team member. Can you put your ego aside and work for the betterment of the whole team? If your primary motivation for a leadership role is making more money, you may find that freelancing in technology can pay even more than you would make as a manager. There are other paths to take where you can keep your hands-on technical skills razor sharp and not have to worry about all the people issues that go with managing a team. You don't have to be an IT manager to make money in technology and if you don't want the role, you'll be doing everyone a favor by not taking it.

Don't worry if you fall short in a category or two. If you're not clear on your results, take some time to think about each question and why you're not comfortable. Leadership roles are not something to be taken lightly. They have a lot of impact on the people around you and the company overall. That's a lot of impact you can have, but it can also be positive or negative impact.

HOW TO BE AN IT LEADER WORTH FOLLOWING

What makes a leader worth following? Does likability, by itself, make a great leader? Is it results and getting work done? Is it providing career growth and support for the team? What makes a great leader? There are several common elements that employees cite in leaders they've enjoyed following. One of these attributes is genuinely caring for the people they lead. But being nice is not enough. It's also about getting things done and delivering results. Great leaders are not just nice people, they get the team moving in the right direction and they get things done.

To be an IT leader worth following, it is important to not only have technical expertise, but to work closely with other people. Leaders need to be able to communicate their vision and get buy-in from people. If you want to be a leader worth following, focus on the people you lead as well as the work that needs to be done. You and your team can do great things together by creating a supportive and collaborative environment.

Great leaders seem to have a knack for the coaching style of leadership, which is supportive and empathetic. They are not always visionaries, though of course being visionary doesn't hurt. But keep in mind there are many visionary leaders who are horrible, unsupportive bosses. They want to achieve their goals by any means necessary. Finally, there are examples of demanding visionary leaders that people still want to follow regardless of personality, like Steve Jobs and Elon Musk. These leaders may not be easy to work for but being part of their success is irresistible. Of course, if you're not Steve Jobs or Elon Musk, you're probably going to need a different approach with your management style.

Employees who work for great leaders often cite qualities like "supportive" and "caring." Other attributes include communicating a clear vision, being decisive, and sharing credit with their team. They set performance expectations and consistently provide feedback. The best leaders also seem to be good at getting to know employees on a personal level. They typically make work just a little bit more fun.

The best leaders also seem to create a lot of other leaders. The growth and experience employees receive under nurturing leaders set them up for their own future leadership role. This may come from being in a supportive environment and the development efforts that most great leaders encourage. Great leaders know that when everyone improves their skills, everything gets easier.

Remember that being a good leader is not only about making decisions and giving orders. You need to be able to empathize with your team and understand their needs. You need to develop and mentor your own future leaders. You need to forge better relationships that boost and support the team. If you want to be a leader worth following, start by being a good role model. Show your team that you are committed to the organization and its goals. Be authentic and passionate about your work and let your energy and commitment inspire them.

Action: who are some leaders you've admired and what makes them stands out to you? One of my favorite leaders was Franklin D. Roosevelt (FDR). FDR was an American president who led the country during some of its darkest years, including the Great Depression, the Dust Bowl, and World War II while overcoming his own challenges from being crippled by polio at age 39. He was a great communicator and gave people hope at a time when the outcome was far from certain.

Action: are you learning the right subjects?. As one develops into a more effective leader, the mastery of business skills becomes increasingly crucial. If you're spending all your self-education time on nothing but technology training, consider adding communication, presentation skills, or business skills to your training list.

THE PATH AHEAD

Many people end up in a leadership position and choose to coast. Maybe they're not sure of what to do in the role, so they just react to whatever is going on around them. But great leaders seem to push themselves farther and more efficiently than everyone else. They learn the right skills and practice the techniques that help them the most. They are genuine and they show up as their best self, determined to make a difference. Great leadership requires some work and dedication, but those who choose to lead can make a real difference. They can leave the world, or at least their company, a better place.

Thomas Edison once said that people miss opportunity because it shows up in overalls and looks a lot like hard work. It's hard work leading people. I've been under some bad leaders and I'm glad I didn't leave my career in their hands. I would have missed the opportunity to make my own impact on the world and become a better person along the way.

The University of Georgia performed a study to find out what makes someone an "asshole." People had no problem recognizing these people in their lives. The main traits of an asshole included being aggressive, entitled, and manipulative. The study also found that half of the assholes cited were either family members or former bosses. No matter what you do, at least try not to be *that* boss.

SUMMARY

In this chapter, we've learned that being a great leader requires more than just making decisions and giving orders. You also need to be able to empathize with your team and understand their needs. We've also learned:

- One way to become a great leader is to keep learning and growing. This can be done by practicing, being determined to improve, and gaining experience.
- Leadership and management are closely related. The best managers are leaders and the best leaders are usually good managers. One without the other is usually not enough.

- No one aspires to a leadership position thinking how they will enjoy encountering all the challenges, roadblocks, and problems that lie ahead of them. Be honest with yourself if you really want to be in a leadership role.
- A good leader is someone who can get things done by working with others. They have a clear vision and communicate it effectively to gain buy-in from their team. They are supportive and care about their employees, setting performance expectations, and providing feedback. Leaders also tend to create other leaders by developing skills on their team and providing a positive work environment.

REFERENCES AND FURTHER READING

Schein, Edgar H., and Peter A. Schein. *Humble Leadership: The Power of Relationships, Openness, and Trust.* Berrett-Koehler Publishers, Inc., 2018.

Sharpe, Brinkley M., Courtland S. Hyatt, Donald R. Lynam, and Joshua D. Miller. "They Are Such an Asshole": Describing the Targets of a Common Insult Among English-Speakers in the United States. *Collabra: Psychology*, 2022, 8 (1): 32552. Online.ucpress.edu. Feb. 2022, https://doi.org/10.1525/collabra.32552.

Manager Demographics and Statistics. Number of Managers in the US, 18 Apr. 2022, https://www.zippia.com/manager-jobs/demographics/.

Chapter 3

Master your mindset

We like to think of our champions and idols as superheroes who were born different from us. We don't like to think of them as relatively ordinary people who made themselves extraordinary.

Carol Dweck
Mindset: The New Psychology of Success

WHY YOUR MINDSET MATTERS

Having the right mindset is essential for your growth. A positive mindset sets you up for success, while a negative mindset holds you back. Your mindset determines your attitude and how you approach challenges. People with a positive mindset approach challenges with confidence and believe they can be overcome. Your attitude keeps you focused and helps you keep you going when things get tough.

In the book, *Mindset: The New Psychology of Success*, author Carol S. Dweck defines two mindsets (see Image 3.1). The first is a growth mindset, which is where you believe that change is possible and that your ability to improve isn't limited. If you believe that you aren't good at something and never will be, this is called a fixed mindset. People with a fixed mindset don't try to improve because they feel it will be impossible. These are the people who say that it's too late for them to learn a language, too hard for them to learn how to code, or that they could never be a public speaker.

Since you are reading this book, I imagine you have a growth mindset. But think about it for a moment: where might some of your own beliefs be holding you back? Where are you saying things like "I'm not good at remembering names" or "I'll never be a good writer." As Henry Ford once said, "*Whether you think you can, or you think you can't–you're right*." You can improve anything with the right focus, effort, and practice. But your mindset is going to limit how much effort you put into improving in the first place.

Leadership involves navigating uncertain outcomes. Having a positive, growth-oriented mindset is essential to navigate these challenges. You must believe you can make things better before anyone else is going to believe it. We all recognize negative leaders. These are the people who are nearly impossible

DOI: 10.1201/9781003314707-4

Two Mindsets

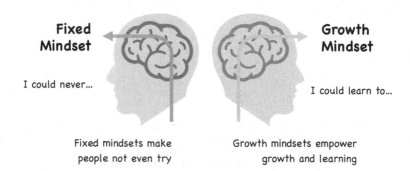

Fixed Mindset

I could never…

Fixed mindsets make
people not even try

Growth Mindset

I could learn to…

Growth mindsets empower
growth and learning

Image 3.1 A growth mindset fosters a belief in the potential for future learning and development, enabling leaders to embrace challenges, learn from mistakes and continuously improve.

to follow. In fact, it's hard just being around them. They bring a cloud of negativity and cynicism over the people they manage and to everyone around them.

Fostering a growth mindset isn't complicated, it starts with being curious. Learn to be curious about the world around you and how things work. Kids have a natural curiosity, which often disappears as we grow older and stop asking questions. Be open to learning new things and exploring different viewpoints. While there are many benefits in being curious, the best one is that it's the cure for boredom. There's always something new to learn when you're curious. I taught myself options trading, how to play guitar, and cybersecurity by pursuing my curiosity. Being curious keeps you stay engaged at work and in the world around you.

Aside from being curious, here are a few other ways to foster a growth mindset:

- **Be open to change.** Be open to new ideas and concepts and new ways of doing things. Challenge your assumptions. Don't be afraid to ask questions and probe deeper into any subject. Try different methods of learning and don't be afraid to experiment. I like using First Principles thinking to help reframe my thinking and come at problems from a different angle. First Principles thinking entails breaking a problem down to the most basic level and then working up from there. This can help you see things in a new light and find different ways to solve problems.
- **Embrace challenges and setbacks as opportunities for growth.** Many people view challenges and setbacks as negative experiences that should be avoided. However, if you can embrace challenges as opportunities for growth, you will learn ten times faster. Make sure you are capturing your challenges and setbacks and try to learn from them. When things work out right, capture what you could have done even better. Make setbacks, obstacles, and challenges an integral part of the learning process.

- **Take an active role in your own development.** No one is going to hand you a learning plan for your success. Find the tools or access to information that you need to grow in your role. As a bonus, this helps you stay engaged in your role and with your organization. You'll also want to make sure you're developing your team, which I cover later in this book.
- **Get feedback.** There are several ways to get feedback, including 360-degree reviews and informal conversations with people who know you well. If you're looking to improve your leadership skills, it's important to get feedback. Most people in leadership positions think they are more strategic than they really are, when they are really lost in the weeds of operational problem-solving. Feedback helps you improve your emotional intelligence and discover your blind spots.

Remember that even if you have a strong growth mindset, it may not be present in all aspects of your life. Sometimes a fixed mindset shows up in subtle ways. "I don't have time to...," "it's too late for me to ...," "that's too complicated" are all more subtle thoughts that reflect a fixed mindset. Our beliefs about our abilities and limitations all start with our thoughts. It is far more empowering to believe that you can accomplish anything than it is to give up before you ever even start with self-defeatist thinking.

Action: do you have a growth mindset or a fixed mindset? What limiting beliefs could be holding you back? How are you fostering a growth mindset in your team? Do you offer your team training in business subjects including leadership development and public speaking skills?

Action: what could you learn that would help you perform better in your current position? I encourage you to develop a strong interest in your business and begin learning more about how it operates, where its revenue comes from, and what factors are crucial to its success. If reading faster would help you, take a speed-reading course. Pick a skill that, if mastered, would make you great at your current job.

ESTABLISHING YOUR LEADERSHIP PHILOSOPHY

Having a leadership philosophy provides a sense of being grounded, aids in decision-making, and offers direction when things don't go your way. Your leadership philosophy provides the basis for your actions and decisions. This means it's important to spend some time understanding which way your leadership compass points.

There are many different leadership styles, and while it's helpful to think about what kind of leader you are, this also brings the risk of implying that your style is set in stone. There are times where you might need to change your style as the situation demands. For example, in a systems outage or

The Six Leadership Styles

Based on Six Leadership Styles by Daniel Goleman (2002)

Image 3.2 Different situations require different approaches. One of the key skills that separates effective leaders from everyone else is the ability to adapt their style to different situations.

cybersecurity event, you might temporarily adopt an autocratic style, but revert to your default style when the incident is over. Adaptive and situational leadership styles form the concept of leadership agility, which is a key theme of this book.

In his book *Six Leadership Styles*, author Daniel Goleman defines several common styles people use in leadership situations (see Image 3.2). These include autocratic, visionary, affiliative, democratic, pacesetting, and coaching. Let's examine each in the context of technology leadership.

- **Autocratic:** these are the "Do as I say" leaders. Generally, an autocratic leader makes all the decisions with little input from their team. There are times, such as in the military, where this style is perfectly appropriate. Financial institutions, technology companies, and other competitive industries may also use this style of leadership quite a bit. Steve Jobs is an example of an autocratic technology leader. He was said to be a demanding boss who was not afraid to show his displeasure. Advantages of an autocratic leadership style includes fast decision-making, clear direction, and tough decision-making. Disadvantages include disempowerment of the team and a lack of diversity in the decision-making process.
- **Visionary:** visionary leaders are authorities on a subject and articulate a shared vision that inspires others into action. Founders of start-up companies are often visionary leaders who have no trouble creating a sense of inspiration. Their excitement can be contagious. The downside of visionary leaders is that ego can sometimes get in the way. This leadership style can also alienate employees who don't share the exact vision.

- **Pacesetting:** pacesetting leaders are often high achievers and expect their team to keep up. They have a clear vision of what needs to be done and how it should be done. However, they don't micromanage their team's every move. Instead, they provide expectations and let their team figure out the details. They expect a high standard of work and performance. The advantages of the pacesetting leadership styles include having a clear vision, high standards, and the ability to motivate employees. The disadvantages include the potential for micromanagement and the very real possibility of employee burnout.
- **Democratic:** democratic leaders want to include everyone in the decision-making process and share power with the team. This style of leadership often appears in less competitive organizations, such as schools, non-profit organizations, and smaller businesses. The advantages of democratic leadership styles include employee empowerment, high engagement levels, and diversity of thought with decision-making. The disadvantages include the potential for slower decision-making, as well as a lack of clarity in direction if there's no consensus.
- **Coaching:** coaching leaders focus on developing their team's skills and abilities. They believe that everyone has the potential to improve and grow. This style of leadership is often used in sports, but also in business and education. The advantages of coaching leadership styles include greater employee development, the ability to motivate employees, and lifelong learning. The coaching mindset requires leaders to stop seeing themselves as the ultimate fixers and help everyone else figure out solutions by asking the right questions. The disadvantages include the potential for employees to become overly reliant on the coach, as well as lack of direction if the coaching leader doesn't ask the right questions.
- **Affiliative:** of all the leadership styles, the affiliative leadership approach is the most focused on the emotional needs of the team. Affiliative leaders build relationships and create harmony. They believe that happy employees are productive employees. The advantages of affiliative leadership styles include stronger relationship building and high employee morale. The disadvantages include the potential for a lack of direction, as well as the possibility getting stuck if there's no consensus. Ultimately, affiliative leaders want *everyone* to be happy.

The most effective leadership style depends on the situation, the people, and the company. The best leaders adapt their style to meet the needs of their team and for the task at hand. For example, I'm autocratic during a security incident, but I prefer the coaching style overall since it supports team development the most. Developing the team that you already have is important when you can't find enough people to do the work. It also helps me build a resilient team that isn't dependent on me always being available to make decisions for them.

Culture and other factors also contribute to how well your leadership style is going to go over at your company. I once had an autocratic leader who came into a flat organization establishing hierarchies and trying to change the culture to what he wanted it to be, rather than taking the time to understand what it was. It ended badly for everyone involved and this leader was ultimately forced out of the organization after having joined with a lot of fanfare. Company culture is an important topic I cover later in this book.

After examining your personal beliefs about leadership styles, you should also consider the needs of your team. What impact do you want to have on them? What do they need from you to be successful? A junior team may benefit from a more autocratic style, a team of seasoned technologists might work best in something closer to a laissez faire approach. Your leadership philosophy should be concise, no more than a few sentences. It should also be something that you can remember easily. Keep it positive and actionable, focusing on what you *will* do rather than what you won't do. And most important is to make it reflective of who you want to be as a leader.

Action: think about the following questions and begin forming your own leadership philosophy. Reflect on these questions:

- Who are your role models when you think about what great leadership looks like?
- Which leadership style resonates the most with you, and why?

Once you've formed a personal leadership philosophy, be sure to write it down and reflect on how your daily actions align to it. For example, if you said that your leadership philosophy is "people come first," be sure to ask yourself how your actions reflect this belief. Are you spending time getting to know your team and do you understand their individual needs? If being a people-first manager is important to you, make sure you are creating the time and habits to be that person.

GOOD FOLLOWERS: THE OTHER SIDE OF LEADERSHIP

> He who cannot be a good follower, cannot be a good leader.
>
> Aristotle

If you're not the CEO of your company, you probably have a boss. Your boss may also have a boss. CEOs of private companies answer to venture capitalists. Most people answer to someone, even if it's just the person in the mirror. As far back as 400 BC, Aristotle suggested that good leaders were also good followers. This means that leaders must be able to sometimes put their own ideas and opinions aside and follow the lead from others.

A study at Harvard Business Review identified five types of followers. These include survivors, sheep, yes people, alienated followers, and effective followers. Survivors do what it takes to get by. Sheep are passive, lacking both initiative and a sense of responsibility. Yes people do what they're told to do, but are otherwise unmotivated. Alienated followers are critical thinkers who would rather be doing something else, so they are passive in their role and wait to be told what to do. Effective followers are self-starters who think for themselves and carry out their assignments with energy and assertiveness. Effective followers have accountability, initiative, and analytical thinking. An organization with effective followers performs well because more employees take ownership and initiative.

Good followers have loyalty for their leaders and a strong commitment to what the organization is trying to accomplish. They also believe in their own contribution to help get there. They keep their egos in check and do what's best for the team. If you have effective followers on your team, keep your eyes on them, because they will likely become your future leaders. Effective followers aren't sheep or yes people though. If something conflicts with their sense of right or wrong, they aren't going to blindly follow orders without raising concerns.

There are a few key things you can do to be a better follower and make your boss's life easier. First, be reliable and dependable. Your boss should be able to count on you to get your work done and do it well. This means being punctual, meeting deadlines, and carrying out your responsibilities without being reminded. Second, take initiative. Don't wait to be told what to do, think for yourself, and figure out what needs to be done. If you see something that needs to be done, do it. This not only shows your boss that you're capable and independent, but it also makes their job easier. Third, be a team player. No one likes a prima donna who always must have their way. Be flexible and willing to compromise. When you work well with others, it makes the whole team more effective. Finally, be positive and upbeat. No one wants to work with negative people. A positive attitude is contagious and makes the workplace more enjoyable for everyone.

Being a good follower is equally as important as being a good leader. You can make your boss's life easier and contribute significantly to the team by being dependable, proactive, honest, and positive.

Actions: are you supportive and proactive with your boss? Have there been times when you were being a survivor, a sheep, a yes person, or an alienated follower? How could you be a better follower?

THE SMARTEST ONE IN THE ROOM

Another big mindset challenge that many information technology (IT) leaders have is the need to be the smartest person in the room when it comes to their subject matter expertise. To preserve this image, they sometimes hold their team back for fear of looking stupid. It may even happen unconsciously. A few years ago, I was working on a project with a very senior engineer. He was an expert in his domain and he knew the ins and outs of this technology better than anyone else on his team. However, he also had a habit of

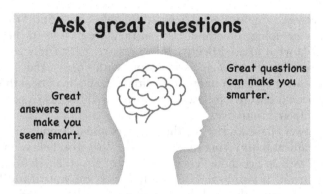

Image 3.3 The ability to ask great questions is important for technology leaders because it allows them to gain a deeper understanding of complex issues, identify underlying problems and develop innovative solutions.

interrupting people during meetings, especially when they were presenting their own ideas. It got to the point where people were afraid to speak up, for fear of being interrupted or shot down. The leader was a smart person with valuable insights, but his behavior prevented the team from functioning. No one wanted to warn this person that the project was likely to fail, which it ultimately did. Effective leaders create environments where people feel comfortable speaking up and sharing honest, candid feedback.

Instead of trying to be the smartest person in the room, strive to be the best thinker in the room (see Image 3.3). The best thinkers don't have all the answers. Instead, they ask the best questions. They know when to defer to others who might have a deeper understanding of a subject. Asking questions shows that you value other people's insights and that you're open to new ideas. It also demonstrates your willingness to learn, regardless of what stage you are at in your career. The best leaders are always learning. They're confident in their abilities, but they don't let their ego get in the way of the work. They know that it's not about them, it's about the team and the company. If you're uncomfortable not being the smartest one in the room, ask yourself why.

Companies don't just sell products or services anymore; they sell platforms, ecosystems, and experiences. To be successful in this environment, IT leaders need to understand and navigate a complex web of relationships between customers, partners, investors, and regulators. Industries are also becoming more global. Companies are operating in markets all over the world and they need leaders who can navigate different cultures, laws, and business practices. Finally, doing business is more competitive than ever. Technology leaders need to be able to not only out-innovate their competition, but also out-execute them. It's one thing to have a great idea and another one completely to deliver a quality product with timely execution. You are never going to be a master of every subject, which means you need to depend on the subject matter experts.

Today's technology leaders need a strong foundation in both technical and business skills. They need to be able to understand and solve complex problems, but they also need to build and execute a vision. Leaders need to be adaptable and able to operate in all environments and adjust their approach as the industry and markets change. Business acumen is becoming a skill that is increasingly more important for all technology leaders, not just for senior executives. The ability to think strategically, navigate change, and build relationships is essential for all IT leaders who want to be successful in today's business environment. You're not going to do it all alone. You need to build a team of experts who can help you navigate these challenges.

Action: do you need to be perceived as the smartest person on your team? How could you start letting go of this image and instead focus on becoming the best thinker?

TRUST AND INTEGRITY

> The supreme quality for leadership is unquestionably integrity. Without it, no real success is possible, no matter whether it is on a section gang, a football field, in an army, or in an office.
>
> Dwight D. Eisenhower

Your most important possession as a leader isn't your technical knowledge (your credibility), it's your integrity. Without integrity, there is no trust, and without trust, there is no leadership. A leader who can't be trusted won't have support from the teams they lead. Leaders who act with integrity build trust faster. Integrity means being honest and doing the right thing, even when no one else is watching. Leaders who have integrity make decisions based on what is best for the organization and their team, not what is best for themselves. They put the needs of others before their own needs.

It takes time and effort to build a good reputation, but this can be quickly destroyed by negative behavior and it's hard to build trust back again once it's gone. You are setting an example as a leader to your peers, your team, and everyone around you. Your behavior influences the company's reputation, so it is important to always act responsibly, respectfully, and ethically. Philosopher Friedrich Nietzsche said it best when he said: "I'm not upset that you lied to me, I'm upset that from now on I can't believe you."

American businessman and philanthropist Warren Buffett is widely considered to be the most successful investor of the 20th century. When he's hiring new leaders at Berkshire Hathaway, he cites integrity, intelligence, and energy as a candidate's most important qualities. But he also warns that if you don't have integrity, the other two qualities will kill you. The logic is simple: if you hire someone who doesn't have integrity, you'll want them to be dumb and lazy.

Intelligent, energetic people who don't have integrity can destroy an organization. If you're not comfortable with someone, don't hire them. It's so much harder to get a person out of the organization afterward. But watch your own integrity as well. Make sure that you are always honest with yourself and others and be consistent in your words and actions. People who lack integrity say one thing and then do another. People with integrity follow through on their commitments, both big and small. Guard your integrity carefully, most companies have a zero-tolerance policy when it comes to issues with integrity, trust, and ethics regardless of how high up you may sit in the organization.

There's no instant fix to either build or strengthen your integrity. It's an ongoing journey that starts with baby steps and little decisions made each day. Building integrity starts with being honest with yourself and then being honest with others. When you make a commitment, keep it. Show up on time and do what you say you're going to do. The reward is a strong foundation for leadership that will last a lifetime.

Action: where can you set a better example for your team and your peers? Ask yourself:

- Am I accountable for my behavior and decisions?
- Do I take responsibility for my mistakes?
- Am I setting a good example for my team and my peers?
- Do I follow through on my commitments and promises, both big and small?

STAYING GROUNDED

So far, we've explored important elements of your mindset including growth mindsets, establishing your leadership philosophy, being a good follower, and maintaining trust and integrity. Next is staying grounded. Grounded leaders make level-headed decisions even when things are chaotic or stressful. Being grounded also means controlling your ego. Leaders with big egos are usually either annoying to work with or dangerous because they are more likely to make bold decisions that are based on their own self-interests rather than what's best for the company. One of the benefits of staying grounded is that you're able to better connect with people on a personal level. This connection is essential for building trust and respect. When people feel like they understand and can relate to you, they're more likely to follow your lead. People see through false personas and using one will only damage your credibility if no one thinks they know the real you.

When you're grounded and genuine, it's also easier to stay focused on goals. You won't be as easily distracted by things that don't matter or by small problems that don't reflect the big picture. It's important to have both your head and your heart in the right place and staying grounded is the best ways to make sure that this happens. We all have an ego. It's human nature. But when our ego gets out of control, it can lead to problems in our personal and professional lives.

Think about your own ego for a moment. If you've accomplished a lot in your career, you might come off as a little arrogant to some if you're always talking about it. Leaders with big egos tend to talk about past accomplishments, the quality of companies on their résumé, and anything that elevates them above everyone else. These people aren't fun to be around since it's all about them. Here are a few tips to help you keep your own ego in check and stay more grounded. I remember one tone deaf leader I worked with who simply couldn't stop talking about himself, past achievements, and how much more mature his previous company was than where he was now. He even did this with business leaders. He came off not only as a prima donna but as someone who couldn't let go of his past and perhaps even someone who deep down felt they had made the wrong decision coming to a less-mature company. Regardless, it's a bad look on a leader. Watch out for ego, it makes you make dumb decisions and lose track of the reality that's in front of you right now. The best ways to guard against ego issues and stay more grounded include:

- **Being self-aware.** The first step in being better grounded is to be aware of when your ego is getting the best of you. If you're starting to feel arrogant or superior, take a step back and check yourself. Are you so much better and smarter than everyone around you?
- **Not taking it personally.** If someone criticizes you, don't let it get to you. Instead, look for the kernel of truth and use it to improve yourself or ignore it completely if it's baseless. Too many leaders get offended at some comment or slight that diminishes their self-image. Criticism is either true or it's not. If it is true, accept it and learn from it. If it's not, ignore it and let it go.
- **Practice humility.** Don't boast about your accomplishments or put yourself above everyone else. Humble leaders are easier to relate to as people. All your past achievements and other companies you've worked for aren't that important in the grand scheme of things. It's what you're doing right here and now that counts.
- **Listen more than you talk.** Another way to keep your ego in check is to listen more than you talk. When you're always talking, it can come across as arrogant and presumptuous as if you were the only one who knows what they're talking about. Instead of talking all the time, listen to everyone else and learn something new. As legendary interviewer Larry King once said, "I never learned anything while I was talking."
- **Don't compare yourself to everyone else.** Theodore Roosevelt once said, "Comparison is the thief of joy." We compare ourselves on social media, in the office, and with friends. There's enough success for everyone, so try to be happy when someone else succeeds rather than a little envious that someone else is getting the attention. Grounded leaders celebrate success everywhere they see it, especially in others.
- **Admit when you're wrong.** It takes a big person to admit when they're wrong. If you make a mistake, don't be afraid to admit it, own it, and make it right. It shows that you're humble and willing to learn from your mistakes. Better yet, if you learn from these mistakes, you just leveled up your game for next time.

Grounded leaders have a life. They spend time with their families and close friends, getting physical exercise, and giving back to the community. Work is important, but it's not the only thing. They expect their employees to do the same. Well-grounded leaders have a steady and confident presence. They don't show up as one person one day and another the next. This takes some discipline and practice, especially during stressful times when it's easy to slip into bad habits.

Action: do you consider yourself a well-grounded leader? If not, what can you do to become more grounded? Take some time this week to focus on being present and keeping your ego in check. The better you get at this, the more grounded you'll become.

THERE ARE NO SOFT SKILLS

I hate the term soft skills. The word soft conjures images of squishy, feel-good topics that make technical and engineering types cringe. At a minimum, the term devalues the benefits that soft skills offer. The word "soft" sounds synonymous with pliable or yielding readily to pressure. But an IT leader with excellent communication abilities and who can read people will be tough in their negotiations and effective in their role. Similarly, the term "soft" also makes the topic sound "easy," which it's not. Soft skills are really business skills. If you are going to operate a business, you're going to need to communicate, work in teams, influence people who don't report to you, and handle all the technology components. The most effective IT leaders are almost indistinguishable from the business leaders, aside from maybe having a deeper understanding of the technology.

Peak performance IT leaders need both technical skills and business skills, but the emphasis now is now more on business skills (see Image 3.4). This has been especially apparent in cybersecurity, where Chief Information Security Officers (CISOs) now need to brief the board of directors and CEO. But it's also required in agile development environments and is becoming more prominent across all of areas of IT. Understanding technology is now considered table stakes. Communication, strategy, and the ability to work with cross-functional teams are the new differentiators. Business skills help you communicate more effectively with everyone around you, not just with other technologists. IT professionals need to understand how to work with business units including finance, marketing, and sales, to ensure that the right technologies are in place to enable the business to function efficiently and effectively. Jobs that only require hands-on technical knowledge are prime targets for offshoring, outsourcing, or automation both now and in the future.

A recurring concern I hear from new technology leaders is that they're worried about keeping their technical skills sharp while spending time developing new skills. They find it difficult to engage with non-technical training since they don't see the value. It's hard to measure soft skills effectively

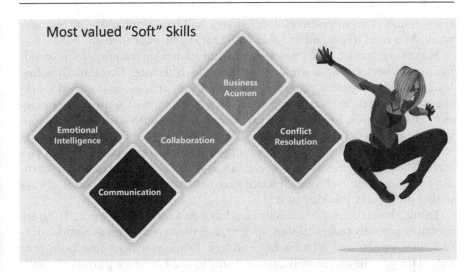

Image 3.4 Soft skills are important for IT leaders because they enable communication, relationship building and collaboration, which then drives innovation.

and improvement takes time and practice, unlike technical skills which you either have or you don't have. You can get certified in knowledge and hands-on technical ability, but no certification or degree will ever guarantee good leadership. This is because leadership lives at the intersection of the arts and sciences. You can learn the required elements of being a painter, but it's the artist who makes a great painting. You can study up on all the theories of being a great salesperson, but it's the artistry of persuasion that closes the deal. The same is true for leaders. You can read all about the characteristics of an effective leader, but it takes more than that to become one. It's the art of leadership that sets the great ones apart from the good ones. But art takes time and patience. Picasso is estimated to have completed 13,500 paintings and around 100,000 prints and engravings. Not all of them were winners and many of them likely served as practice leading up to his true and lasting works of art.

Better business and soft skills help you influence business leaders. As a result, your technical recommendations are more likely to be accepted and you'll be able to sell your ideas better. As you progress with your career, you'll find that the further you move from coding and hands-on computer work, the more your people skills and communication are going to determine how far you go with your career.

Even leaders who see the benefits of developing business and soft skills are concerned about losing their "technical edge" as they move up the management chain. This is a very personal decision and you'll have to strike your own balance. Ask yourself how much technical knowledge you really need in a senior role. What got you promoted to your current job may not be what keeps you there. As you progress in your career and take on larger teams, your day job will become much more about communication, conflict resolution, and relationship building than it will be about hands-on computer work. You need to get comfortable with that if you want to lead.

Make time for soft skills development and leadership training. Even spending just an hour or two a week can make a big difference. Enroll in an online leadership development program, read books or articles, and attend workshops or conferences. Stay humble and keep learning. Soft skills require practice, not just book knowledge. I can intellectually understand every step in what it takes to deliver a great presentation, but that doesn't mean I'm going to deliver a great presentation. Seek opportunities to practice the skills you learn. Speak at conferences. Embrace an argument on your team as a learning experience for everyone. Practice may not make perfection, but it always makes progress if you keep at it.

Think about the most successful leaders you know and respect. They are probably not only technically competent, but they are also great communicators, motivators, and relationship builders. While you may have been promoted for your technical skills, you're going to need to develop your soft skills and balance them with your own definition of "enough" technical knowledge to be effective in your role.

Action: how would you assess your business and soft skills? Where could you improve? Pick one thing, such as getting more comfortable with public speaking, and see if you can find opportunities to get out of your comfort zone and start practicing more.

LEADERS ARE READERS

Not all readers are leaders, but all leaders are readers.

Harry S. Truman

The final step in getting your mindset right for leadership is to realize that leaders are readers and need to keep learning. Studies suggest that reading makes you smarter, creative, insightful, and improves your vocabulary, knowledge, reasoning, and empathy skills. But the average American reads only four books a year. The average CEO, by contrast, reads about 60. That's five books a month. What do they read? They read biographies, history, and business books. But they also read novels, self-help, and other subjects as well. Why do they read so much more than the average person? It's because they know that reading is one of the best ways to learn new things and gain new insights. In fact, reading is a shortcut to success and for the time invested, there is no single better way to learn from smarter people than you.

People say they don't read because they don't have time. Yet some of the most successful people seem to find quite a lot of time for reading. Mark Cuban reads for more than three hours a day. Warren Buffet estimates that he spends 80% of his working day reading and thinking. Bill Gates stated that

Leaders are readers

The average American reads 4 books a year

The average CEO reads 60

Image 3.5 Reading provides access to a wealth of information, ideas, and perspectives that can enhance knowledge, creativity, and critical thinking skills.

even though he can go anywhere and meet with anyone, he primarily learns new things through reading. The good news is that you don't need to carve out hours a day from your busy schedule. But if you aren't carving out any time to read at all, you're shortchanging your learning potential. The bottom line is that successful people have time to read because they make it a priority (see Image 3.5). There's no more mystery to it than that.

You can learn just about anything by reading. Reading taught Elon Musk how to build a rocket ship. One of the best things about reading is that you can learn at your own pace. You can re-read sections or chapters and you can go as fast or as slow as you like. Reading is a great way to learn new information without feeling overwhelmed. But the human adult attention span is shrinking every day, leaving many people feeling unable or unwilling to read books in their free time.

In the book *The Shallows: What the Internet is Doing to Our Brains*, author Nicholas Carr argues that the Internet has turned us into the equivalent of lab rats constantly pressing levers to get tiny pellets of social or intellectual nourishment from social media and bite-size Internet content. It's taken away our ability to focus. He goes on to add that people who read without distraction "made their own associations, drew their own inferences and analogies, fostered their own ideas. They thought deeply as they read deeply."

You may think that you read a lot on the Internet and that that's enough. Short articles and blog posts will give you information faster than reading books. But the average blog post is written in an hour or two. There's even a whole cottage industry using artificial intelligence (AI) to write much of the content you're reading online. Authors on Facebook, LinkedIn, and other platforms are publishing superficial or regurgitated material in the never-ending effort to monetize your attention. Yes, you can find some good technical content online, but it's probably not going to go deep enough for you to really understand any truly complex subject. Books can take years or even lifetimes to write. I could not have written this book 20 years ago; I simply didn't have the experience or perspectives yet. Trying to condense everything into a few online pages might give you a taste for something, but it won't give you a satisfying and nourishing meal.

Reading can obviously make you smarter, but it can also help create empathy, spark curiosity, and provide different perspectives that can help you better understand the world around us. As a technologist, you'll want to also make sure you're keeping up with your own industry and trends that are driving the future. Reading business books will also give you an edge. But you make sure you broaden your perspective and read biographies, fiction, and other genres. The most successful people seem to read very broadly and make connections between different topics that many people wouldn't see.

Leadership is about influence, but you can't influence others if you don't have a good understanding of the world around you. Reading helps you gain that understanding. It exposes you to new ideas and different perspectives. It makes you a better thinker and helps you manage stress since it's an active form of active recovery, a topic I will cover later in this book. In short, reading makes leaders better informed and well-rounded. Minute-for-minute there is no better investment of your time.

I keep a library in my pocket with Apple Books and Amazon's Kindle app on my phone. Instead of doom-scrolling the news or reading Facebook posts, I spend a lot of my downtime when I'm stuck on a grocery line or in transit by reading a book on my phone. It helps me turn downtime into something that helps make me better and smarter.

Wondering what book to read next? Here are a few of my favorites that had a big impact on my life:

- *Essentialism: The Disciplined Pursuit of Less*, by Greg McKeown. Are you doing too much and feeling overwhelmed? This book helps you focus on what's essential in your life and helps you achieve more by doing less. While you're at it, read: *Effortless: Make It Easier to Do What Matters Most*, also by Greg McKeown. Effortless had a big impact on me. Making progress doesn't have to be hard and the puritan work ethic is overrated. We overcomplicate things in our mind without asking if there is an easier way. Thanks to this book, I'm constantly looking for the easy button throughout my day, recognizing that being done is better than being perfect.
- *Peak Mind: Find Your Focus, Own Your Attention, Invest 12 Minutes a Day*, by Amishi P. Jha et al. This book completely flipped my perspective on mindfulness and meditation. I practice meditation every day now and how much better off I am now than when I did inconsistent, "when I feel like it" meditation. If you're skeptical about the benefits of mind training, mindfulness, and meditation, read this book.
- *The Art of Impossible: A Peak Performance Primer*. Building on cutting-edge neuroscience and more than 20 years of research best-selling author and peak performance expert, Steven Kotler lays out the blueprint for

performance improvement. I found the concept of the "corporate athlete" intriguing. This is a fantastic book with tons of great research behind it.

- *Factfulness: Ten Reasons We're Wrong About the World - and Why Things Are Better Than You Think*, by Hans Rosling. Ever feel like the world is going to hell? Well, it turns out we're better off now than ever before. We overestimate how bad things are and underestimate the progress of humanity. We believe the world is more divided and violent than ever before, without understanding what things were really like at the dawn of civilization. This book helps you look at the world with a new perspective and puts a strong emphasis on facts that will help you understand the role of technology and the progress of civilization. This book is also a top Bill Gates recommendation and helps us attack our own confirmation biases.

Action: still not convinced you have the time to read? Follow this simple three-step process to start a reading habit.

1. Block out 15 minutes in your schedule for reading every day.
2. Choose a book you really want to read. While I generally prioritize nonfiction titles, it's fine to use fiction if it's a quality author. Whatever your choice, make it something you're excited about reading. If your book is a physical book, keep it easily accessible and visible.
3. Celebrate a small victory when you're done. Neuroscience shows us that even a short fist pump helps release neurotransmitters including dopamine that help habits stick over time. Strive to be consistent and continually increase the amount of time as much as possible and soon you'll have a reading habit.

Keep a running list of the books you'd like to read next, and you'll never have to think about what to read. Keep track of what you learned by keeping notes or journaling. Smart phones and tablets are great for keeping a lot of books handy, but also keep in mind that they are full of distractions. You may sit down intending to read and find yourself checking email and surfing the web. I use a Kindle Paperwhite when I want to have a lot of books with me, but don't trust myself to focus on reading them. Real books work even better for keeping your attention in one place.

If you're still struggling with reading, you can always use audiobooks. Audible.com and Scribd.com are both great places to get your favorite books in audio format. Audio books are especially good for long commutes, but you can also listen to books while you're doing the dishes or other simple activities. I'm a big fan of audio books, but it can be harder to make sure you're capturing important points in notes.

Action: how many books do you read in a year? If the answer is zero, why not start a reading habit today?

SUMMARY

It's important to get your mindset right so that other things you do will fall in place and you'll be positioned for success. This chapter covered several key topics, including:

- A growth mindset increases engagement and your chance of success. Be open to learning new things, embracing challenges, and taking an active role in your personal and career development.
- The most successful IT leaders have technical competence, but are also great communicators, motivators, and relationship builders. To be an effective leader, focus on developing both your technical skills and soft or business skills.
- To be an effective follower, be a critical thinker and have a high level of engagement and enthusiasm. Effective followers take initiative and are proactive.
- Leaders with integrity make decisions based on what is best for the organization, not themselves. They put the needs of others before their own needs. They show respect and act responsibly, respectfully, and ethically.
- People can relate to grounded leaders. Being genuine, honest, and humble are key components of earning respect.
- Reading is a great way to improve your knowledge and understanding of the world around you. Not only do books help you learn new things, but they also help you gain new perspectives.

REFERENCES AND FURTHER READING

Carr, Nicholas G. *The Shallows: How the Internet Is Changing the Way We Think, Read and Remember.* Atlantic Books, 2010.

Dweck, Carol S. *Mindset: The New Psychology of Success.* Robinson, 2017.

Jha, Amishi P. *Peak Mind 12 Minutes a Day to Find Your Focus, Meet the Challenge and Be Fully Present When It Matters Most.* Piatkus, 2021.

Kelley, Robert. *In Praise of Followers.* Harvard Business Review, 1 Aug. 2014, https://hbr.org/1988/11/in-praise-of-followers.

Kotler, Steven. *The Art of Impossible: A Peak Performance Primer.* HarperCollins, 2021.

McKeown, Greg. *Effortless: Make It Easier to Do What Matters Most.* Currency, 2021.

McKeown, Greg. *Essentialism: The Disciplined Pursuit of Less.* Virgin Books, 2021.

Rosling, Hans, and Anna Rosling. *Factfulness: Ten Reasons We're Wrong about the World - and Why Things Are Better than You Think.* Flatiron Books, 2020.

Chapter 4

IT leadership peak performance

> I often tell leaders that what makes leadership so hard is dealing with people, and people are crazy. And the craziest person a leader has to deal with is themselves...
>
> Jocko Willink

WHAT IS PEAK PERFORMANCE IT LEADERSHIP?

You probably instinctively have a good idea how leadership works. Create clear, prioritized goals, communicate your goals, and then start leading. Leadership is simple, but that doesn't mean it's easy. People have issues. Problems show up in our lives that throw us off track. It could be family drama, health issues, boss problems, or any number of life's other challenges. When a problem shows up and disrupts your leadership rhythm, it can be difficult to get your head back in the game. And when your head isn't in the game, it's going to be hard to lead anyone else.

Even without the outside drama, we screw things up and make mistakes that can throw us off track. Anxiety causes us to mess up an important presentation. Not listening carefully to a colleague causes an argument. Getting lost in thought during a meeting ends in embarrassing moments when someone asks you a question. Peak performance is all about showing up as your best self every day. Some people refer to this as "leading yourself," but that term is over-used and doesn't really catch the spirit of what you need to do as a leader. Peak performance is about bringing your best self to every interaction, every time. It's about being fully present and engaged with what you're doing, no matter if you're leading a team or just living your life.

Peak performance isn't just for athletes, it's for everyone. To achieve peak performance in any field, you need to be both physically and mentally fit. You need to have the right mindset and you need to be able to push yourself when it matters most. But peak performance isn't about working harder. It's about being intentional with your time and zooming in and out from strategic plans to tactical implementation details. To do this, you need a clear vision of what you want and be able to communicate it to your team and motivate them to

DOI: 10.1201/9781003314707-5

act. You also need to be willing to take some risks and experiment a little along the way.

SYSTEMS: THE ALGORITHM OF SUCCESS

> You do not rise to the level of your goals. You fall to the level of your systems.
>
> James Clear

Peak performance requires being efficient and effective with your time and your energy. This means knowing when to push yourself and when to back off. It requires having a clear understanding of your goals and then showing up every day engaged and present to make them happen. You need to be physically and emotionally strong, which means taking care of yourself – getting enough sleep, eating well, and exercising regularly. You also need to have a positive outlook and be mentally tough, which means being able to manage stress, stay calm under pressure, and keep your focus when things get tough. Finally, you need to be able to deal with setbacks and failures and learn from them so you can keep moving forward. Winston Churchill had a great definition of success that incorporated both wins and losses. "Success consists of going from failure to failure without loss of enthusiasm." He also said, "If you're going through hell, keep going." Both quotes show that Churchill understood that success is not always a straight line. There will be plenty of problems along the way, but it's important to keep going and not get discouraged.

Obviously, a big part of success is having clear goals. Without having a goal, you won't have anything to aim for and it will be very difficult to measure progress. But having a clear goal is not enough. You also need to be willing to put in the hard work to make it happen. This is where systems can help. Goals help you focus on a desired outcome. They are important for planning the future, but they do not tell you what you need to do today to get there. Systems focus on what you need to do every day to make progress toward goals. Systems keep you on track and help ensure that your goals will be achievable. Small, consistent steps are the secret to creating big, sustainable changes and making massive progress.

For example, you might have a goal to get in better shape. But instead of just setting the goal, focus on the system that supports the goal. A system is what you need to do every day to make progress toward that goal. Systems can make progress an easy part of your life that you don't need to think about much. A simple system to support getting in better shape might be sleeping in your workout clothes and having your gym bag visible and ready to go every morning. This system might also include creating some exercise routines, so you don't have to waste time deciding what to do in the gym every day. Using systems helps makes almost anything a habit and eventually a routine that becomes part of who you are.

People talk about being consistent, but few of us really are. Showing up as your best self every day is one of the most groundbreaking habits that will not only help your leadership ability but will upgrade every single aspect of your life. Everyone can be consistent when they feel motivated, but you'll need to embrace the fact that most of the days, you're not going to feel motivated and that's okay. We want to be effective and productive, but we aren't robots. It's better to build systems that embraces our laziness and still make it easy to succeed.

Action: design a simple system that helps set you up for success in two simple steps:

1. Identify an important goal or task you want to accomplish.
2. Design a system that either automates the task or makes it easier to succeed.

Here are a few ideas to get you started:

- Automate recurring tasks like bill payments or investing.
- Learn how to script or to use Apple Shortcuts or Windows PowerShell (neither one is that hard!) and automate common tasks like starting and ending your workday. I have a simple script that opens email, Teams, and my other work tools every Monday morning, which gives me the freedom to exit all these tools on the weekend without thinking about it.
- Schedule daily or weekly reviews on your calendar and create a checklist of what a weekly review means to you. I like doing a review every Friday that looks at the past week and what was accomplished as well as the week ahead and what I need to start planning.
- Create a personal productivity system to keep track of your important goals. I like Kanban boards, which can serve as visual reminders of work that's in progress and a view of what's coming up next.

Morning and evening routines

One of the best systems you can put in place to show up as a stronger leader is a morning and evening routine. Developing solid routines will change your life and help you show up more present, engaged, and aware. In his book, *The Miracle Morning: The Not-So-Obvious Secret Guaranteed to Transform Your Life: Before 8AM*, author Hal Elrod states "If you want to achieve your full potential ... the single most important thing that you can do is improve how you start your day." Hal was hit head-on by a drunk driver in a truck traveling 80 mph the wrong way on the highway. He was in a coma for six days and the doctors told him he might never walk again. He used the transformative power of morning routines to completely turn his life around.

Morning and evening routines are important because they help you focus on what's important and set you up for success during the day. When we know what we're going to do each day our brains can enter a state of flow more easily. Flow is a state of peak performance where we are so focused and engaged in what we're doing that time itself seems to disappear.

How do you wake up each day? Do you spring out of bed, ready to tackle the day? Do you slowly ease into your day, taking time to enjoy a cup of coffee? Do you jump right into email? Regardless of how you start your day, it's important to have some sort of routine in place. A morning routine sets the tone for the rest of the day and helps you to be more productive. Just like a musician warms up by practicing scales, a morning routine helps you get yourself ready for the challenges of the day ahead.

What does a good morning routine look like? It varies by individual preferences, but there are a few basic elements to consider.

- **Wake up at the same every day**: this may seem like a no-brainer, but it's important to establish a regular sleep schedule. When you go to bed and wake up at the same time each day, your body naturally falls into a rhythm, and you'll feel more rested. I use Apple Watch to monitor my sleeping habits and you can really see and feel the impact the next day when you didn't get a good night's sleep.
- **Exercise**: taking some time to get your heart rate up and break a sweat is a great way to start your day. Exercise has been shown to improve mood, increase energy levels, and boost productivity. I like doing heavy bag work and TRX suspension training, but I also mix it up on off days by hiking. The important thing is to pick something you like doing so that you'll keep up with it.
- **Journaling**: if you could spend five minutes a day centering yourself, planning your day and setting yourself up for success, would you do it? What if that same exercise improved your mindset and helped you become a better writer at the same time? The benefits of journaling include reflection, emotional release, capturing ideas, and gaining a deeper understanding of yourself. See this book's appendix for some journal prompts if you don't know how to get started.
- **Meditation, breathwork, or contemplation**: consider adding a meditation or mindfulness practice to your morning routine. Taking even a few intentional minutes to connect with yourself first thing in the morning helps you focus on your goals and manage stress. Give yourself permission to do nothing, even for just a few minutes and connect with the miracle of life.
- **Eat a healthy breakfast**: starting your day with a nutritious meal will give you sustained energy throughout the day. Skip the donuts and go for something that includes protein, healthy fats, and complex carbohydrates. I've done intermittent fasting and other methods that claim to improve performance, but my experience is you're best off with a good breakfast that isn't loaded with sugar.

If all this sounds like a lot to get done every day, remember that you can scale up and down as your time allows. My morning routine includes journaling, breathwork, and meditation followed by an intense workout and a cold shower. On rush days when I'm heading to the airport, I can get it all done in 30 minutes. If you can't carve out 30 minutes for yourself, you don't own your time and you're probably just reacting to everything going on around you. See if you could wake up 30 minutes earlier. Doing your morning routine every day is important, but it's also important to find the right routine you can sustain. If you pick something that's too much, it may feel like a burden. But even just a few minutes each day can make a big difference in the lives of those around us when you show up clear-headed and ready to go.

At the end of the day, evening routines can help you to wind down and prepare for a good night's sleep. Too many of us end our days bored and exhausted watching Netflix. This is called passive recovery. Passive recovery means doing something that doesn't require any effort. This compares to active recovery, where light or low-intensity activity helps your body recover from the day's challenges. Just like our muscles need to recover after a hard workout, our brains need it too. A good evening routine helps you release the stress of the day and begin to relax. It's a way of signaling to your body that the day is done and it's time to wind down.

Evening routines don't need to be complicated. Consider incorporating a few elements such as:

- **Unplug from technology**: give yourself some time to disconnect from devices and screens before bed. The blue light from screens disrupts your sleep cycle and makes it harder to fall asleep. It's also critical to unplug from technology when you work from home to help prevent burnout. Checking work email right before bed can also put you in a very bad zone for sleep if you become aware of a problem.
- **Reading**: I already discussed the benefits of reading, and the evening is a great time to do it. Remember that your phone and tablet might not be the best evening devices since the blue light may keep you up at night. Most smartphones now have settings to reduce the blue light on the computer screen. Make the change to "night mode" automatic so you don't have to think about it.
- **Stretching or light exercise**: taking some time to do some gentle stretching or yoga can help to release tension from the body and prepare you for a restful night's sleep. If you want something a little more active, try qigong or tai chi. Qigong is a great way to reduce stress, increase energy, and improve your overall sense of well-being. Tai chi is a bit more challenging, but it has many of the same benefits as qigong. The Shaolin monks from China practice qigong daily. Even badass warrior monks need some form of active recovery.
- **Journaling**: the evening is a great time to reflect on your day. You can journal about your successes, challenges, and gratitude. This is also a great time to set your intentions for tomorrow. I've included some evening routine journal prompts in the appendix of this book.

Morning and evening routines help you to optimize your performance no matter what you're doing. The routines you establish should be based on your own needs and preferences. If you're not a morning person, don't force yourself to wake up at 5 am because you think that's what successful people do. Find what works for you and stick to it. Your routines should be something that you can commit to and something you look forward to. They should make you feel good, not stressed. When you have the right routines in place, your whole day falls into place.

Whatever you do, resist the temptation to work into the night every night. You might think you're getting more done, but you're not. This is the rule of diminishing returns, where more effort results in less progress. Give your brain a break and come back fresh tomorrow. I confess that I still struggle with my evening routine, but I've learned to minimally implement a "pencil's down" time around 8 PM and have also learned to recognize when I'm working harder but getting less done. If I have something that's still in progress and it's getting late, I try to capture exactly where I left off so I can pick up tomorrow at the same spot without any fuss. Then I spend time clearing my mind and I focus on unwinding so that I don't take the problems of the day to bed with me. I'm sure they will all be waiting there for me tomorrow.

Action: do you have a morning and evening routine? It can be hard to establish one if you have kids or a large family but carving out even a little quiet space and making sure that you're getting exercise and clearing mental space will help ensure that you're showing up as a leader and not just reacting to whatever's in your inbox or the crisis of the day.

Action: put down the phone in the evening and turn off the computer. Use do-not-disturb and airplane mode to draw your boundaries. Focus on active recovery activities like reading, exercise, or spending time with your family. If you're used to nonstop phone notifications, this can feel unusual at first. But in time, you'll see how jarring it is to have all those interruptions on in the first place.

MANAGING EMOTIONS

Napoleon's definition of a military genius:

> The man who can do the average thing when everyone else around him is losing his mind.

In her book *My Stroke of Insight*, Jill Bolte Taylor explains that emotions last just 90 seconds, but when we keep fueling them with our thoughts, they can last for 10 or 20 years. As a leader, it's important for you to manage your emotions. The further you progress in your career, the more you will be put in charge of important things. When important things don't go well, you'll need to make sure your emotions don't get the best of you. Decisions made in poor emotional states tend to be universally bad ones. When you learn to control your emotions, you'll be able to stay calm under pressure and make thoughtful decisions from a neutral place.

I'm not suggesting that emotions are unimportant. In fact, positive emotions help you as a leader. For example, feeling excited about a new project helps motivate your team to give their best performance. But watch out for your negative emotions. Anger, frustration, and envy can all lead to destructive behavior. A good leader is aware of their emotions and knows how to manage them. But you should also be aware of the emotions of your team members. If you see someone who seems angry or frustrated, take the time to talk to them and see if there's anything you can do to help.

Eventually, you are going to run into situations that provoke strong emotional responses. Someone else got the promotion. Someone on your team messed up an important project. The boss is mad that you missed a deadline. Everyone has their hot buttons, but at work, there's an expectation that your reaction remains professional. Watch for your own negative emotions including:

- **Frustration**: a project is moving at a glacial pace. Your boss isn't supportive. Your team is arguing among themselves. Frustration can come up at any time. Try to take a step back and understand why you're feeling frustrated before saying or doing something you'll regret. Journaling about your frustration can help you internally process why you feel the way you do while giving you some perspective that whatever it is will eventually pass.
- **Anxiety**: a looming deadline. A presentation you're not prepared for. Anxiety shows up in many ways at work. Anxiety can get out of control if you allow it, which usually makes the problem you were worrying about a self-fulling prophecy. The antidote to anxiety is action. Make a list of what is causing your anxiety and then start taking steps to address each issue. Prioritize problems and then get to work on the most important things. Don't try to do everything, do the most important things.
- **Anger**: of all emotions, anger often provokes the response you're going to regret the most. This is true at work and in our lives. We all get angry and it's normal. But it's important to understand why you're feeling angry before lashing out reactively at someone. If you find yourself getting angry, take some deep breaths and a mindful pause to try and understand the source of your anger. Is it really about the situation or is there something else going on? It's OK to go regroup and come back when you're in a better zone.
- **Aversion**: we all work with people we may not like. If you find yourself in these situations, remember that everyone has different communication styles and experiences. Just because someone rubs you the wrong way, doesn't mean they're a bad person. The antidote to aversion is

compassion. You see a coworker going through a tough time. A customer is upset and taking it out on you. In these situations, it's important to remember that we are all human beings going through our own struggles. A little compassion can go a long way in diffusing a tense situation.

- **Disappointment**: disappointment is a productivity killer. When you suffer a major disappointment, such as shutting down a favorite project or not getting a promotion you've been working toward, it might feel like the whole world is crashing down. Major disappointment can leave you not trying as hard in the future or make you give up altogether. Disappointment can also lead to depression if left unchecked. Recognize that disappointment is temporary and focus on whatever comes next. Find something to get excited about even if it's outside of work. This helps you shift negative thought patterns to more positive ones.

As a leader, it's important to be aware of your emotions and the emotions your team may experience. When negative emotions start to take over, manage them in a way that doesn't impact your productivity or decision-making skills. The best leaders know how to stay in control during a crisis and keep their teams focused on the important things. We all experience strong emotions at some point. The key isn't to ignore them or hope they'll pass, but to take some time to understand your feelings and transform them into something more productive.

STRESS, BURNOUT AND THE MYTH OF WORK-LIFE BALANCE

Work sometimes takes precedence over everything else in our lives, which can be especially true for leaders. But having a harmonious work-life balance is important for our career and for our life. The term "balance" suggests there is some invisible scale between Work and Life buckets. When you hear "work-life balance," you probably imagine having an extremely productive day at work and leaving early to spend the other half of the day with friends and family. This usually isn't plausible, so instead strive for a realistic schedule that prioritizes the important things in your life.

Being out of balance with your values causes stress. Stress is a natural response that comes from difficult situations. But when stress becomes chronic, it leads to health problems and burnout. Burnout starts in the mind. It's a state of mental and physical exhaustion caused by excessive and prolonged stress. It leads to feelings of cynicism, detachment, and hopelessness. The first step to avoiding burnout is to recognize its signs and symptoms. Burnout is real and you shouldn't ignore it. If you're feeling disconnected from your work, like it's never-ending, or that you're just going through the motions, you might be experiencing burnout.

Performing leaders are especially at risk for burnout since they have high-pressure jobs with many responsibilities. They push harder and try harder. As a leader of an information technology (IT) function, you may have to work into the night to fix a critical system problem or be on-call 24/7 in case of an emergency. Remote work means the lines between work and a personal life have become more blurred, making it even harder to disconnect and recharge. Fortunately, there are several things you can do to help prevent burnout and gain some sense of balance in your life:

- **Set boundaries:** set your personal boundaries and stick to them. It's important to have things you enjoy outside of work, so that you don't resent your job. Setting boundaries also means saying no to additional work commitments when you're already feeling overwhelmed. Schedule time for your hobbies and make sure that you have time to spend with your family and friends. This helps you recharge and come back to work feeling refreshed.
- **Take breaks throughout the day:** get up and walk around every hour or so or and take a few minutes to clear your mind. Neuroscience proves that knowledge work benefits from frequent breaks. In addition to physical activity, try to mix up your routine. If you always eat lunch at your desk, try going for a walk or eating lunch somewhere new. I let my Apple Watch remind me to get up every hour and walk around. The whole "close your rings" campaign did a great job of gamifying healthy habits.
- **Delegate:** you can't do everything yourself. If you're feeling overwhelmed, it's time to delegate some of your tasks to your team. This doesn't mean dumping all your work on someone else and hoping for the best. But it does mean finding someone who can help alleviate the workload.
- **Speak up:** when you need help, ask for it. Talk to your manager about what you're experiencing and how you're feeling. They may be able to lighten your workload or give you additional resources to help.

Finally, accept that you can't get everything done. I've given up on concepts like inbox zero, only made me neurotically check my inbox even more than normal. I don't strive for perfect, I just do my best. If you're feeling overwhelmed, take a step back and assess your priorities. What's most important? What can wait? Don't try to do everything at once. I've learned to look at my inbox at the end of the day and ask myself what will have lasting consequences if I don't get to it tonight? The answer is almost always nothing.

Many executives have too much stress simply because they work too long. Recognize that there are diminishing returns that come from overworking. When you work too long, you will feel like you're under constant pressure. While it's good to be dedicated to your job, there are diminishing returns that come from overworking. This means that more effort will not translate to more results and those last few hours will barely be productive at all.

Very few people talk about burnout in the technology industry. In the US, managers sometimes glorify overwork and being constantly busy as a sign of their importance. In Japan, they have a word, Karoshi, which basically translates into "overwork death" or dying at your desk. The more hours worked gets more results strategy isn't sustainable, accurate, or healthy. We need to talk about burnout and the toll it takes on our mental and physical health. Over time it will make you resent your job and possibly your career. Many lawyers and finance professionals quit six or seven figure jobs, citing the time demands, burnout, and lack of freedom as their reasons.

If you're starting to feel burnt out, take a step back and reevaluate your priorities before it becomes overwhelming. Make sure you're taking time for yourself and not letting work consume your entire life. Talk to your boss about your concerns and see if there are ways to lighten your load. See if you can hire more resources. If you're struggling, don't be afraid to ask for help from colleagues or friends. Of course, when your boss is working harder and longer than you are, it can be difficult to have this conversation. But if you're in a leadership position, you want to set the example for your own team. They're not going to take your advice if you're not following it yourself.

Only you can define what makes a good work-life balance. When a parent says "my family is my life" we respect them for it. When someone says, "my work is my life," we get concerned because they only focus on their job. Neither view is wrong. It's your life and it should be a life that includes work but is not defined by it. Find the balance that works best for you and expect to make frequent adjustments as priorities change.

Action: time flies while you're writing replies. The average professional spends 28% of their time responding to email. There are days I feel like email is my only job. How much time do you spend working on email? Email usually reflects other people's priorities. Are you working on your priorities or everyone else's? How could you spend less time reading email and more time getting important work done?

Action: the average executive attends 62 meetings a month. This is only 2–3 per day, which seems optimistic for many of us. Is your calendar so filled with meetings that you don't have time for any other work? Where could you start blocking out time for important tasks like relationship building, career development, innovation, and strategic planning? Google allows their employees to have 20% of their time for projects that are outside of their core role. While 20% might be difficult for you, aim to at least have a few hours a week for development and encourage your team to do the same.

IMPOSTER SYNDROME: TAMING THE INNER CRITIC

Imposter syndrome is a condition where people feel like they aren't good enough or qualified enough to do something or be in a certain job. Harvard Business Review describes impostor syndrome as: "a collection of feelings of inadequacy that persist despite evident success." Imposter syndrome is relatively common in high achievers. High achievers are constantly stretching past their limits and comparing themselves to everyone else. They also go after bigger roles, which can sometimes leave them wondering if they took on more than they can handle.

When I was interviewing for my first security job at Merrill Lynch back in the late 90s, I was the fourth best candidate for the role after an initial phone screen. The hiring manager only wanted to see the top three candidates in person, but at the last minute one of them accepted another offer and I wound up in the interview queue. The recruiter gave me some helpful and honest feedback. I wasn't confident enough. Since I didn't have much security experience, I doubted I would even get the role which stopped me from trying as hard as I should have been. I went to the interview with more confidence, found out that many of my doubts were unfounded, and learned a valuable lesson on how your thoughts can undermine your actions and ultimately your performance.

People think imposter syndrome is more common among women than men. I'm not sure this is true, but I do know that men aren't immune. I was impressed by one of my mentors freely admitting to his whole team that he felt like an imposter in a recent senior business executive meeting. This was someone I really respect who has led teams of hundreds of people. As Chief Information Security Officer (CISOs), we need to act and communicate at the highest levels of the organization. Presenting to the board of directors has become a huge stumbling block for many CISOs. Who wouldn't feel like an imposter sitting around a table that often consists of former CEOs and senior business executives? But senior IT leaders are going to need to deal with senior business executives and eventually you might start feeling a bit out of your league, especially in a large company.

If you are a leader who feels like an imposter, you are not alone. Many successful people feel this way at some point in their lives. The important thing is to not let imposter syndrome hold you back from trying your best. You need to believe in yourself before anyone will believe in you. Overcoming imposter syndrome requires recognizing the thoughts and feelings that contribute to it and reframing them.

A great way to deal with feelings of imposter syndrome is understanding the competence/confidence loop. We all recognize that our success accelerates when we are confident. The simplest way to become more confident in something is to become more competent at it. As we become more competent (skilled), our confidence grows and we get better at what we do. When I started my first security job, I felt like an imposter because I didn't know enough about the subject. But as I learned, I grew confident enough to take on bigger roles and eventually got to the point where I felt confident enough to build programs for Fortune 500 companies and protect a state government as their CISO.

The Confidence-Competence Loop

Image 4.1 The confidence-competence loop works in a self-reinforcing cycle where acting helps develop competence, which leads to better confidence and ultimately leads to better competence.

A key theme in this book is that you can train for anything, and that you get what you train for. You can train your way into being a better speaker, a calmer person, or a more strategic thinker. You can also train your way into being a worrier, a people-pleaser, or a perfectionist. So, if you want to be a better speaker, start by practicing speaking. Get comfortable using your voice and saying what you have to say. If you want to be calmer, start by practicing meditation or mindfulness. And if you want to be more strategic, start by learning how to think through problems and make complex decisions. By training your mind, you can change your life.

You need confidence to lead, but even confidence is a skill you can develop. Competency builds confidence and confidence begins by acting like the person you want to become. If you want to be more confident, start by taking on small tasks and challenges that stretch you outside of your comfort zone. As you accomplish more, your confidence will grow. And as your confidence grows (see Image 4.1), you'll be able to take on bigger challenges and it becomes a virtuous cycle.

Of course, I might be confident in my computer skills, but maybe not so much with my cooking abilities. You don't have to be confident in everything, but no matter the subject, some skill and practice helps. I'm not a great cook, but I've learned a few techniques including knife skills that make cooking more interesting and fun. This means I'll probably do it more, which will also make me more likely to get better at it over time. The great news is this works for any skill from being a better leader to cooking a better dinner.

Action: imposter syndrome is really a confidence issue. But confidence and competence are closely linked. If you're not feeling confident about some aspect of your job, how could you become better versed on the subject? Put together a learning plan and make sure you track it to completion.

DISTRACTIONS WILL MAKE YOU MEDIOCRE

"If you seek tranquillity, do less." Or (more accurately) do what's essential—what the logos of a social being requires, and in the requisite way. Which brings a double satisfaction: to do less, better. Because most of what we say and do is not essential. If you can eliminate it, you'll have more time, and more tranquillity. Ask yourself at every moment, "Is this necessary?" But we need to eliminate unnecessary assumptions as well. To eliminate the unnecessary actions that follow.

Marcus Aurelius
Meditations

Technology leaders are expected not only to lead their team, but also to solve complex problems that don't have straightforward solutions. Showing up with energy, focus, and attention gives you a huge edge over everyone else. Of course, it's not easy being present in a world full of distractions and instant messages, a deluge of email, and wall-to-wall meetings. It's easy to respond reflexively to distractions when you're supposed to be focused on something else.

The cost of distraction is huge. On average, it takes 25 minutes to refocus after an interruption. While you can limit self-imposed interruptions like social media, personal email, and text messages, you can't control everything. If you're in a meeting, and your phone rings, do you answer it? The decision needs to be made quickly, but it's also one that will have an impact on how effective you are. Studies before the pandemic found that even when people were in the office, 60% were not paying attention at any given moment. Some even see meetings themselves as a form of distraction that takes away from getting "real work" done. Yet we still fill up our calendars with back-to-back meetings and the day slips by with very little to show for it.

As a leader you are expected to be at meetings. I used to let my calendar get so full that it was hard to get a bathroom break, much less a lunch break. The problem with this is that it leaves you with no time to do deeper work, which can make you resentful of all the demands on your time. Elon Musk co-founded six companies including electric car maker Tesla, rocket producer SpaceX, and tunneling startup the Boring Company. He's clearly a productive person. He also advised his Tesla staff in a memo that they should "walk out of a meeting or drop off a call as soon as it is obvious you aren't adding value. It is not rude to leave, it is rude to make someone stay and waste their time." It's not about doing more, it's about doing fewer things better. It means making sure that you are focused on the right things and only the right things.

The most effective leaders aren't the ones who spend the most time working. They are the ones who have mastered the art of focus and who work on only the right things. They say no to distractions and demands on their time that don't align with their goals. If you want to be a more effective leader, start by learning to say no to things that distract you from your goals. Doing too much and trying to fit more in every day is stressful and leads to burnout.

Leaders need to do big things, but they don't need to do everything. If you don't focus on the big things, you'll only have small things to show for your effort.

Productivity comes from setting priorities and focusing on the most important thing. Sounds easy, right? Your productivity as a leader has a direct impact on the success of your team. The more you try to do everything yourself, the more you'll get bogged down in the details and the less time you'll have to focus on the important things. Effective leaders are great at their personal productivity, which is how they take on more responsibility without getting overwhelmed. They prioritize their time and energy so they can focus on the most important things. They delegate or push back on the rest. Many of the most productive people also seem to have perfectly healthy personal life outside of work. In fact, productivity is not about the number of hours worked. The eight-hour workday doesn't consider that people have different energy levels at different times of day. It also ignores the reality that most people in office are interrupted many times a day, which makes it hard to get into a flow state where deeper work is possible. In an office setting, many workdays are a mix of low value work like responding to email followed by unnecessary meetings and then being peppered with distractions like instant messages and people stopping by to talk. It's no wonder that people can't seem to get anything done and stress levels are higher than ever.

Take some time to review your personal productivity. Are you working on the right things? Do you have a system for prioritizing your time? Are you being interrupted too often? If you can make some changes to improve your personal productivity, it will have a big impact on your leadership effectiveness. Here are a few things that can help you be more productive and take ownership of your workday.

- **Set specific, achievable priorities for the day**: people who consistently do high value work tend to start each day with a surprisingly short list of tasks. At first glance, it seems like they're not being ambitious or hard working enough. In fact, their superpower is their focus, not the length of their to-do list. When you start your workday with an unreasonable and unachievable list of work, you cripple your ability to make progress because subconsciously you know it can't do it all. Make sure you have no more than three clear priorities for what a successful day looks like for you. This can be small progress on big projects or just knocking out some small, easily achievable tasks. If you have something big going on that day, like a management offsite, that's your priority. Stop pretending you're going to get a lot more than that done for the day.
- **Start with your most important task**: once you know what your priorities are, start with the most important one. This is the task that will have the biggest impact on your day and getting it done will give you a sense of accomplishment and motivation to keep going. In the book, *Eat That Frog!: 21 Great Ways to Stop Procrastinating and Get More*

Done in Less Time, author Brian Tracy discusses some important keys to productivity. The main idea of the book is to focus on the most important task of the day and do it first thing in the morning. The day invariably doesn't go according to plan and this way you've still made some progress.

- **Take breaks:** our bodies have natural cycles that ebb and flow throughout the day. You can use this to your advantage by working in intervals and then taking a break. When I need to work for a long time straight like when I'm writing, I like to use the Pomodoro Technique. I work for 25 minutes of distraction-free work followed by a five-minute break. After four of these cycles, I take a longer break. This helps me stay focused without burning out in the process. There are tons of apps out there that can help you use the Pomodoro Technique. My favorite is Pommie, though there are many others. Alternatively, any old timer will do.
- **Single-tasking, not multi-tasking:** you've heard it before, but if you start single-tasking, it will change your life and your productivity in amazing ways. Multitasking doesn't work, but we keep doing it anyway. We are all guilty. We check chat messages during meetings, reply to email, and we get distracted. Try to do one thing at a time and make it a daily practice. You'll get better at it over time.
- **Have an upper limit on your work hours:** we covered the diminishing returns of overwork, but they deserve to be emphasized. One of the most important things you can do to boost your productivity is to have an upper limit on your working hours and use your newfound free time for activities that help you recover and come back fresh tomorrow.

Distractions are everywhere and they will make you ineffective. As simple as it sounds, having only three priorities for the day and posting it as a note on your monitor can keep you focused. There's no need for complicated apps or other productivity tools and I have tried them all. As technologists, we look for new software to help us, but sometimes a pencil and paper is all you need, and the notes have an advantage of always being visible. It's the simple strategies that are the most effective and sustainable over time.

Action: do a time audit. One of the easiest ways to improve your productivity is by taking unnecessary meetings off the calendar. If necessary, speak up to your boss and let them know which meetings are diverting attention from your more strategic work and see if someone else could cover them. Repeat this process often, meetings have a way of sneaking back in and some may start out as useful and their importance fades over time.

COGNITIVE LOAD AND DECISION FATIGUE

The concept of cognitive load solved a lot of mysteries for me. It helped me understand why we get overwhelmed, why introverts don't like big parties, and why multitasking doesn't work. Cognitive load theory describes the way

Excess cognitive load makes everything harder

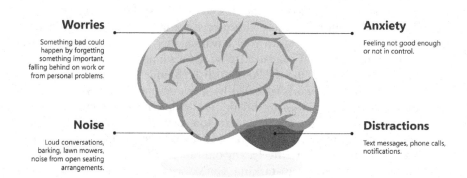

Worries

Something bad could happen by forgetting something important, falling behind on work or from personal problems.

Anxiety

Feeling not good enough or not in control.

Noise

Loud conversations, barking, lawn mowers, noise from open seating arrangements.

Distractions

Text messages, phone calls, notifications.

Image 4.2 Excessive cognitive load hurts performance, impairs learning ability and increases stress as the brain struggles to process too much information at once.

we process information as having three parts: sensory memory, working memory, and long-term memory. You are bombarded with sensory information every day and your brain filters out the most important items to keep in working memory. But this working memory doesn't hold very much, usually only a few thoughts at a time. Think of it like random access memory (RAM) on a computer versus using your brain's long-term storage for memories you can recall later.

Cognitive load theory (see Image 4.2) is built on the premise that the brain can only do so many things at once and therefore we should be intentional about what we ask it to do. If we overload our working memory, we can't process information as efficiently and we are more likely to make mistakes. Cognitive load has important implications on how we learn and how we work and why open seating arrangements can be disastrous for work that requires concentration.

Multitasking is a waste of both time and energy. People think they are great multi-taskers, but we don't really multitask anyway. Instead, we quickly change contexts from one thing to another and then back again. The problem is that the brain has trouble keeping up with the changing contexts and trying to force it to keep up increases your stress. Clifford Nass, a communication professor at Stanford, explains that the more you multitask, the less you're able to learn, concentrate, or even just be nice to people. Yet multitasking has become a norm in society, with people believing that they can do more by doing more things simultaneously. Research shows that multitasking decreases our cognitive ability, stunts our emotional intelligence, stifles our creativity, and makes us ineffective leaders. When we multitask every day, our brain changes its patterns and sustaining attention on any one thing becomes nearly impossible. When we read our email during meetings or try to carry on two conversations at once, we are overloading our working memory and it affects our ability to process that information. I used to be one of those people with two phones to my ear or reading email while someone was trying to talk to me. I never do this anymore and I'm far more productive now than I ever was back then.

Productivity expert David Allen, author of *Getting Things Done* and *Making it all Work*, summarizes the situation as "the mind is for having ideas, not for holding them." Where can you begin to free up cognitive load in your life? I like to get organized using David's "capture" process where you get anything and everything that has your attention out of your head and into a single place. This starts the process of clarifying and focusing your priorities.

In *How to Focus*, Zen master Thich Nhat Hanh says "Intellectually we know we should live in the present moment. Yet we're always being pushed by our habit energy of rushing around. We've lost our capacity to be in the present moment. This is why practicing mindfulness and concentration is so important; talking and reading about it is not enough." Being more present at work is being more present in life. Lower your cognitive load by clearing your head, reducing or eliminating distractions, and doing one thing at a time can perform miracles not only at work, but everywhere in your life. So many technologists work with two or more monitors and with tons of windows and system processes running. Just like a computer that's running spyware, our minds go into unproductive thought loops that burn energy and take away from more important tasks.

It turns out that making decisions also requires a lot of energy. A study of over 1,100 cases looked at judge's decisions and found that at the beginning of the day a judge was more likely to rule in the criminal's favor, but this likelihood steadily decreases as the day goes on. It didn't matter what the crime was. In the beginning of the day, there was a 65% chance of a favorable ruling, a number which fell close to zero as the morning progressed and then jumped up to 65% again after a lunch break. By the end of the day, it was back to zero. Judges weigh a lot of information and make difficult decisions all day, so it's not surprising that they get tired as the day goes on. This is called decision fatigue.

Decision fatigue is related to cognitive load in that making decisions can be exhausting and cause people to feel overwhelmed if there are too many decisions to make. The idea is that after making too many decisions, your ability to make more decisions gets worse as the day progresses. In other words, the more decisions you make, the harder it will be to keep making good decisions.

Silicon Valley has known about decision fatigue forever. Steve Jobs used to wear the same outfit every day to reduce decision fatigue. Mark Zuckerberg and many other highly successful people wear similar outfits every day to limit their decision fatigue. But it's not just making a decision that can be draining. Letting decisions linger for too long also creates cognitive overhead. You spend both conscious and unconscious energy ("background processing") thinking about something rather than freeing up your mental energy to concentrate on the present moment.

Many people think that time is our scarcest resource, but it's really energy. Everyone gets 24 hours a day, but our energy wanes when we use it poorly. When we work our brain too hard by multitasking and making too many decisions, we need to give our brains a rest and recover. We are only starting to understand how the brain works and I'm sure we will learn much more about how we process information over time. Until then, make sure that you're working in a way that optimizes your time and energy by focusing on one thing at a time, making fewer unnecessary decisions and taking more breaks.

Action: do a simple experiment and try to listen to an audiobook or podcast while you're reading an email. You'll be surprised at how much harder it is to pay attention to either one in any meaningful way. This is the difference between hearing and listening. Sometimes we hear that someone said something, but if we're distracted, we may not be able to process what they said. If you've ever tried to have a conversation with someone absorbed in using their smartphone, you'll know exactly what I mean.

Action: where can you reduce your cognitive load and free up your working memory to solve bigger problems? Music with lyrics, other people's conversations, and multitasking can all strain your working memory and reduce your effectiveness. Where can you start living your life in full screen mode?

THE PATH TO PEAK PERFORMANCE DOESN'T END

> Over more than 300 years of history, the only predictable factor that drives individual earnings potential is skills and knowledge.
>
> Economist Thomas Picketty

The path to peak performance never ends. No matter how successful you become, there will always be room to improve. Circumstances change, people change, and what worked once may not work in the future. Instead of making drastic changes in the hopes of achieving perfection, try making small, incremental daily improvements. This practice is called Kaizen and it was developed by American businessmen to build new armament factories for World War II before it was introduced in Japan. Just like an athlete who stops training, peak performance skills erode without practice. There are a lot of difficult topics to master in this chapter, but if there was only one thing that you could do starting today that would help with all of them, it would be establishing a consistent meditation or mindfulness practice.

In his book *Tribe of Mentors*, Tim Ferriss interviewed hundreds of successful people, including Arianna Huffington and Ray Dalio. Tim was searching for what some of the world's most successful people attributed to their success. Ray Dalio, founder, chair, and co-Chief Investment Officer at Bridgewater Associates (the largest hedge fund in the world), cites meditation as "*one of the best or most worthwhile investments"* he ever made. In fact, 80% of the people interviewed by Ferriss appeared to have some sort of meditation or mindfulness practice. This makes absolute sense if you see the ability to focus and own your attention as a prerequisite for being successful. The most successful people in the world seem to take active steps to quiet their mind rather than leaving it to chance.

Meditation helps you take a step back and realize that you are not your thoughts. It helps you gain new perspectives on stressful situations, increases your general self-awareness and empathy, and helps you focus on the present moment. Meditation has been practiced for thousands of years. It was originally intended as a spiritual development tool, but these days, it is commonly used for relaxation and stress reduction. And who couldn't use more of that?

Of course, not every meditation leads to a blissful or mystical state. Just know that there are no good or bad meditation sessions and that being consistent will always be more effective than if you do it now and then. You'll also build grit and discipline when you sit through difficult emotions and thoughts. Meditation is a process of getting to know yourself on a much deeper level. You won't feel like doing it most days, you'll be too angry some days, too excited, too bored, too overwhelmed with work. Sit anyway and see how your mind operates. Bonus: once you get insight on how your own mind works, you'll understand why everyone else behaves the way they do, which helps you build empathy.

There are plenty of great books, courses, and apps that teach meditation as well as many free guided meditations online. There are also many forms of meditation, so pick whatever works best for you. Guided meditations include apps like Calm and Headspace. There are also mantra-based meditation techniques like Transcendental Meditation®. If you're simply not the type of person who can sit still, you might try some form of moving meditation like walking meditation, yoga, or qigong. Sitting still and doing nothing turns out to be one of the hardest things we can do.

A simple breath awareness meditation is included in the appendix of this book.

SUMMARY

This chapter is intended to encourage you to show up as a leader by establishing practices that will help you excel. The most important thing is maintaining a growth mindset, which sets you up for success. A growth mindset is where you believe that almost any change is possible. This is an important concept that holds many people back and keeps people from trying in the first place.

- Leading yourself is one of the hardest aspects of leadership. Showing up as your best self every day, managing stress, and avoiding burnout are all important skills that can be practiced.

- Emotions will come up at work. Make sure that you're managing them and not letting them impact your team or your performance. We remember the leaders who didn't lose their cool under stress as well as the ones who did. Who would you rather be? Regulating your emotions allows you to act from a more neutral state where you can make better decisions.
- Imposter syndrome is a common condition where people feel like they are not good enough. Overcoming imposter syndrome requires recognizing the thoughts and feelings that contribute to it and then reframing them.
- Disconnecting from the workday is easier with a wind-down routine. The extra hours in the evening generally provide diminishing returns with an increased chance of burnout or resentment of the job.
- Showing up as your best self every day sets both you and your team up for success. Making the time to ensure you're not overworking, overstressed, or overdistracted at work is an important part of showing up as your best self every day.
- Peak performance doesn't mean trying to do everything. In fact, it means you do fewer, but more important things.
- Overworking increases the chances of making a mistake and it will take longer to finish simple tasks. Fortunately, an abundance of productivity advice boils down to a few key themes: take care of yourself physically and mentally, set the right priorities, stay focused on them. Delegate or say no to everything else.

REFERENCES AND FURTHER READING

Allen, David. *Getting Things Done*. Penguin Publishing Group, 2015.

Collins, James C. *Good to Great*. Harper Business, 2001.

Elrod, Hal. *The Miracle Morning: The Not-so-Obvious Secret Guaranteed to Transform Your Life before 8AM*. Hal Elrod International, 2019.

Eyal, Nir, and Julie Li-Eyal. *Indistractable: How to Control Your Attention and Choose Your Life*. Bloomsbury Publishing, 2020.

(ILT), Hanh, Thich Nhat/Deantonis, Jason. *How to Focus*. Random House Inc., 2022.

Kotler, Steven, and Jamie Wheal. *Stealing Fire: How Silicon Valley, the Navy Seals, and Maverick Scientists Are Revolutionizing the Way We Live and Work*. Dey St., 2018.

Kotler, Steven. *The Art of Impossible: A Peak Performance Primer*. HarperCollins, 2021.

Meier, J. D. *Getting Results the Agile Way: A Personal Results System for Work and Life*. Innovation Playhouse, 2010.

Sapolsky, Robert M. *Behave: The Biology of Humans at Our Best and Worst*. Penguin Books, 2018.

Sullivan, Dan, and Benjamin Hardy. *Who Not How: The Formula to Achieve Bigger Goals through Accelerating Teamwork*. Hay House Inc., 2020.

Tracy, Brian. *Eat That Frog!* Berrett-Koehler Publishers, 2017.

Part II

Leadership in action

At this point in the book, you should understand that you've never "made it" as a leader and that leadership development is a continuous process. You should also understand that improvement is possible when you have a growth mindset and that if you're going to be better than average, you'll need to work harder than average. You should also understand the importance of peak performance in terms of your general health and well-being, your mental health, and your personal productivity systems.

The next section of this book takes these skills back to the office. Far too many leadership books serve as pep talks or offer theoretical techniques that seem to work better on paper than they do in the real world. Leadership takes practice and refinement. Leadership has more to do with what you do every day than it is about acquiring more knowledge about leadership. This is why believing that there might be some sort of degree or certificate program to make great leaders is faulty reasoning.

The rest of this book takes the foundational elements from part I and applies them to leading teams and getting things done. This section examines topics including orienting yourself in a new role, defining a strategy, and executing that strategy by building a high-performance team. Finally, it looks at the future of work and what will continue to drive change in the technology industry.

Before we get into the business of leading people, it's worth exploring two more concepts: volatile, uncertain, complex, and ambiguous (VUCA) and the OODA loop. Let's begin by trying to understand the world through the lens of the VUCA framework.

LIVING IN A VUCA WORLD

The world is messy. Work is messy. High-flying tech stocks have come down to earth and the white-hot tech job market has turned into layoffs in a period of only a few months. It may change two more times by the time this book is published. The United States and other global economies are on the brink of recession. COVID, war with Russia in the Ukraine, inflation, recession supply chain, and other issues promise to keep the world a volatile place for the foreseeable future. This makes for an uncertain world that is difficult to

DOI: 10.1201/9781003314707-6

The VUCA World

- Volatility
- Uncertainty
- Complexity
- Ambiguity

Image II.1 Understanding VUCA helps leaders navigate rapidly changing business environments and make informed decisions in the face of ambiguity and uncertainty.

predict or even understand. This is our VUCA world (see Image II.1). VUCA is an acronym that stands for volatile, uncertain, complex, and ambiguous.

Change is certain, but we live in an age where the speed of change and the number of factors that can initiate change are unprecedented. How are you supposed to lead in such an unpredictable world? The first step is to acknowledge you can't understand or predict everything that's going to happen and that change isn't always going to be in your favor. If you're going to navigate this environment, you need to be flexible, adaptable, and comfortable with ambiguity. You need to have a clear vision for what you want to achieve and adapt to change when things don't go as planned.

Understanding the concept of VUCA will help you navigate change and develop leadership agility. It will also help you develop a flexible perspective toward change. You'll learn to see change as just change, neither good nor bad and always with lessons to be learned. Eventually, you may even learn to see the opportunity in change. And there is always opportunity with change.

Let's break down each component of VUCA:

- **Volatile**: change is rapid and unpredictable. Change can be sudden and dramatic, or it can be gradual. Change can be due to geopolitical factors, economic conditions, or it could be a technology change such as the move toward cloud computing which has left many people wondering if the concept of the corporate data center is dead.
- **Uncertain**: the future is uncertain. You can't always predict what will happen next and surprises will spring up that you never saw coming. Hurricanes, war, 9/11, financial crises ... this is the age of the Black Swan event, and the future is always in flux.
- **Complex**: the world is increasingly complex and interconnected. Problems with a third-party suppliers can have devastating consequences on a business. The world chip shortage brought automobile production to a standstill and delayed product launches.
- **Ambiguous**: information is everywhere, but insights are hard to find. Information is usually incomplete or even contradictory. We live in the age of misinformation and fake news. It can be difficult to understand what is happening and why and what it all means.

Making decisions with incomplete information in the face of uncertainty and adapting as circumstances change is an approach not taught in many business schools. Instead, we're taught to plan thoroughly. We're taught not to fail. We're taught to do our research and not act unless the facts support our conclusions. The methods are slow but safe. The problem is that the world moves at a much faster pace now. In 1965, the average life of companies on the S&P 500 was 33 years. By 1990, it was down to 20 years as companies became more short-term focused. By 2026, it's expected to shrink to 14 years as the business landscape continues to evolve. At this rate, half of the S&P 500 may be replaced over the next 10 years by businesses that don't even yet exist yet. We need to consider more agile approaches that change as the world changes around us.

Effective leaders attack VUCA; they don't wait. They expect to fail and iterate, but they get started, which is key. Leaders who wait for VUCA to disappear before they act are only exacerbating the problem. Acting in the face of VUCA helps you gain information more quickly and make more productive decisions based on reality and what's working. Believing that things will eventually get clearer is only setting yourself up for disappointment. When you're able to accept that volatility, uncertainty, complexity, and ambiguity are constant factors, you can operate as if they were business as usual. Doing so helps you get information more quickly and make better decisions under pressure because decisions don't need to be perfect.

Change can be difficult, but it doesn't have to be scary. Understanding the concept of VUCA helps you to be better prepared for change and can help you to develop an agile and adaptable management style. If you're wondering how to navigate change and uncertainty, the best approach to a VUCA world is the OODA loop.

THE OODA LOOP: THE ROSETTA STONE FOR LEADERSHIP AGILITY

To survive and thrive in the VUCA world, you need a decision-making process that is both efficient and effective. The OODA loop provides such a process. The OODA loop is a learning system and is an amazing framework for dealing with uncertainty. The OODA loop helps you deal with changing and challenging circumstances and still come out on top by constantly re-orienting to new realities and new information. The OODA loop consists of a series of actions observing, orienting, deciding, and acting in a continuous cycle. It was developed by military strategist and United States Air Force Colonel John Boyd. It in an incredible tool when you take some time to understand it properly. The model was based on the observation that smaller, seemingly less capable aircraft were able to outmaneuver what should have been superior competition.

The OODA proposes that to achieve a goal, an individual must constantly be reevaluating and redefining their perspective. One should be constantly creating and destroying their view of the world and re-orienting to new

The OODA Loop

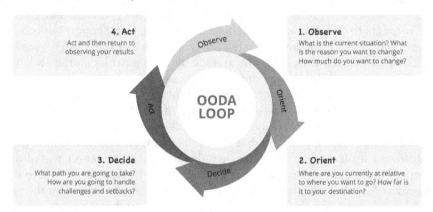

Image II.2 The OODA loop, consisting of Observe, Orient, Decide, and Act, can aid in navigating complex situations by facilitating agile decision-making through continuous feedback and iteration.

realities as things change. The OODA loop (see Image II.2) is the key to leadership agility and agility in just about any situation. Let's examine how it works in practice.

In the observing phase, you take in information around you. Observe people, behavior, and any other inputs. During this phase, more information is better as it will help with the next phase: orienting. During the orienting phase, you start to make sense of what you observed. Use experience and mental models to interpret data from the previous phase and start to see the patterns. Next, find the best action based on the information gathered in the first two phases. Next, you act on your decision. Many people who have heard about OODA loop often miss the next step, which is to go back and observe the results of your actions and iterate through the loop again and again.

The OODA loop is often misunderstood or oversimplified. The four steps are often taught as if they are linear, when in fact they are not. The loop is meant to be a continuous process, with each step feeding into the next. A few keys to getting the OODA loop right include:

1. **Understanding you will never have complete data.** In the observation phase, you are probably looking at incomplete or imperfect information. You might even have too much information to process. This is where judgement is important. Don't get stuck continually looking for more or perfect data. When you see the patterns emerge, you can move on to the next phase. When you get paralyzed looking for more data, you won't make decisions and ultimately won't act. This is called analysis paralysis. Do the best you can with the data you have at the time. Don't wait for 100% certainty, when 80% certainty is likely more than good enough. Errors can be dealt with later in the cycle if your initial hypothesis was wrong.

2. **Orient properly.** Orienting is the most important phase of the OODA loop. Orientation shapes decisions and actions for the rest of the loop, which influences future iterations. Orienting correctly compounds positively, while orienting incorrectly compounds negatively. Successful orientation means seeing things exactly as they are and then acting on correct information. Unsuccessful orientation is when your biases and ego get in the way, and you see only what you want to see. Orienting incorrectly is like doubling down on a bad bet.

3. **Iteration in a continuous cycle.** Remember that OODA is a *loop*, not an end-to-end process. When you act on your decisions, go back and observe the impact of your actions and start the whole process over again. The faster you can iterate an OODA loop, the faster you can make progress even in the absence of perfect information. According to Boyd, the ability to orient effectively and quickly is what separated the winners from losers in a battle. Faster decisions led to faster actions, which led to faster victory.

When you're continuously re-orienting yourself, you won't cling to solutions that don't work anymore. The OODA loop is an amazing tool, but you do need to use it properly. When we fail to observe properly, we don't see problems that are right in front of our face. We might have plenty of information, but we become paralyzed with indecision. We might decide something, but then fail to act on that decision or act too slowly and miss the opportunity. Finally, when we act but fail to observe the consequences of our actions, we fail to see the impact of a wrong decision until it is too late.

The OODA loop is a powerful tool for managing uncertainty and ambiguity. It helps us to orient quickly and act in response to changing circumstances. The OODA loop helps you get busy when everyone else is only thinking about where to start.

Action: while the OODA loop is good for many situations, I enjoy using it to keep up with my busiest days. This doesn't need to be a long process. Try the following exercise and see if it works for you.

- **Observe**: what's coming up on your calendar including several days ahead? Do you need to do anything to get ready? Is there anything critical in your inbox that needs immediate attention?
- **Orient**: what absolutely needs to be done today? What's high priority, or urgent and important?
- **Decide**: what is the best thing you could do right now? Helpful hint: keep your cognitive load low by picking *only* one thing. Don't let a long list distract you from the item you pick. In other words, keep the most important thing the most important thing.
- **Act**: get back to work. Nothing happens without action. Give the task your full attention. And when that urgent call from your boss comes? It's probably time to start the loop all over again.

SUMMARY

- Life is VUCA. Information technology (IT) leaders need to be agile and adaptable to navigate through these changes. Embrace change and learn to see the opportunity in the chaos.
- The OODA loop is a decision-making process that helps leaders quickly orient themselves to new situations and make decisions in the face of uncertainty. The loop never ends, which allows leaders to continually refine their decisions. The key to success with the OODA loop is keeping the loop going, continuously refining your decisions in the face of new information and observations.
- No company is immune to change. Leaders should embrace change and use it to their advantage by being open to new ideas, trying new things, and taking new risks.

REFERENCES AND FURTHER READING

Coram, Robert. *Boyd: The Fighter Pilot Who Changed the Art of War*. Back Bay Books/Little, Brown, 2004.

Ferriss, Timothy. *Tribe of Mentors*. Houghton Mifflin Harcourt, 2017.

McKay, Brett, and Kate McKay. "The Tao of Boyd: How to Master the OODA Loop." *The Art of Manliness*, 2021, https://www.artofmanliness.com/character/behavior/ooda-loop/.

Chapter 5

Starting a new job
How to thrive

The average person stays with their employer for about four years. For workers between ages 25 and 34, the median tenure is just over three years. This means that at some point in your career, you are likely to be switching employers yourself, even if you're happy where you are right now. People on your team are also likely to come and go. This is the new reality. Companies no longer offer lifetime employment (if they ever really did) and employees have taken note.

Starting a new role always brings some anxiety. You may have to travel more or work longer hours. You should be prepared for those changes and try to manage your expectations so that you're not caught off guard. If your new role is a promotion at the same company, this can be a big change too. You may have more responsibilities, a new team to manage, and a new boss. Even simple promotions at the same company can come with their own unique set of challenges, such as managing a former peer.

Starting a new role is a cause for celebration. You may feel sad about leaving the comfort and safety of what's familiar, but new opportunities are exciting and full of promise. There will always be positives and negatives with any big change. You might be excited about the new challenges and opportunities, but on the other hand, you may feel nervous about leaving your comfort zone making a good first impression. You may also have some doubt that you made the right decision. Take the time to process your feelings and remember that embracing change is an important part of personal growth.

BEFORE YOUR FIRST DAY AT A NEW JOB

If possible, I recommend taking some time off before starting a new role. Going from one company to another over a weekend is exhausting. So is winding down an old position and saying goodbye to friends and colleagues. Taking time off before your new job starts helps you prepare, clear your mind, and be ready for the new role to begin. Of course, you should be aware of any health insurance implications, so you don't wind up with any unpleasant surprises.

DOI: 10.1201/9781003314707-7

Relocation comes with a host of other issues and challenges. While paid relocation seems to be on the decline, it's still offered by some companies as an incentive to attract top talent. If you're relocating for your job, be prepared for some bumps in the road and all the stress that can come with moving. It's also a good idea to get an idea of the commute from your potential home to the office. If you have children, you'll need to research schools in the area. And if you're moving from a small town to a big city, get a feel for the neighborhoods that would be best for you. If you already know someone from the company, now might be a good time to take them out to lunch.

Don't underestimate the stress introduced from changing jobs or starting a new role. I've had more than ten company changes in my career and a few of those included changing industries. If you're feeling anxious or stressed about an upcoming job change, it's perfectly normal. Don't try to bottle up your emotions or tell yourself that you shouldn't feel anxious or stressed. Acknowledging your feelings can help you deal with them in a healthy way.

YOUR FIRST WEEK ON THE JOB

You walk into your new job on your first day and don't know what to expect but you're ready. You've prepared yourself as best you can, but there are always surprises. You take a deep breath and step into the unknown. You're introduced to your team and shown to your desk. You sit down and look around. Everyone seems friendly enough, but you can tell that they're all busy with their own work. You're not sure how well you're going to fit in this new environment, but you're eager to get going and make an impression. Those first few days in a larger company are mostly spent just getting orientated and gaining access to systems. You'll have a lot of reading, training, and paperwork to do. There are lots of new names and faces to remember. Of course, if you were hired directly into a remote role, your onboarding experience might be very different.

You spend the first few hours getting to know your team, your boss, and your new surroundings if your job is in an office. It's a lot of information to take in, but you know you're up for the challenge. By the end of the day, you're exhausted. At this point, you're either excited and can't wait to see what tomorrow brings or you're anxious to know if you made the right decision. Maybe both. Either way congratulations, you made it through your first day!

I remember starting a senior role at a large bank. On my first day, I found out that my position had been replaced annually for several years running. People greeted me with a universal "good luck!" and I admit I was a bit nervous that there seemed to be such a high body count that had come before me. It took me months to realize that it was due to a combination of leaders with insufficient technical background and basic inability to get things done in a large organization. There were also a high number of audit issues that already had my name on it, so clearly expectations were high. Ultimately, I was successful in the role, but it gave me a lot to worry about in those first few weeks.

You probably won't get a lot done in your first week on the job other than basic relationship building and access to systems and that's OK. It usually takes a few weeks to get into a rhythm, iron out systems access issues, and start meeting people outside your team. Obviously smaller companies take less time to get organized. Take your time, be patient, and you'll get there. It's normal to feel a little bit lost at first. Just know that things will start to make sense eventually.

Starting a new job may not be a true VUCA activity, which as you'll recall stands for volatile, uncertain, complex and ambiguous. But starting a new job comes with enough uncertainty and ambiguity that the observe, orient, decide, act (OODA) loop can be helpful. In the example of starting a new job, your OODA loop might look something like:

1. **Observe**: take in as much information as possible. For example, you might want to take some time to observe how your team interacts with each other. You'll want to notice the little things that might not be immediately obvious. How do people dress and speak to each other? What's the morale like? All these things give you clues as to how you will need to operate to get things done. While the OODA loop is iterative, in the first few days, you'll want to mostly observe and orient and refrain from making too many decisions or taking too many actions. Leaders who come in eager to make immediate changes and prove their value are often unsuccessful because they haven't had enough time to properly orient themselves to make the right decisions.

2. **Orient**: orientation is a gradual process when you're starting somewhere new. You might be able to orient on small things like where the coffee machine is and if you're lucky you might orient on bigger things like understanding the company's business model and the basics of the culture. Get a feel for what your day-to-day work schedule will be like. Start to understand what is expected of you in your role and answer some questions. What does this company do? How does it make money? Who are its customers? What are its core values? The more information you have, the better equipped you will be to make decisions later.

3. **Decide**: once you've gathered enough information, you can begin making some simple decisions. You'll need to use judgement to decide what's the best course of action but remember that there may be more than one right answer. Try to make the best decisions you can with the information you have. The bigger the decision, the more you want to make sure that you're properly oriented first. Remember, orienting compounds positively in future decisions but orienting poorly compounds negatively and can send you off track quickly.

4. Act: this is where you put your decisions into action and start getting things done. Don't be afraid to ask for help when you need it and lean on peers, mentors, and your team. Nobody expects you to know everything, so don't be afraid to ask questions along the way in case you need to make course corrections.

5. Iterate: OODA is an iterative framework, which means that after you act you need to go back to the observation phase and start the process all over again. Leaders who don't check the results of their actions are tone deaf until things go wrong, and by then course correction can be difficult. If you see problems with a decision or action, try a different approach and keep iterating until you get it right. The goal is to learn and grow from your experiences as quickly as possible.

There it is, the OODA loop in action. Use it to help navigate your first week in your new role and deal with all the uncertainty. Remember, the key is to act and then use feedback to improve your future decisions. The goal is to get into a virtuous cycle where you're quickly making decisions, acting, and doing it over again. The more you do this, the faster you'll be on solid ground making progress.

The OODA loop is a decision-making framework, not a leadership style. You can use it regardless of your leadership style or philosophy. The key is to use it in a way that works for you and your team. If you're too aggressive, you'll end up micromanaging your team or being perceived as domineering. If you're too passive, your team will lose faith in your leadership and ability to make decisions. Even after you feel settled in your role, never lose sight of the big picture. Leaders who don't monitor their progress and adjust as necessary will be caught off guard eventually.

YOUR FIRST 90 DAYS MATTER, BUT NOT AS MUCH AS YOU THINK

There's a lot of emphasis on the first 90 or 100 days of a new job for good reason. Those first few months can set the tone for the rest of your time with the company. This is especially true for senior leadership roles that come with high expectations. The traits you demonstrate during the first few months will either build trust and confidence or create an environment of skepticism that you're the right person for the job. You want to hit the ground running, learn about your new job quickly, make some initial decisions, and start executing on your vision for the role – all while getting to know your team and starting to build relationships (see Image 5.1).

In the book *Master Your Next Move: The Essential Companion to The First 90 Days*, author Michael D. Watkins explores eight typical career transitions and their challenges. Watkins' framework for transitioning to a new role includes negotiating success, achieving alignment, building your team, securing early wins, creating alliances, and managing yourself.

Simple 90-Day Plan Objectives

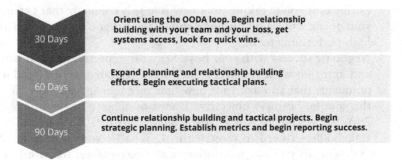

30 Days	Orient using the OODA loop. Begin relationship building with your team and your boss, get systems access, look for quick wins.
60 Days	Expand planning and relationship building efforts. Begin executing tactical plans.
90 Days	Continue relationship building and tactical projects. Begin strategic planning. Establish metrics and begin reporting success.

Having a plan to hit the ground running will help you
gain momentum for your next 90 days and beyond.

Image 5.1 Having a 90-day plan allows you to establish clear goals, build relationships, identify potential challenges and establish credibility.

Transitioning to a new role can be a difficult process but following his process can help make it easier. Let's look at each step.

1. **Accelerate your learning.** Learn as much as possible about the new role and its challenges. Watkins advocates asking lots of questions, reading relevant materials, and talking to people in similar roles. One way to keep track of all this is to create a "learning board" with three columns: what you need to learn (questions), where you will get your answers (resources), and your timeline for completing each item (**see Image 5.2**).

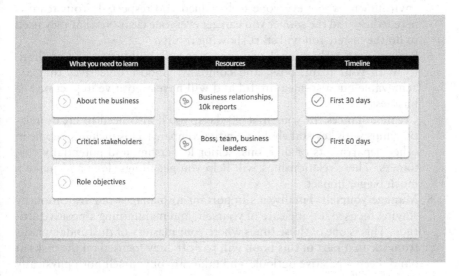

What you need to learn	Resources	Timeline
About the business	Business relationships, 10k reports	First 30 days
Critical stakeholders	Boss, team, business leaders	First 60 days
Role objectives		

Image 5.2 Creating a learning board can help you stay organized when you're starting a new job.

2. **Match your strategy to the situation.** There are right and wrong ways to approach a transition, so find an approach that works for you. For example, if you're taking on a new role in a company that's struggling, your focus will be on different things than if you're joining an already high-performing team.

3. **Negotiate success with your boss.** Set clear expectations with your boss and agree on what resources you'll have available to you. Watkins recommends that you ask your new manager four questions: 1. What are the specific business objectives I need to achieve in the first 90 days? 2. What resources will I have available to me? 3. Who are the key stakeholders I need to meet with? 4. What is your management style and how do you like to communicate? Remember, the word "negotiate." Objectives and criteria should be mutually agreed on, and if you feel expectations are unreasonable, now is a great time to help reset those expectations. Chief Information Security Officers (CISOs), Chief Information Officers (CIOs), and other senior roles are often set up to fail from the start because management expectations and available resources are completely out of sync.

4. **Achieve alignment.** Once you set clear expectations with your boss, it's time to start aligning your team with these goals. Creating a shared vision, setting priorities, and building trust are great starting points. You want to make sure that everyone understands the objectives and why they're important.

5. **Build your team.** One of the most important things you can do in your first 90 days is to build your team. If you need to hire, start the process since this takes time. But you also want to use the team you have wisely by delegating effectively and providing clear direction. Create a positive environment where everyone feels valued and respected. Your team is here to help and the sooner you can get everyone clear on what they need to do the faster, you will start showing results.

6. **Secure some early wins.** Early successes help build trust and credibility with your team, boss, and company. Choose objectives that are achievable but also meaningful and will have a positive impact on the business.

7. **Create alliances.** In your first 90 days, you'll also need to create relationships with key stakeholders in the company. This includes people in other departments or divisions, senior leadership, and potentially customers. These relationships will help you get things done and make a much bigger impact.

8. **Manage yourself.** Finally, it's important to manage your transition by staying focused, taking care of yourself, and maintaining a positive attitude. This is one of those times where your mastery of the fundamentals from the first part of this book will pay off. Stay focused on the tasks at hand, keep a positive outlook, and take care of yourself both physically and mentally.

Make sure you plan out your first 90–100 days carefully. It's important to be realistic about what you can achieve in this period. Many people stress themselves out over a new job because they put far too much pressure to perform right from day one. Focus on a few things that will have a meaningful impact. Your new boss probably doesn't want you jumping in and solving big problems right away because you're likely to ruffle feathers and do more harm than good. Your first few moves should be weighed carefully. The size of your company, team, and the authority of your role will also influence what you can get done in 90 days. You don't want to come in like a bull in a China shop and try to change everything without properly orienting yourself. You'll make an impression but won't be the one you want.

Transitioning to a new role can be stressful, but with a little effort and planning things will go easier. Learn as much as possible about the new role, set clear expectations with your new manager, focus on a strong team, and you'll be on your way to success quickly. Remember to stay focused and positive throughout the transition process and lean back on your mastery of the fundamentals from the first part of the book to help manage stress.

Action: if you are starting a new role, what challenges do you anticipate? How can you use the eight-step process outlined above to be ready?

PRIORITIZE RELATIONSHIP BUILDING

Strong relationships make it easier to communicate effectively, which is essential when trying to solve problems or make decisions (see Image 5.3). Relationships create a positive work environment, which encourages employees to be more productive and engaged. Relationships are also how you will get information

Relationships are critical

No matter if it's your boss, your team or your colleagues: your relationships matter.

Lead by example

Listen more than you talk

Value input and opinions from others

Image 5.3 Relationships are important to technology leaders because they facilitate collaboration, build trust, and foster innovation, all of which are critical to driving success.

and build a strong network of people who can support and help you in your career and in the efforts that you lead.

Effective leaders focus on building relationships right away with their boss, their colleagues, and their team. Humans are naturally social creatures and good relationships with colleagues also make our jobs more enjoyable. But a good work relationship requires trust, respect, self-awareness, inclusion, and open communication. These characteristics are essential for working together effectively and for finding solutions based on collaborative insight. Relationships also help make sure that cross-functional projects stay on track.

Relationship skills are critical in the workplace. Good relationships allow for a leader to bring a team together and get a project accomplished. However, collaboration is only an effective workplace tool if the people who are collaborating can get along with each other. Don't wait until there's a need or a crisis. Relationships are best made under casual and relaxed circumstances. Here are five points to remember as you start building your relationships at work.

1. **Get to know people as individuals**: if you can, take the time to get to know your colleagues on a personal level. What are their interests? What motivates them? What are their strengths and weaknesses? The better you know your colleagues and your team, the easier it will be to work together in the future. If you want others to trust you, start by being vulnerable and sharing something personal about yourself first.

2. **Be inclusive**: it's easy to get caught up trying to impress senior stakeholders and neglect your more junior colleagues. Remember that everyone on your team is important and that a good reputation is built across all levels of the organization regardless of reporting lines. Lower your cognitive load by treating everyone with the same level of respect and you can stop thinking about who's going to get you ahead or not. As a bonus, you'll start seeing the potential in people who may become future leaders.

3. **Be seen**: it's hard for people to engage with you if they don't know who you are. Attend meetings prepared and be willing to share ideas. If you're working remotely, make sure to have your camera on, especially early on in your tenure. This way people can get to know you better and put a name to the face.

4. **Be proactive**: when you join a new team, your colleagues will be keen to see what you can deliver. Offer your knowledge and experience to group challenges and find ways to help. Just be careful about overcommitting and spreading yourself too thin, as this leads us to the next item: follow-through.

5. **Follow through**: a lack of follow-through is one of the quickest ways to damage your reputation. It leads to missed opportunities, strained relationships, and a loss of trust. If you find that you're unable meet

your obligations, be open and honest about it but don't just ignore it and hope it goes away. Don't trust your memory to remember requests that require follow-through. Write them down, get them out of your head, and manage them to completion.

Building and maintaining good working relationships with your team, co-workers, manager, and other stakeholders also require some maintenance. Don't be that person who only connects when there's a problem or new work that needs to be done. Although you should build and maintain good working relationships with everyone, some relationships deserve extra attention, including the relationship between you and your boss, which is covered next.

Action: if you're new at a company or even if you've been there a while, it's helpful to assess your relationships. Where do you want or need more support? Who do you want to get to know better? Put some casual "sync up" meetings on the calendar with no hidden agendas.

GET TO KNOW YOUR BOSS

There's no one at work more important to your success than your boss. People often have bad relationships with their boss because they didn't bother trying to build a good one from the beginning. There is something that can make you just a little nervous or edgy when you're meeting with your boss. After all, this person decides if you get a raise, a bonus, a promotion, or if you'll keep your job at all. And guess what? You are also someone's boss if you manage a team and you probably make everyone just a little bit edgy as well. It's helpful keeping perspective.

A good relationship with your boss gives you a solid foundation for a productive, positive working environment and can obviously help with your career advancement. Building a positive relationship with your boss is one of the most important aspects of starting a new job. Silence your inner critic and remember that if your boss hired you, they have faith in your ability to do the job and they want you to succeed. If they didn't hire you directly, they might already have a pre-existing opinion of you. In this case, you'll need to work on either maintaining that opinion or repairing it as needed. No matter what the situation, a good working relationship is a critical part of your success. Going against your boss always ends badly and going aggressively against your boss will result in termination in most companies.

Get to know your boss's communication style as a first step. Some bosses want big picture plans, while others want to see numbers and data. Your boss probably likes to get information a certain way. Do they want every detail? Do they want to be copied on every email? Do they only want to know about potential surprises? If your boss sends email evenings and weekends, do they expect a response right away or is that just their way of catching up on email? Everyone has a different style and you need to understand how they prefer to receive information and how much. The easiest way to get this right is to simply ask.

Aim for a somewhat neutral tone with your boss during your first few weeks at a new job. You're both getting to know each other and you don't want to come on too strong with opinions or be overly negative or pessimistic. Be patient, it takes time to get to know someone's work style. Your boss isn't used to you either, so give them some time to adjust. If you're replacing someone, it may also take a while for your boss to get used to the fact that you do things differently than your predecessor. Also remember that your boss has a boss as well, and they may be going through their own relationship challenges.

If you're having difficulty managing your relationship with your boss, regardless of how long you've been working together, here are a few tips to help get things back on track:

1. **Find common ground.** Finding common ground helps people build trust and rapport. This can be something as simple as sharing a common interest in a hobby. It can also be as simple as saying hello in the morning, catching up on small talk during breaks, or taking the time to ask about their weekend. Don't make the conversation only about small talk though, your boss has a lot of competing priorities and you don't want to be perceived as a time waster.

2. **Communicate openly and regularly.** Once you understand your boss's communication style, make sure to keep communication open. You should have a recurring 1-1 meeting with your boss either weekly or bi-weekly, but again be respectful of their time. Your boss is the one person who's probably busier than you. Communication goes both ways. If your boss asks for your opinion on something, give them an honest answer even if it's not exactly what they want to hear.

3. **Anticipate problems.** Small problems have a way of growing into big ones fast. If you know that something may be an issue soon, it's a good idea to give your boss an early heads-up and include your plan to manage the situation. No boss likes surprises, especially bad surprises.

4. **Ask for help.** If you're having trouble with a project or don't understand something, tell your boss. They can't help you if they don't know there's a problem. Your boss can help you navigate obstacles, remove roadblocks, and offer advice on company culture, just like you're going to do for your own team. But you have to ask first.

5. **Be yourself.** At a minimum, be professional and cordial when interacting with your boss. Some bosses take a long time to warm up before they'll make themselves vulnerable and share personal information with you. Be proactive, but don't go overboard the first few weeks. Relationships and trust take time to build.

6. **Bring solutions, not more problems**. Bosses are typically bombarded with challenging problems, both large and small. If you're going to approach your boss with a problem, make sure you also have a solution in mind. Better yet, offer to take something off their plate. I love it when my team does that and I'm willing to bet your boss will too.

7. **Don't take it personally**. Sometimes, things happen that are out of your control. If your boss is having a bad day, it may not be about you. I remember one particularly difficult conversation I had with a former boss about a trivial issue. It turned out he was already in a bad mood from the meeting before mine and I never stood a chance. Shrug off the occasional bad interaction or two.

Although it may seem difficult with some people, developing a good relationship with your boss is important for both your career and your overall work satisfaction. With a little effort, you can learn to communicate effectively and build trust. Remember to be yourself, stay positive, and offer solutions. Take feedback from your boss seriously and act on it. Finally, never take it personally. Bosses are just people too and when you succeed, they succeed.

Action: even if you've been in your role for a while, don't take the relationship with your boss for granted. How is your relationship now and how could you improve it? Even if the relationship seems good, what's one small thing you could do to make it even better?

GET TO KNOW YOUR TEAM

A strong relationship with your team is one of the most underrated benefits of being a leader. It's not always easy being in charge and it's even harder to be a leader without the trust and respect of your team. If you want to be effective, you need to build a good working relationship with your team. But trust is earned, not given away freely. Building trust with your team starts with being honest and transparent. Your team needs to know that they can rely on you to have their back and that you have their best interests at heart. When you're honest with your team, they'll be more likely to trust you and follow your lead. Think about what you want from your boss for a moment, since that's probably what your direct reports want from you. Do you want someone who's always honest with you? Or do you want someone who's constantly trying to manipulate you and be elusive?

Unless you have a very large team, chances are you will get to know your team members very well over time. You'll have a good idea of their strengths and weaknesses and you can use this knowledge to build better relationships with them and help them map out their career path. Take the time to get to know your team members as individuals. Find out what motivates them and what makes them tick.

I hope by now that you realize that micromanagement is a losing strategy. It affects morale, destroys confidence, and crushes the ability for people to work autonomously. If you want your team to be successful, give them the freedom and some space to do their best work. This doesn't mean that you shouldn't provide guidance or that you should accept mediocre results. It just means that you should trust your team to do their jobs and resist the urge to get involved with *how* they do their job.

Building trust and getting to know your team takes some time. Here are six daily habits to foster better relationships.

1. **Keep an open-door policy.** In the age of remote work and open office seating, this may not mean a literal open door, but it does mean making yourself available. Moving meetings, jumping on calls, and inserting yourself in the middle of tense exchanges all show support for your team. If they need you somewhere to get the right attention on something, be there. Your team needs to feel like they can come to you with problems, concerns, and ideas. This is especially true if you travel extensively. Making yourself available for problems and questions helps ensure that work doesn't grind to a standstill while you're away.

2. **Lead by example.** Your employees will take their cues from you, so it's important to set the right tone. If you want your team to be collaborative, make sure you're working collaboratively with them. If you want them to be innovative, show them that you're open and supportive to new ideas.

3. **Use mindful listening.** Good leaders listen to their team and value their opinions. Use mindful listening when your team is trying to tell you something. Showing up with your presence and attention lets them know they can count on you rather than having problems fall on deaf ears. Active listening techniques, such as rephrasing what the speaker has said and asking follow-up questions, let the speaker know you value their input and better yet make sure you're actually hearing what they're saying.

4. **Be approachable.** If you want to run a team well, you must be able to receive and deliver bad news. Part of your success as a leader comes from being approachable by your team and colleagues and being transparent with both good news and bad. I've had leaders so unapproachable that no one wanted to tell them good news, much less bad news. Inevitably, they only find out about problems the hard way when something blows up.

5. **Show appreciation.** Good bosses appreciate a job well done. They know how to give credit where it's due and how to make their team feel valued. Showing appreciation is one of the easiest ways to build good relationships with your team. You won't always be able to show your appreciation with bonuses and promotions but at least thank people for doing a good job and show them that you value their contribution.

6. **Be kind**. Aim to develop kindness so it becomes your automatic response to everything. Start by identifying unkind acts and refraining from them and retraining yourself toward kindness. Shaunti Feldhahn, a kindness researcher, developed a Thirty Day Kindness Challenge to do just that. When her team implemented it in workplaces, they found 89% of relationships improved. This happened in every workplace and environment, a startlingly consistent result. The more kindness you develop, the better your relationships will be both at home and at work. Kindness means being sincere, so treat team members as people to engage with rather than just giving them orders to follow and problems to solve. Lead with your heart and the rest is sure to follow.

These six daily habits will help you build trust, respect, and better communication with your team so that you can lead them better. Building relationships takes time, trust, and effort. However, even small improvements can make a difference. It's what you do every day that counts the most. Try to get 1% better a day and let it compound over time.

Action: what's your initial assessment of your team? Do they seem jaded? Excited for new leadership? What concerns do you have? Where are the opportunities?

SUMMARY

No matter if you're starting a new role or trying to improve the one you've been in for years, building better relationships is the cornerstone of being more effective at work. Your relationships with your boss, your direct reports, and your colleagues all have a huge impact on how successful you will be. We also covered:

- Take time off between jobs, if possible. This helps you clear your head and start fresh in the new position.
- Starting a new job is a VUCA activity, which means it's volatile, uncertain, complex and ambiguous. The OODA loop is a good framework for navigating. The OODA loop is a four-step decision-making process that includes observing the environment, orienting, and making sense of what you see, deciding what to do next and then acting accordingly.
- Your first 90 days are important, but not that important. People become stressed over a new job because they put far too much pressure on themselves to perform. Focus on a few things that will have an impact and don't try to change everything all at once.
- The most important thing a new leader can do is to start building relationships with colleagues. This requires trust, respect, self-awareness, inclusion, and open communication. Remember that a good reputation is built across all levels of the organization, not just management.

- A good relationship with your boss gives you a solid foundation for a productive, positive working environment. Your boss wants you to succeed, so take advantage of their willingness to offer help and guidance.
- Five daily habits will help build better relationships with your employees. These habits are keeping an open-door policy, leading by example, using mindful listening, being approachable, and showing appreciation.

REFERENCES AND FURTHER READING

Arneson, Steve. *What Your Boss Really Wants from You: 15 Insights to Improve Your Relationship.* ReadHowYouWant, 2014.

Dewett, Todd. *Managing Your Manager.* LinkedIn, 2014.

Sutton, Robert I. *Good Boss, Bad Boss: How to Be the Best... and Learn from the Worst.* Piatkus, 2017.

Watkins, Michael. *Master Your Next Move: The Essential Companion to the First 90 Days.* Harvard Business Review Press, 2019.

Watkins, Michael. *The First 90 Days: Critical Strategies for New Leaders at All Levels.* Harvard Business School Press, 2003.

Chapter 6

A crash course in strategic planning

WHY STRATEGIC PLANNING IS IMPORTANT

Strategy without leadership is wishful thinking and leadership without a strategy has no direction. Leading without a strategy means you're either maintaining the status quo, reacting to whatever comes up or just hoping that things will get better or stay OK under your watch. People are sometimes put off by the term "strategic planning" or "strategic thinking." Just like leadership, the word strategy means different things to different people and comes with some baggage. If the word "strategic" puts you off, just think about "planning." Planning is a straightforward idea that implies that success isn't just luck and that its destiny can be influenced by picking the right goals and then working toward them.

Strategic planning typically involves thinking about a three-to-five-year horizon. As a technology leader, you're probably already thinking about the future. What new technology will disrupt your industry? How can you stay ahead of the curve? It doesn't matter if you lead an operational function, a software development team, or a team of systems engineers, strategic planning is important. Having a good planning process helps make sure you stay proactive and have a vision for the future. A strategic plan offers clarity and serves as a roadmap to help reach business goals. And business goals require technology to get there, so aligning the two is important.

Some technology managers feel that their role is operational and therefore doesn't need a plan, but even an operational function needs a vision for the future. In an operational function like desktop support, you might have a goal to improve help desk response time by 30%. But you still need a high-level strategy and plan of *how* you're going to do that.

Strategic planning is important for information technology (IT) leaders because it helps them set priorities, allocate resources, and align their team's efforts with business goals. Strategic planning provides a framework for making decisions about where to invest money and time and which priorities are more important than others. When we don't have a strategic plan, we wind up chasing the latest technology fads or investing in tools that doesn't help meet business objectives.

DOI: 10.1201/9781003314707-8

There are many ways to go about creating a strategy. But most IT leaders follow a basic process:

1. Understand and define the problem.
2. Analyze the operating environment.
3. Form a plan.
4. Gain support for the plan.
5. Execute and course correct as necessary.

We will dive into each of these steps in more detail, but first let's understand how strategic planning differs from general project work or day-to-day operations.

HOW STRATEGIC PLANNING IS DIFFERENT FROM MANAGING A PROJECT

Strategic planning is the process of setting goals, identifying and assessing external threats and opportunities, and developing an action plan to achieve objectives. In contrast, project management is the process of planning, executing, and monitoring individual projects to ensure that they are completed on time and within budget. While both strategic planning and project management are important to the success of organizations, they are distinct processes. Strategic planning focuses on the big picture and setting long-term goals, while project management is focused on the day-to-day execution of a specific project

Many technology functions include at least some operational and project work that may not be aligned to a bigger strategy. These day-to-day projects still need to be done, but they don't directly support a strategic vision. A few key attributes of a strategic plan include:

- **Strategic plans have a longer time horizon**: strategic planning is future-oriented, usually in the 3–5-year range, which may seem like an eternity in technology. If you're leading a commercial software development function, an example goal might be: "In three years' time, we want to be the market leader." If you're leading an operational support organization, a goal might include migrating away from a legacy software platform and onto a new system.
- **Strategic plans need broad stakeholder support**: strategic plans usually require input from multiple stakeholders, including business leaders, employees, and business users. This is different from a project, which usually has a single sponsor or business owner. You might also need new funding and resources to achieve strategic goals. Strategic plans should be bigger and more ambitious than individual projects.
- **Strategic plans are flexible:** because a strategic plan has a longer time horizon, they need to be flexible. Plans may change as new information comes up or as the business climate changes. Strategic plans should be living documents that are revisited on a regular basis.

- **Big picture thinking**: strategic planning involves taking a step back from the day-to-day work and thinking about the bigger picture. You can't just focus on one project or one initiative, you must think about how all your initiatives fit together. This can be difficult for technology leaders who are immersed in day-to-day operations. Strategic planning requires a different mindset, some creativity, and a big picture view of where you're going. People overestimate how much they can get done in a year, but they underestimate how much they can get done in a few years. Strategic plans help you focus on more ambitious, but achievable goals.

When you don't have a strategy, you are working on a collection of unrelated projects. A technology strategy provides a roadmap and helps you prioritize efforts so that you can achieve your objectives faster. There are many ways to go about creating a strategy and the process you use will be determined by the size and complexity of your organization. Here's a general framework that can help get you started.

DEVELOPING A STRATEGY

While there are many approaches to creating a strategic plan, this simple five-step process will help you if you don't know where to start. This process includes understanding the problem/opportunity, developing a hypothesis about how you can best solve the problem, and gaining support for it within your organization. It also includes executing the strategy and adjusting things as necessary along the way.

Step 1: understand the problem or opportunity

The first step in creating a strategy is to define and understand the problem or opportunity. An example might be improving customer satisfaction or entering a new market. It could be a cloud migration or a digital transformation. It could also be your own plan for what you want to do with your team or function. When I joined the State of Connecticut, I put together two strategic plans: one for a "whole of state" approach to cybersecurity and one that was exclusively focused on internal state systems. The whole of state plan was focused on technology as an enabler and influencing the security of entities that were not directly under our control. The state other plan was more about internal process improvements and products that support what we are doing with Digital Government. In both cases, I had to clearly articulate where we were going strategically and get support from many stakeholders. As with this example, your plan should be tailored to your audience.

Completely understanding the problem is vital for a successful strategy. All too often, technology leaders jump into solutions mode without taking the time to really understand the problem (see Image 6.1). You may only see

Planning includes risk management

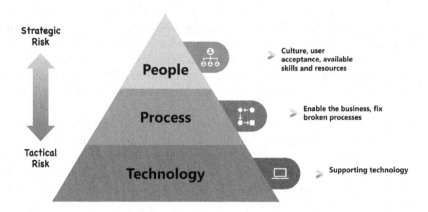

Image 6.1 Accounting for risk in the strategic planning process enables leaders to identify potential threats and opportunities and develop contingency plans.

one part of the problem and assume it's enough to get started. This leads to sub-optimal solutions that don't address deeper issues or challenges. Spend some time speaking with stakeholders, doing research, and looking at the problem from different angles. Get input from subject matter experts, no matter where they report in the organization. Only then will you be able to develop a comprehensive view.

The best way to make sure you've thoroughly understood a problem is to ask a lot of questions. One helpful way is the 5 "Why's." This is a simple technique that is used in manufacturing to get to the root cause of problems. The idea is that you keep asking "why" until you can't ask it anymore, which is usually about five times. For example, if your goal was to enter a new market, your "why's" might include "Why do we want to enter this market?" and "Why is now the right time to enter the market?" Each time there's an answer, you ask another why to go a layer deeper.

Other questions you may want to consider as you put a strategy together include:

- **What is my business outcome?** It's easy for technologists to get caught up in the technology itself. Make sure you understand the business objectives that technology is supporting and that everything is in alignment. Example business goals could include increasing revenue, improving customer satisfaction, or entering new markets. Business context helps you understand why technology is there in the first place.
- **What are the benefits of the outcome?** What are the benefits of a successful outcome? Why should the business support your plan with time, people, and money? This is a simple "so what" question that many

business leaders ask? What is the impact if you don't execute on this strategy?

- **Who are my stakeholders?** It's important to understand who you're trying to solve the problem for. This could be internal customers, external customers, or both. When you're thinking about technology solutions, it's important to understand what processes they will be supporting. Will this effort require changing business any processes? What are the pain points in the current process? Are there any bottlenecks or other areas where technology could help improve efficiencies? Automating a bad process results in an automated bad process. Fix the process first and then support it with technology.

- **What are the risks associated with this problem or opportunity?** Any new initiative has some risk associated with it. Make sure you understand what those risks are and have a plan to mitigate them. Many people try to avoid taking risks, but if you don't take any risks and try to plan for every contingency, you'll be too paralyzed with planning to even start the real work. The idea is having a plan to manage, but not eliminate your risk.

- **What does "done" look like?** This is probably the most important question to ask when you're developing a technology strategy. What does success look like? How will you know when you've achieved your goals? Make sure you have a clear understanding of this right from the beginning. This will help you develop better solutions, control project scope, and track progress. Work that don't have a boundary becomes infinity work that never ends. Digital transformations and large projects often suffer from this problem. No one knows when it's finished or even how much further there is to go. This is why 84% of digital transformation projects fail.

By taking the time to understand a problem or opportunity thoroughly, you'll be in a much better position to develop an effective strategy. Asking questions and understanding the problem is just the first step. Now that you have some idea of what you're trying to accomplish, it's time to analyze your environment.

Step 2: analyze the environment

Engineers like to jump straight into building a solution when they see a problem. This approach doesn't account for all the headwinds you will face and how business and technology trends might derail your efforts. When you're analyzing your environment, consider both the current state and the future state. Where is the technology market going? What trends are emerging that could impact your solution? I was at a firm that bet heavily on OS/2 Warp Server at a time when it was clear that Windows NT was going to be the winner. Betting heavily on the wrong technology puts you and your organization in a bad place.

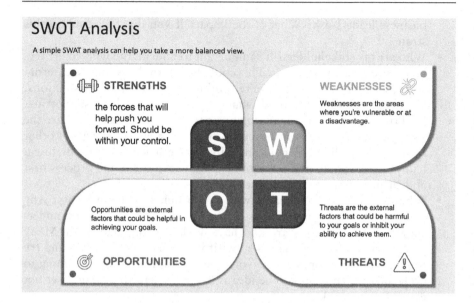

SWOT Analysis

A simple SWAT analysis can help you take a more balanced view.

STRENGTHS

the forces that will help push you forward. Should be within your control.

S

W

WEAKNESSES

Weaknesses are the areas where you're vulnerable or at a disadvantage.

O

T

Opportunities are external factors that could be helpful in achieving your goals.

Threats are the external factors that could be harmful to your goals or inhibit your ability to achieve them.

OPPORTUNITIES

THREATS

Image 6.2 A SWOT analysis provides a structured framework for evaluating strengths, weaknesses, opportunities, and threats that can help leaders make better decisions and anticipate issues.

It's helpful at this point to do a SWOT analysis (see Image 6.2). SWOT stands for strengths, weaknesses, opportunities, and threats. A SWOT analysis will help you understand the current environment and give insight into potential opportunities and roadblocks. One benefit this process provides is encouraging you to take a more balanced look at the forces that will help you or hold you back. This keeps you from being too optimistic or too pessimistic in your approach. A SWOT analysis is done on a 2 × 2 grid with one square for each view.

Step one of a SWOT analysis is to list your strengths. These are the forces that will help push you forward. It could include a great budget or great people with free bandwidth to help. Your strengths should be under your control and should be something you can use to your advantage. Next, list your weaknesses. These are the areas where you're vulnerable or at a disadvantage. This could include a lack of experience in a certain technology or a limited budget. Third, list your opportunities. Opportunities are external factors that could be helpful in achieving your goals. They could include an emerging technology or a new regulation that creates market demand for your product. Last are your threats. These are the external factors that could be harmful to your goals or inhibit your ability to achieve them. Threats might include a competitor with similar technology or a change in industry trends that decreases the demand for your product, such as when the cryptocurrency market crashed and people lost interest in most projects tied to this technology.

A SWOT analysis is a useful tool for managers because it allows them to identify the strengths, weaknesses, opportunities, and threats affecting their strategy. This information can then be incorporated into the plan.

Step 3: form the plan

Next, it's time to start developing a detailed plan. This is where you'll take all the information that you've gathered in the first two steps and put it into a coherent strategy. After examining your strengths, weaknesses, threats, and opportunities, you will want to build on your strengths, boost your weak areas, head off any threats, and exploit every opportunity. The bigger the program, the more time it will take to implement and the more moving pieces that you'll have to manage. Planning helps you understand what needs to be done, who will do it, when it needs to be done by, and how you'll know if it's successful.

Review the SWOT analysis from the previous step. How will you capitalize on your strengths? How will you mitigate your weaknesses? What opportunities can you take advantage of? How will you watch out for your threats? Your strategy should include budget and resource assumptions. This includes not only the money you have to spend, but also the people and skills you'll need. Part of the plan may require obtaining new resources that don't exist today. If that's the case, you'll want to make sure that you have a solid business case for why those resources are needed. You should be able to articulate how new resources will help you achieve goals faster and better. Write down people, technology, or consulting resources that may be required and be prepared to have enough detail to defend your estimates and justify the expense. Other elements to capture in your plan include timing and milestones. When do you need to have certain things done by to stay on track? Where are the project dependencies? What are the major milestones that you can use to gauge progress?

Forming a plan is specific to you, your company, and your technology needs. There is no one-size-fits-all solution. By taking the time to do a thorough analysis and develop a well-thought-out plan, you'll be in a much better position to execute on your strategy.

You'll likely go through several iterations before settling on a final plan. Because of the pressure we put on ourselves to be perfect, it may be hard to decide when your plan is ready to be shared with a wider audience. These questions will help you know when you're ready:

- **Is your plan aligned with the business?** New technology does not translate directly to business value. If you can't articulate the business value of your plan, there's a good chance it may not have any value and therefore won't be supported or funded. If you can't demonstrate business value, start over again until you can.
- **Can you articulate your plan simply?** If you can't explain your plan in simple terms, it's probably not ready to be shared. Worse yet, your

plan may be too complex for people to be able to understand which will lead to poor execution. You should be able to articulate the plan and its business value in a few sentences, sometimes called an "elevator pitch." The idea of an elevator pitch is that you should be able to explain something in the time it takes to ride an elevator with someone. Apple's elevator pitch for the Mac is simple: "Easy to learn. Astoundingly powerful. And designed to let you work, play, and create in ways you never imagined." Anyone can understand the value proposition without getting lost in the technical details.

- **Are you confident in your ability to execute the plan?** If you're not sure you can pull off the steps in your plan, you may need to do more work. Building confidence comes from having a complete understanding of all the moving parts and being realistic about what you can achieve. Striving for perfection can be paralyzing. Directional certainty is good enough. At this point, you should have engaged subject matter experts to make sure that what you're planning is realistic. Most times, the people who are slated to do the work are in the best position to point out the problem areas. Don't assume you understand all the variables and try to go it alone writing the plan.

- **Are your timelines and milestones realistic?** Having an unrealistic plan makes it hard to follow through, which will in turn cause you to underperform and disappoint your stakeholders and team. Your boss might also lose confidence in your abilities. Your plan needs to be realistic. A common problem in IT is an over-reliance on key subject matter experts. Have you reviewed their availability? Will they be 100% dedicated to your work or are they juggling many other priorities? Procurement can also introduce lengthy delays. Make sure you are mapping out project dependencies and assumptions so they can be discussed and tracked.

- **Can you justify new resource requests?** If you need to hire people or buy new software, do you have a solid business case for it and an idea of the cost? Expenses will get a lot of attention from your boss and other decision makers. Make sure your boss is on board with new resource requirements before sharing your plan more widely, because they will likely have to help you defend it.

- **Do you have a contingency plan?** In technology, there's always the risk that something will go wrong. Technical problems happen and sometimes they can't be avoided. Supply chain issues arise. Key resources quit or move on to another job. Technology tools don't always work the way they were advertised. Have a contingency plan in place for when things don't go as expected including alternate vendors or tools.

When you can answer "yes" to all these questions, then you're probably ready to share your plan. But remember, a good plan is never finished. You'll want to use OODA loop thinking to iterate with what's working and what's not when it's time to execute and adjust the plan. Now, it's time to go get support and possibly funding for your plan.

Step 4: getting support for your plan

Once you've developed a plan, it's time to confirm buy-in from the people who will be responsible for executing it or who need to be informed about it or fund it (see Image 6.3). The best way to gain support from key stakeholders is to clearly articulate the business value of your technology initiative and how it will help achieve the company's overall goals. Start by re-confirming full support from your boss. If your boss is not on board with the plan or even elements of the plan, you'll need to go back to the previous step and adjust. Your boss will be instrumental in helping you gain support from other key stakeholders when you might not have enough political clout in the organization. Larger initiatives may have to be "sold" all the way up to the CEO and board of directors and your boss will have a hand in those marketing efforts.

Once you have your boss's full support, it's time to share your plan with other stakeholders. Depending on the size and scope of your technology initiative, this could include people like the Chief Information Officer (CIO), Chief Financial Officer (CFO), or other peers. These are people who have a vested interest in your initiative and can help you ensure its success. No one likes surprises and very few strategic plans can be done in a silo without help from other areas, so make sure you have the right people on board with what you're proposing.

The best way to gain support from everyone is to be clear and concise about your plan and its value. Resist the urge to go deep into technical details and be prepared for questions. The last thing you want to do is be caught off guard by obvious questions you can't answer. If you do get a question you can't

Gaining support for your plan is critical

❖ Objectives
❖ Funding
❖ People
❖ Skills
❖ Timelines
❖ Deliverables

Image 6.3 Technology leaders must communicate and advocate for their ideas which helps increase a sense of purpose and collaboration among team members.

answer, be honest about it and say you'll get back with an answer and then make sure that you do.

Be prepared to adjust your plan based on feedback. If you don't take feedback seriously, you won't have full support from everyone. If you're not a natural communicator, now is the time to start practicing. The success of larger technology initiative rests heavily on effective communication and making sure everyone is supportive from the top down. If there are detractors who don't want to support your plan, try to understand their position and see if there's a way to address their concerns and win them over. If it's a critical stakeholder, such as the leader of a team that will support your efforts, you need to work all the way through your differences.

The most common concern you may encounter with an ambitious plan includes a lack of understanding about how it's going to succeed. Most IT leaders have their own plans, so they may not have the time or bandwidth to help you with yours. Explain how your technology initiative intersects with their goals and how it fits into the bigger picture of company success. The easier you make it for others to understand exactly what you need from them, the more likely they are to help you. Your plan will also seem less overwhelming to them if you can show that you only need them for a smaller part of it.

Put together a well-organized and professional presentation that outlines your proposed actions, the reasoning behind them, and the expected results. Visual cues work better than just talking, especially if numbers, percentages, and complex ideas need to be represented.

Gaining support for a plan isn't always easy. This is especially true when you're working with business leaders who may not understand the technology involved. Keep in mind that you know a lot more about technology then they do and strive to make it easy for them to understand. This means no acronyms, buzzwords, or technical jargon. Speak in business terms and show business value. Remember the concept of cognitive load and that executives have their attention span pulled in many directions. Use a bottom-line up-front approach and limit the technical detail.

Step 5: execute, monitor, and measure

After you've created a plan and gained support from key stakeholders, it's time to execute. This is where the rubber meets the road and you put your plan into action. Keep track of progress and ensure that everything is on track with regular updates. Executing a plan is a big subject that you will read more about in Chapter 7.

CULTURE EATS STRATEGY FOR BREAKFAST

There's a saying that culture eats strategy for breakfast. No matter how well-thought-out and well-executed your plan is, it will ultimately be unsuccessful if the company culture is not supportive of it. Technology initiatives are often met with resistance because they require change and people may be uncomfortable with change. Companies often think they embrace change when they don't. They may have a mission statement that says they value change, but in reality, they often reward people for maintaining the status quo.

One way to overcome resistance is to get people involved early in the process. If they feel like they have a say in the direction of your technology initiative, they're more likely to give buy-in and support it. Another way to overcome resistance is to present the ideas in your strategy in a way that resonates with the company's core values. For example, as the State of Connecticut moves toward a digital government, my security conversations often revolve around how security provides the trust element that our citizens need for an all-digital government to succeed. Rather than implementing security for security's sake, this helps make it an integral part of digital government, which has clear benefits for our citizens.

Culture is a complex topic that is often overlooked in strategic planning because it's not easy to address. If you're new to the company, you'll want to move very cautiously and look to your boss to provide guidance and possibly some air cover if there are headwinds. A good plan being implemented in the wrong culture is doomed to fail. It's one thing to declare you're going to revolutionize electric vehicles and another thing to be Tesla. The difference is in creating and executing on a good strategic plan that fits the culture and gets everyone on board with the vision.

Culture shapes how people interact with each other and with technology. It can have a big impact on your strategy and on execution. Failure to adapt to culture can make you fail as a leader. A positive culture brings out the best in people, and it can make technology more user-friendly and effective. A negative culture does the opposite, making it difficult to get things done.

When we talk about cultural fit, what we really mean is how the person aligns with company values and behaviors. Culture can be difficult to define and isn't going to be written down somewhere. It's something that needs to be experienced. Culture includes the traits of each employee and how they interact at work, creating an organic whole that describes what it means to "work here."

Corporate culture can be the fuel that turns a vision into reality or what makes your plan dead on arrival. Experts agree that it can be hard to change company culture in a large organization that come with complex office dynamics. In a big company, each department or business unit may have its own unique culture. You'd be surprised at the number of leaders who would rather research and study other corporate cultures than simply ask their team what it will take to improve their existing culture. Culture change happens slowly and takes sustained effort over a long time. If part of your plan involves going against your company's culture, you have a bad plan.

If you're relatively new to an organization, and even if you're not, you should spend time trying to get and know your corporate culture before attempting large, cross-functional projects. Some cultures lean toward autonomy and emphasize individual action and competition. Others lean toward integration and teamwork, emphasizing relationships and coordinating group efforts. Every culture is unique, so there really is no way to learn your company culture other than to experience it yourself.

Whatever your company's culture looks like, you are responsible for the culture on your team. Your actions and behaviors set the tone for the team regardless of what the overall corporate culture looks like. Setting the right culture for your team can be the beginning of change for the larger corporate culture, especially if your team is delivering results in a way that's worth emulating.

Action: at the State of Connecticut, we are working to change the culture through three values: owning the outcome, making it better, and being one team. These are values we felt would help build the culture we wanted to see. By rewarding these behaviors when we see them and pointing out where we don't, we are slowly and steadily changing our culture.

Does your company have a published values statement? A values statement outlines core principles and philosophical values that inform corporate decision-making and behavior. Finding and understanding your company's value statement is a great starting point for understanding your corporate culture. Just keep in mind that some companies may say one thing and do another.

Become an impartial observer of your company culture as if you were filming a documentary. Watch how people interact with each other. How do they handle conflicts? Is there a culture of support or one of blame? How do senior leaders interact with the rest of the firm? Is the organization relatively flat or very hierarchical? Keep a running list of what you observe and begin to form a comprehensive picture.

Here are some excerpted examples of corporate value statements.

Hyatt: we care for people so they can be their best.

Teachable: autonomy and attitude: we're a team of self-starters who take serious pride in our work – and it shows.

Meta: live in the Future: live in the Future guides us to build the future of distributed work that we want, where opportunity isn't limited by geography. This means operating as a distributed-first company and being the early adopters of the future products we're building to help people feel present together no matter where they are.

Ping Identity: one Ping. We win or lose together. Nothing here is a spectator sport.

Wayfair: we Hustle and Take Big Risks: we move quickly and we're not afraid to make mistakes. Here, smart risk-taking is encouraged – even if it fails – and every team member is empowered to tackle challenges in exciting and innovative ways.

Zoom Communications: care: for community, customers, company, teammates, selves.

SUMMARY

Strategy means starting from where you are right now, then determining where you want to go and how you're going to get there. In this chapter, we learned:

- You need a good strategy and leadership to succeed. Strategy without leadership is wishful thinking and leadership without a strategy has no direction.
- Present technology plans in a professional and well-organized way that outlines proposed actions, the reasoning behind them, and the expected results. Business value trumps technology tools every time.
- Address concerns that people may have and be prepared to answer questions up front. Make sure everyone is aware of their role and responsibilities.
- Quarterly and yearly reviews are common for technology planning, but timing should be flexible and tailored to the needs of a company.
- Culture can derail great strategies and halt otherwise good execution. Take the time to understand your company's culture in the context of how it will affect your ability to deliver results.

REFERENCES AND FURTHER READING

Day, George S. *See Sooner, Act Faster - How Vigilant Leaders Thrive in an Era of Digital Turbulence*. The MIT Press, 2019.

Kim, Gene. *Phoenix Project, 5th Anniversary Edition: A Novel about It, DevOps, and Helping Your Business Win*. IT Revolution Press, 2018.

Rogers, David L. *The Digital Transformation Playbook: Rethink Your Business for the Digital Age*. Columbia Business School Publishing, 2016.

Sacolick, Isaac. *Driving Digital: The Leader's Guide to Business Transformation through Technology*. Amacom, 2022.

Saldanha, Tony. *Why Digital Transformations Fail: The Surprising Disciplines of How to Take off and Stay Ahead*. Berrett-Koehler Publishers, 2019.

Siebel, Thomas M., and Condoleezza Rice. *Digital Transformation: Survive and Thrive in an Era of Mass Extinction*. RosettaBooks, 2019.

Chapter 7

Building a high-performance team

> It is the responsibility of leadership to work intelligently with what is given, and not waste time fantasizing about a world of flawless people and perfect choices.
>
> Marcus Aurelius

No matter if you inherited a team or built one from scratch, as a leader, you are responsible for that team's success. Leaders set the tone, build trust, motivate team members, and help them grow. Your team and your ability to manage that team effectively will determine if you succeed as an information technology (IT) leader. It doesn't matter how great of a leader you are if your team isn't performing well. As the leader, you need to ensure that your team has the resources and support it needs to be successful. You also need to be able to manage conflicts and keep your team focused on the task at hand.

This chapter looks at building a great team by attracting and retaining great people and by developing the people you already have. Developing your people helps build a sense of loyalty and dedication that is difficult to obtain in the marketplace. If you're not looking to build a team from scratch or hire anyone new, this chapter also discusses taking the team you have from good to great by improving communication, establishing trust, and creating a shared vision.

ATTRACTING GREAT PEOPLE: WITH OR WITHOUT A BIG BUDGET

Technology workers are expensive. The average IT salary in the United States is $208,626 as of May 27, 2022, according to Salary.com. Of course, salary ranges can vary widely depending on many factors, including position, education, certification requirements, technical skills, and experience. But there's no disputing that technology workers command some of the highest salaries in any profession with top Chief Information Officers (CIOs) from Fortune 500 companies earning seven-figure compensation packages.

DOI: 10.1201/9781003314707-9

Regardless of their cost, technical people have an expertise that companies need and they help put systems in place that ultimately make the business money. And technology is everywhere now from refrigerators and cars to watches and cellphones. The spread of technology into industries that have traditionally been technology averse means that there is more competition for technical talent. Technology also isn't easy or fast to learn. This means that database administrators, software engineers, cloud architects, and web developers are all going to cost a lot to attract and retain. The number of companies looking for these qualified and competent technology employees is skyrocketing. This means you might get some sticker shock when you ask candidates for their salary expectations. Employees with in-demand skills get to pick and choose the companies they work for.

Depending on your company and industry, you probably won't have a blank check to attract and retain top technical talent. Even well-heeled industries like financial services compete for top talent with more than a paycheck by offering perks and great benefits. But what about smaller firms, the public sector, and non-profit organizations that can't afford to pay top dollar for technology talent?

When I joined the State of Connecticut coming from the financial services industry, I knew I was going to have a challenge hiring people. In financial services, it's common for leaders to come in and clean house to make way for their friends and colleagues from previous firms. These leaders tend to ignore the talent right in front of their faces, opting instead to bring in colleagues from their previous companies. Sometimes this works and sometimes it results in very interesting culture clashes. Industry veterans from Amazon and Google are trading executives at prestigious financial services firms including Goldman Sachs and others and it has a big impact on the environment because of different ways of thinking.

Working in government gave me a different perspective on recruiting tactics and how to find the best talent. When we hire at the state, we emphasize our strengths: great work-life balance, a clear mission of public service, and a stable work environment. Of course, money is important, but it doesn't have to be everything (see Image 7.1). When you play to your strengths, you can attract people with more than just a paycheck.

You should do your best to ensure that you are paying market rate to attract talent or at least the best that you can within corporate parameters. If your company is paying below market rate for an in-demand technical niche like cloud computing, you're going to struggle to attract. But don't neglect the team that you already have from a salary perspective either. I've seen plenty of companies where the loyal person who has been in place 20 years is making a fraction of what new people are being hired for. If you have a solid employee who is paid dramatically below market rate, you have an obligation to fight for a market adjustment to their salary even if you don't win. Good leadership means doing the right thing.

Hiring great people

Salary isn't the only thing. Employees also want:

1. Meaningful work
2. Benefits and perks
3. Location flexibility
4. Training and development
5. Latest technology
6. Good company culture

Image 7.1 To attract and retain top talent in the technology industry, leaders can offer career development, a positive work culture, and flexible work arrangements.

A few things that can help attract employees outside of offering a competitive salary include:

- **Encourage a good company culture:** corporate culture is important. Is yours inviting and nurturing? Or is it known for 100-hour workweeks and a constant churn of employees? There are a lot of firms that rely on big paychecks to make up for toxic work environments. Those days aren't over yet, but they are an endangered species. Many millennials and generation Z employees prefer purpose over paycheck and expect a lot more from their career. Remember, even if you are at a company that has a bad reputation that doesn't mean that your team needs to inherit the reputation. Focus on what's under your control and make sure you're running a positive and inviting environment. Remember that different generations may have different motivations and perspectives. Don't assume everyone thinks the same way you do.
- **Use wider searches:** "Post and pray" is not a great recruiting strategy any more unless your company is in the top echelon of employers. Even then, some roles are so specific in their technical requirements that there may only be a handful of candidates out there. Hopefully, your company is leveraging social media tools including LinkedIn (https://www. linkedin.com) to find candidates. LinkedIn is a great platform for connecting with professionals in various industries. Facebook groups and Twitter can also help reach potential candidates. There are many groups dedicated to specific industries or professions that can also be a great way to reach potential candidates. Ask your team for referrals. Good people tend to know other good people. Also, don't forget that people will be looking up your background as the hiring manager. Make sure

your social media profile is inviting and provides enough information to give someone a feel for their potential new boss.

- **Know when to call in the professionals**: technology is still a fast-growing market and hot skills are always in demand. For senior roles and high-demand technical niche skills like cloud computing or cybersecurity, you might be better off using a recruiter. The best technical recruiters are great communicators and negotiators. Retainer basis recruiters become an extension of the client's team and focus on the quality and appropriateness for the position rather than just matching skills on a résumé with a job posting.

- **Develop the employees you have**: invest as much as you can into employee development and training programs. Sir Richard Branson has a great view on employee development: "Train people well enough so they can leave and treat them well enough so they don't want to." Leaders should listen to their employees and give them what they want and need for development. Make the time to support your team to attend conferences, take advantage of vendor-provided training, and create an environment of continuous learning. If you want to multiply that impact, have team members discuss key takeaways they've learned from a conference with the team. Just make sure you're giving equal training opportunities to everyone.

- **Offer good work-life balance**: work-life balance became a game-changer for many during the pandemic. Commutes vanished, leaving some with hours of found time every day. Suddenly, work wasn't such a big deal. Now firms are trying to aggressively bring those employees back to the office, presumably to keep a better eye on their productivity. Hybrid and remote work arrangements not only make you a preferred employer for most, but they also give you a much larger candidate pool to tap.

- **Provide a good work environment**: if your employees work in an office, make sure your office space is as comfortable and inviting as possible. So many firms moved to open seating environments in the name of improving collaboration and (the real reason) for saving costs on office space. It turns out that these open space environments decrease productivity, with one in three workers saying that they find these environments challenging for their concentration and productivity. Many companies think that open seating arrangements encourage more collaboration. But a 2018 study published by the Royal Society showed that open architectures decreased the number of face-to-face interactions. The study specifically noted, "rather than prompting increasingly vibrant face-to-face collaboration, open architecture appeared to trigger a natural human response to socially withdraw from officemates and interact instead over email and IM." While it may not be possible for you to personally change your corporate seating strategy, try to make your office space as inviting as possible and remember the concept of cognitive load. Noise and distractions are not facilitators for work that requires concentration.

Whatever way you go about attracting talent, don't compromise when you're hiring someone new. Hiring someone who isn't a good performer will drag your whole team down. Hiring difficult people creates disharmony and makes it difficult for your team to function. It's better to wait for the right employee than to hire someone who isn't a good fit, regardless of their technical talent. Turnover, productivity, and morale are all impacted when you have difficult people on your team. The best way to avoid a bad hire is to be selective in the hiring process and to go with your overall gut feeling. If someone feels like they're not going to be a good fit for the team, then they probably aren't, and you should keep looking.

Finally, resist the urge to bring in toxic superstars. Employees who are talented and hardworking but also prone to unprofessional outbursts and immature behavior are detrimental to the organization. They hijack important meetings, treat coworkers poorly, and cause disruption and distraction more than they add value. If a toxic superstar is already on your team causing disruption, consider letting them go regardless of their technical skills. As a leader, you own the culture and tone on your team and the behavior you accept is the behavior you are going to get. While a toxic superstar might be very good at what they do, they won't make up for the negative impact on the rest of the team.

Technology jobs are undergoing an upheaval as I write this book. It is a time of both opportunity and challenge for IT leaders. The "Great Resignation" describes the wave of employees who are leaving their jobs in search of new opportunities. But with markets changing, will the Great Recession change the odds as tech employees are being laid off? It may for some. But the most talented employees still have the upper hand, and supply and demand will remain in their favor.

Offering a competitive salary is table stakes. Skilled employees have more opportunities than ever. Companies need to offer employees meaningful work, flexible work environments and a path for career growth and development. Offices need to be places people want to go, not have to go. Companies that adapt to these changing circumstances will attract and retain the best talent, which will ultimately make them more successful.

Action: how are you recruiting talent in your organization? If you're using the "post and pray" model, what could you do differently to increase your odds of success?

Action: what are your company's strengths and why would someone want to work there? How are you leveraging those strengths to attract and retain talent?

WHAT IS A HIGH-PERFORMANCE TEAM?

Growing a great team takes time, but when all the pieces come together, you have a high-performing team that can achieve great things. Building a high-performance team is not the same as just building a team. You may already have a team and they may already be doing a relatively good job. But what exactly is a high-performance team?

With rare exceptions, nothing big gets done without a team of people behind the effort. Even solo businesses lean on accountants, lawyers, and advisors to help them achieve their business goals. But the concept of a "high-performance team" has captured the imagination of many managers and organizations. The phrase conjures up images of superstar employees who are handpicked to work together on special initiatives. But how can you make sure your own team is simply performing as well as they could be?

While there is no single definition of a high-performance team, there are some common characteristics they tend to share. High-performance teams are innovative in their problem-solving. They communicate and collaborate. They also deliver consistent and great results. A high-performance team has a sense of purpose, ambitious performance goals, mutual accountability, and trust between team members.

Bruce Tuckman came up with a framework (see Image 7.2) to describe the path that teams follow to become high performance. Tuckman's research focused on group dynamics and how teams progressed from their initial forming to becoming a performing team. Here's what happens in each stage.

1. **Stage 1: forming.** When a new team forms, people may not know how they fit in or how they'll work with each another. Creating a shared purpose and common goals helps to create this commitment. A cyber-security team has a very clear purpose and mission. But every team needs to understand why they exist. Even for an established team, it's always a good time to revisit purpose, vision, and strategy. Also don't

Tuckman's Team Development Model

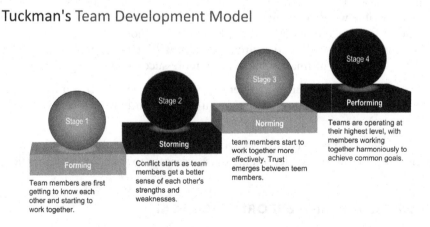

Image 7.2 Tuckman's team development model provides a framework for understanding and improving team dynamics, communication and productivity.

assume that teams that have been together for years know each other well and work together well. Your predecessor may not have had the same leadership perspectives that you have.

2. **Stage 2: storming.** In the storming stage, people start pushing against established boundaries. You might have conflict between team members, especially if roles and responsibilities aren't yet clear. The leader's role is coaching through this conflict and keeping everyone focused on goals. Storming is a normal phase that many leaders dread, but if you don't work your way through your differences, you'll never get everyone on the same page. Never leave team conflict unchecked, but also remember that a little friction can be a good thing.

3. **Stage 3: norming.** A team moves into the norming stage when people start to resolve their differences, appreciate each other's strengths, and respect your authority as a leader. People begin to actively appreciate differences.

4. **Stage 4: performing.** In the performing stage, the team is in flow and performing to its full potential. Members take on roles and responsibilities dynamically, and differences among members are fully appreciated and leveraged to achieve common goals. The performing team is resilient by using each other's unique abilities and talents to collectively get the job done.

Some teams never make it to the performing stage – they get stuck in storming mode, with members constantly bickering and disagreeing. Others coast along in the norming stage, but then never reach their full potential where everyone is working as a team. What's the key to moving into a high-performing stage? Experts believe that psychological safety may be a key ingredient.

CREATING PSYCHOLOGICAL SAFETY

Organizational behavioral scientist Amy Edmondson of Harvard first introduced the construct of "team psychological safety" and defined it as "a shared belief held by members of a team that the team is safe for interpersonal risk taking." Taking a risk around your team members may sound simple. But asking a basic question like "why are we doing this project?" may make someone feel stupid. This is a common problem among technologists, where being right and being perceived as smart are prized possessions.

Fundamentally, creating psychological safety facilitates communication. It supports the belief that you won't be humiliated, rejected, or punished for speaking up with an idea, question, or concern. This creates a climate where people feel they can take risks without feeling insecure or embarrassed for being wrong. Creating a culture of psychological safety has been linked with increased creativity, productivity, and engagement. When people feel like they can take risks and be themselves, they're more likely to come up with innovative solutions and speak up when they see a problem. Teams where there is no perceived psychological safety are characterized by a lack of trust, where team members are afraid to openly give and receive feedback or share bad news. In simpler words, you'll get the best out of people by letting everyone themselves in a judgment-free zone.

Creating psychological safety requires leaders to pay attention to team dynamics and take steps to make sure that everyone can be heard. They need to set the tone and demonstrate that it's safe to take risks and make mistakes. Share your own stories of where you've taken risks and that didn't work out and what you learned from the experience. Encourage everyone to give feedback to each other, without fear of reprisal. Create opportunities for employees to socialize with each other outside of work. Team building exercises, social events, and informal networking opportunities can help people feel more connected.

Psychological safety does not mean that you don't expect people to work hard or be held accountable for their actions. But it does mean you're creating an environment where people feel they can take risks and openly discuss difficult issues. This way, you can tap into the full potential of your team and create a cohesive, productive group.

Action: what phase of Tuckman's model is your team at? Norming, storming, forming, or performing? Is your team performing at their highest potential? If not, how can you help them get there? Have you created an environment where people feel comfortable taking risks and providing feedback? If not, what can you do to change that?

THE LEADER AS COACH

We can't know everything as technology leaders. The rate of change is so fast, and technology is more complex and interconnected than ever. The role of an IT leader must continuously adapt to changing circumstances. IT leaders need to act as a coach now more than ever to help team members grow and keep up with the pace of change. A coach is someone who provides guidance, support, and feedback. The coaching leader's job is to help team members identify their strengths and weaknesses, set goals and develop a plan to reach those goals, and overcome obstacles along the way. Coaching will become an increasingly important leadership skill to help get the most out of the people you already have. The leader as coach is an empowering management style that supports both personal and professional growth in the employee. Coaching encourages collaboration and inspires a high level of engagement. It also helps create a learning culture for your team, which is instrumental in a high-performance team. A coaching leader helps employees learn the right skills they need to be successful, both for now and in the future.

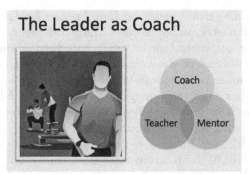

Image 7.3 Coaching leaders excel at managing technologists because they create a supportive and collaborative work environment that encourages open communication, innovation and continuous learning.

A good coach doesn't give you the answers, they help you get to the answers that are already inside of you. The coaching leader listens attentively, gives feedback that is both positive and constructive, and is patient enough to help team members make their own mistakes and grow and learn. Everyone has the potential to become a coaching leader (see Image 7.3), but it's a skill that must be practiced. Coaching leaders focus on developing individuals, supporting the learning process and gaining lasting performance improvement.

If you want to adopt a coaching mindset with your team, one of the best ways to start is by learning to ask better questions. Asking better questions helps you unlock your team's potential and decision-making ability. Better questions are open-ended questions that can't be answered with a yes or no since these questions don't encourage problem-solving. Open-ended questions require you to think critically and come up with your own ideas. Here are a few examples of good open-ended questions designed to spark creative thinking and problem-solving:

- If you could change just one thing about this process, what would it be?
- What are the pros and cons of doing things this way?
- How could we approach this problem differently?
- What other options could we consider?
- Do you think there is an easier way to get the same results?

Asking better questions requires employees to think critically and come up with their own answers. Questions encourage creativity, collaboration, and problem-solving. But many leaders rank the coaching style as one of their least favorites because it takes time and effort to teach their employees. The coaching leadership style is extremely effective, but it does require patience and a willingness to invest in your team's development. But the benefits of coaching are worth the investment since it also leads to a more engaged, productive, and happier workforce.

In his book *Leading with Questions: How Leaders Find the Right Solutions by Knowing What to Ask*, author Michael Marquardt suggests that some of the biggest disasters in corporate America might have been avoided if their leaders had asked questions. Leaders who were aware of, but never questioned, employee actions may have influenced corporate implosions at Enron, WorldCom, Lehman Brothers, and Arthur Andersen among many others. The good news is that asking great questions is yet another skill you can improve with practice.

Aside from creating a safe environment and asking better questions, the GROW framework (see Image 7.4) can also help you develop a coaching leadership style. GROW is an acronym for goal, reality, options and will/way forward. The GROW framework helps ensure that goals are achievable and realistic. It also helps to generate options and create a plan to move forward. The GROW model can be used to help individuals and organizations grow, but it would also work for individual development. Let's look at each step of the GROW process in more detail:

- **Goal**. Start with establishing the goal. For example, you may want your team to be more innovative, so your goal could be framed as, "I want our team to come up with three new ideas we can implement in the next six months." Your personal goal might be getting a promotion over the next two years. Pick something meaningful that will make a difference if you succeed.
- **Reality**. Once you establish a goal, get a realistic picture of where you or your team is starting from. This helps you understand what needs to change and helps you identify obstacles that might be in the way. For example, you might find that your team is already innovative, but they lack the resources to implement their ideas.

The GROW Model

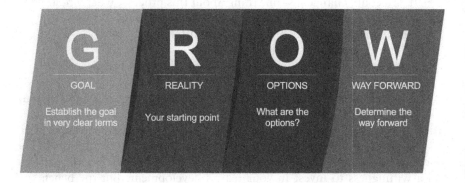

Image 7.4 The GROW model enables technology leaders to take a systematic approach to coaching and goal-setting that enables their teams to reach their full potential.

- **Options**. The next step is to brainstorm options to help reach the goal. Discuss options as a team and decide on the best ones together. Typical questions to ask include: "What else could we do? What if this or that constraint was removed? Would that change things? What are the advantages and disadvantages of each option?" In our innovation example above, you might explore giving your team more resources or setting aside dedicated innovation and "think time" each week.
- **The way forward**. Get your team to commit to specific actions and establish a timeline for progress reviews. This helps make sure they are accountable and will also help you track their progress. Using our innovation example again, you might decide to implement a scheduled innovation time each week. Google's "20% time" is a famous example of this where employees are encouraged to spend 20% of their time working on projects that are outside of their normal job responsibilities. Gmail, Google News, and AdSense all came from following this process.

The coaching leadership style empowers individuals and teams to be their best and do their best. To get coaching right, you need to be able to ask good questions and be equally receptive to answering some questions yourself when the answers aren't clear. A coaching leadership style requires providing clear and actionable feedback, something not all managers are comfortable with. Practice giving feedback and it will become natural. Technology leadership is about so much more than coding or managing software deployments. It's about inspiring people to do their best work and unleashing their creativity to solve problems.

Action: does the coaching leadership style resonate with you? If you don't think this style would work for you or your team, why? What do you think would be more effective? There is no single right answer for everyone and every situation.

MANAGING CONFLICT

Sooner or later, you are going to encounter situations where members of your team just can't seem to see eye to eye. In these cases, it's important to remember that it's not always possible to please everyone and that ultimately the responsibility for the business outcome rests on your shoulders. As a leader, you're going to need to make decisions that are in the best interest of the team, even if it means making some individuals unhappy. When team members aren't getting along, it can have a negative effect on productivity and morale. One of your most important responsibilities is managing conflict and helping team members find a compromise. When conflict arises on a team and the leader doesn't help mediate, it can destroy morale.

Most people try to avoid conflicts, but you shouldn't see conflict as a bad thing. Conflicts represent an opportunity for everyone to learn and grow including you as a leader. Mediating conflicts is one of those leadership skills that takes time and practice. There's more art than science to mediating conflicts, and it helps if you already have trust and respect in place before stepping into the middle of a big issue. If you find yourself in the middle of a heated argument, here are a few things you can do to help defuse the situation:

- **Remain calm and objective**: a leader should be the voice of reason, even in the most challenging situations. It can be difficult to stay calm when everyone's emotions are running high, but it's important to remember that you need to set an example for the team. When you're finding yourself caught up in the moment, take a pause and connect with your breathing. A mindful pause can be performed in as little as 10 seconds and can help you to reset and refocus your mind.
- **Listen to both sides**: it's important to get the full story before passing any judgment. Both parties in the conflict need to be given a chance to share their side. Sometimes people just want to be heard and understood. Once you've heard both sides, don't play favorites. Taking sides in an argument will only make the situation worse and further damage relationships in the team if everyone else is forced to pick sides. Conflict can be uncomfortable, but it's temporary if you take the time to work through the issue.
- **Facilitate a resolution**: the goal of mediating a conflict isn't to just get through tension, but to help find a resolution to the problem. It's usually best to have everyone think through a solution or compromise on their own. But if people are too far on opposite sides of an argument, you may need to adapt a more autocratic leadership style and make the final decision. But don't do it without making sure that everyone's voice is heard first and make it clear that you own the outcome of your decision. Sometimes, people are just afraid that a bad decision will reflect poorly on them, so owning the outcome may put them more at ease.
- **Compromise**: in many cases, the best resolution to a conflict is a compromise. It's important to remember that everyone isn't always going to be happy with the outcome. Of course, as the leader you need to be fully behind the compromise as being the right decision.

Team conflict is natural and normal and is going to happen sooner or later. The key is to not let it get in the way of the team's performance. Help your people learn and grow by working through conflict. By remaining calm, listening to both sides, and facilitating a resolution, you can turn a negative situation into a positive one.

FIVE SECRETS OF HIGH-PERFORMING TEAMS

IT leaders are responsible for keeping the lights on and ensuring that critical systems are up and running, but they're also expected to be innovative and drive digital transformation. It's a lot to ask of any team, let alone one that's dealing with changing technology, budget constraints, and talent shortages. A well-performing team can continue to improve and you can turn around a struggling team with the right effort and focus. Taking a team from good to great usually involves five steps: setting the right vision, learning from mistakes, becoming a learning organization, dealing with tough issues, and using clear communication. Let's examine one in more detail.

1. **Set the right goals and create a shared vision and purpose.** The best teams know what they're trying to do and why it matters. They understand the company's strategy and how their work fits into the bigger picture. This clarity of purpose gives them a shared goal to strive for and a reason to care about their work.
2. **Learn from mistakes and improve.** Great teams are never satisfied with their current performance level and are always looking for ways to improve. They experiment with new ideas and embrace change. They share best practices with each other and strive to do everything better next time.
3. **Develop a learning culture.** High-performing teams have the right skills and knowledge and where they don't, they go find it. They have a learning culture where team members ask for help and share their knowledge with each other. These teams continue learning and growing by dedicating time to technical training. As a leader, you need to recognize that a significant amount of learning occurs informally between team members working together on projects. Make sure to provide opportunities for collaboration. If employees are pursuing certification, create informal study groups and show your support.
4. **Address tough issues.** High-performance teams understand that difficult conversations are a normal and necessary part of work. They also know when it is appropriate to escalate an issue. They take the time to solve disagreements thoroughly before coming to a final decision or settling on an outcome.
5. **Use clear communication.** Performing teams share information openly and frequently. They keep each other up to date on changes, both big and small. They use a variety of communication channels (e.g., email, slack, video conferencing) to make sure that everyone is informed.

It's also important to view team members as distinct individuals with their own unique talents and weaknesses. The best teams know how to play to each other's strengths and help them overcome their weaknesses. They fill in each other's gaps and have each other's backs.

QUIET QUITTING AND OTHER HEADWINDS

Generation Z calls it "quiet quitting" and millennials call it "setting boundaries." Generation X calls it "slacking off." Coasting culture is here and it's a big problem for leaders everywhere. Generation Z and some younger millennials have some of the lowest employee engagement level of all time, according to Gallup data. The Reddit group r/antiwork has more than 2.1 million members and the proclamation, "Unemployment for all, not just the rich!" Proponents of antiwork believe that employers exploit their employees, and that quiet quitting is a legitimate excuse for professional laziness. This isn't a generational problem; employees of all ages are showing less enthusiasm for work than ever before and it's a serious issue for technology leaders.

Quiet quitting rejects the workplace hustle culture, professional burnout, and the presumption that people's jobs should form the basis for their identities. Quiet quitters reject meetings after 5, don't answer phone calls after hours, and let emails sit for days. Some lower-level workers proclaim that they are simply "acting their wage." Quiet quitters are suddenly finding that they are also the first ones being let go during layoffs. Worse yet, they're finding themselves without any marketable accomplishments to help them find their next job.

Before the buzzwords came, we used to just call quiet quitting workplace apathy. Apathy is a lack of feeling or emotion. It's an emotional numbness or sense of indifference. Apathy is characterized by boredom, lack of motivation, and social withdrawal. It usually entails doing just enough to not get fired or to get your boss angry. Apathy has a negative impact on team morale and performance, so it's critical for leaders to be aware of apathy and address it early. Mediocre performance is harmful to the employee's future and to the organization. Apathy is also contagious. When people see other people putting in the minimum effort, they're more likely to do the same.

Apathy comes from being bored and unchallenged. When someone becomes disengaged, they lose motivation. Apathy starts in the mind and then comes out in performance. Addressing workplace apathy starts with the leader. Leaders need to be aware of their own level of engagement and set the tone for their team. If you're not engaged, your team won't be either. Be encouraging and upbeat, give employees a sense of purpose and make sure they feel like they're part of something larger. Delegate your authority and trust your team to do great work. Take an interest in their development and let them know that you're invested in their success. Listen to employee concerns and address them directly. Help them see the connection between their work and the company's mission. Encourage a growth mindset by challenging them to stretch themselves and learn new things. The longer apathy goes unchecked, the more damage it will do to your team's morale and to their performance.

Aside from apathy, other headwinds on the way to building a high-performing team include:

- **Not enough communication.** Team members need to be able to trust and rely on each other. If there is a lack of communication, it will be difficult for everyone to build trust. How much communication is enough? The answer is almost universally "more."
- **Lack of trust.** If team members can't overcome trust issues, it will be hard for them to work together. Look out for subtle trust issues. For example, some companies reward performance in the form of a cash bonus, but you may need to make sure that people aren't undermining each other trying to make themselves look better. While healthy competition is OK, the perception of limited bonus pools or promotion opportunities can sometimes pit teammates against each other.
- **Lack of leadership.** A high-performing team needs a leader who can provide guidance and direction. Leaders need to be able to articulate the team's vision and objectives and help everyone understand how their work fits into the bigger picture. In other words, a high-performing team starts with you.
- **Not valuing diversity.** A team that values all forms of diversity will be more likely to be successful than a team that doesn't. Diversity brings different thoughts and perspectives to the table, which can help the team solve problems better. A team that is homogeneous may have difficulty seeing different points of view and may make one-dimensional decisions. Make sure you're leveraging all members of the team regardless of their experience and that everyone contributes to problem-solving. Calling out an individual for their opinions can help get better insight and can also increase engagement levels.

These are just a few issues that can get in the way of building a high-performing team. Be aware of these roadblocks and take steps to overcome them. Building a high-performance team takes time. It won't happen overnight, but if you're patient and put in the work, you'll eventually see the results.

Action: leaders own the tone and atmosphere of their team. If you are seeing signs of apathy, it's time to act. Start by taking a close look at yourself and see if you might be part of the problem. Are you bored or unchallenged? If someone on your team is bored or unchallenged, help them find ways to reignite their passion or help them find something more inspiring elsewhere.

LEADING THROUGH CRISIS

Mergers, divestitures, and economic problems can throw even high-performing teams off balance. In times of uncertainty, it's important for leaders to be a source of stability. That means having a clear head and staying calm under pressure. It can be difficult to stay calm when things are chaotic, but it's important to remember that your team is looking to you for guidance. If you can keep your head during a crisis, they'll be more likely to do the same. Cool heads solve problems rather than making small problems bigger with emotional reactions.

There are a lot of things that can throw a company into turmoil. Whether it's a sudden change in leadership, a financial crisis, merger, or something else entirely, it's the leader's job to maintain composure and keep things running smoothly. Napoleon Bonaparte once said that a military genius is "the man who can do the average thing when everyone else around him is losing his mind." Most people don't do well with change or turmoil, which means there's an advantage to be gained by people who stay calm under pressure.

As a Chief Information Security Officer (CISO) for 25 years, I've had to deal with a lot of high-pressure security incidents. These events can happen any time of the day or night and there's usually quite a bit of pressure to get answers you may not know. Management wants frequent status updates while you're still trying to ensure that an incident is contained. IT leaders with production responsibilities may run into similar challenges during system outages. A faulty update crashes an important server. The network has an outage. Every second of downtime translates to a financial loss. These high-pressure situations make or break leaders.

Whatever the situation is, an important key to getting through a crisis is remembering that you're not in it alone. Other people have dealt with similar challenges and come out the other side and if you keep your cool, it will be easier to get people aligned on resolving the issue. Also realize that everything isn't under your control. You can't always prevent things from going wrong, but you can control how you react to them.

In a high-pressure situation, your most difficult problem is not only the issue at hand, but your reaction and mental state. Even with strong leadership fundamentals in place, managing your emotions under high stress takes experience. Here are a few tips that may help you stay calm under pressure:

- **Don't take it personally**: it's never about you, it's about the situation. Focus on the present: you can't change the past and the future hasn't unfolded yet. All you can do is control what's happening right now. Worrying about what could happen or what already happened won't help you solve the problem.
- **Focus on what you can control**: you can't control everything, so focus on what you can control and let go of everything else. Focusing on the things that you can directly change helps you feel calmer and more in control of the situation.
- **Take a breather**: if you need to, take some time to step away from tense situations even if it's only for a few minutes. When we're under stress, our breathing becomes shallow and fast. This sends more oxygen to

our muscles and prepares us for fight-or-flight. But it also has the effect of making us feel more anxious. A few deep breaths can help you calm down. Navy Sea Air and Land (SEAL) practice controlled breathing techniques to stay calm and focused under high pressure. This technique is known as box breathing, or square breathing, and it helps regulate your body's natural calming response by slowing down your respiration and decreasing your cortisol levels. It also works by distracting your mind as you count and breathe, calming your nervous system and decreasing stress in your body. To perform box breathing, breathe in for four seconds, hold your breath for four seconds, breathe out for four seconds, then hold for another four seconds, and repeat. You can gradually increase the count as you feel your nervous system relax. Box breathing is simple, but it is also a combat-ready technique. Practicing it when you don't need to will help you fall back on it without thinking during a real crisis. Try some box breathing any time you're feeling stressed and the behavior will become automatic.

• **Keep perspective**: keep a long-term perspective and know that very few IT problems are life-or-death or permanent problems that can't be fixed. If the situation was your fault, try to learn from the experience and make it right. Even if the problem resulted from someone else, like a cybersecurity incident, you own the response and the outcome. Just because something wasn't your fault, doesn't mean that you don't have ownership of the issue.

Action: practice box breathing and mindfulness techniques frequently to stay calm under pressure. The more you practice, the more it will become second nature during a real crisis.

SUCCESSION PLANNING: HOW AND WHY TO OBSOLETE YOURSELF AS QUICKLY AS POSSIBLE

Even the best leaders should know when it's time to step aside. One of the most famous examples was when Steve Jobs handed over the day-to-day leadership duties of CEO over to Tim Cook. Their relationship was far from perfect. Three years before Jobs's death, Cook was quoted as saying that he would never replace him. But ultimately this move helped address Jobs' failing health and did what was best for Apple.

Instead of being threatened by promising talent, groom them and prepare them as your eventual successor. When the time comes for you to step down, you can rest assured that things will be left in good hands. Leaders often think they're too busy to spend time on succession planning or that no one is good enough to replace them. But if you want to build a resilient team, you need to do some form of succession planning for your role and for other key roles on your team.

Succession planning is a strategy in which companies appoint another employee to take over leadership roles. This helps guarantee that the company will continue operating efficiently after somebody leaves for a new opportunity, retires, or passes away. Many leaders see the value in cross-training critical skills on their team, but they forget to include themself. I've only worked in one organization that had a formal succession planning process. As part of the process, you would identify the critical roles on your team and a potential successor for each one including your own role. Potential successors could come from anywhere in the company. You had to rate if that person was ready today or if they needed further development to be a plausible successor. Remember that having a fixed mindset will cause you to create unconscious biases. Even if someone isn't ready today, high-potential employees tend to improve and grow over time and may grow into the role in a few years.

You might think that planning your own succession isn't important and that your company should figure it out after you're gone. But one day you might decide to take advantage of a new opportunity. Maybe you're nearing retirement. It could even be that there's a bigger role within the organization and you want to go for it. I've seen promotions stall because there was no obvious plan to backfill the old role. Succession planning ultimately helps you step out of a role more gracefully.

There are many ways to go about succession planning, but the best way is the one that fits your company's culture. Here's a simple succession planning process:

1. **Acknowledge your company's culture**. Your succession candidate needs to be the right fit from multiple angles. In an aggressive, get-things-done culture, a more laid-back personality who might be technically competent for a role might not be the right personality fit to succeed in the role.
2. **Consider all the alternatives**. Not everyone is trying to move up a hierarchy. Expand your candidates to include peers. Perhaps you could collapse your team under another team. Maybe there's a senior leader ready for a new challenge.
3. **Create and manage a plan**. Succession planning is not about replacing a leader with anyone. It's about replacing a leader with someone who's prepared for the role. The candidate you have in mind may need some development before they are ready to take over a given role. Some roles are also specific enough that there's simply no obvious internal candidates to groom for the position. C-level technology executives may not have a clear heir apparent in the organization. In these cases, you may have no choice but to recruit outside the company if the need arises.

Most leaders have one or two employees capable of really stepping up and doing more. Letting someone act as your right-hand person can keep meetings moving while you're out of the office and eventually help groom them as your successor. I rarely cancel my team meeting since I have two backups who can help keep the cadence going if I'm away. This makes me more flexible covering meetings, but it also gives my leaders exposure to senior management. This helps get senior management comfortable with the idea of this person one day inheriting your role.

Action: who could step into your role one day? How could you start preparing them today to lead your role in the future? Start by giving them opportunities to grow and make sure they're getting some exposure to your boss. If your boss doesn't know who your selection is, they won't support the choice.

SUMMARY

In this chapter, we learned the steps required to build a high-performance team. Creating psychological safety and watching out for workplace apathy are all important to getting the most out of a team. Remember these important points:

- Technology workers are expensive, and the number of companies looking for qualified and competent tech talent across the country is increasing. This means that you might have some sticker shock when you ask candidates for their salary expectations.
- Hiring difficult people will create disharmony on your team and make it difficult for your team to function properly. Avoid hiring toxic superstars and consider the overall needs of the team.
- A high-performing team is one that feels safe to take risks and communicate openly with each other. To create a culture of psychological safety, leaders need to set the tone from the top and demonstrate that it's OK for team members to make mistakes. Leaders also need to encourage team members to give feedback to each other, without fear of reprisal. When team members feel safe taking risks, they're more likely to come up with innovative solutions and speak up when they see a problem.
- Bruce Tuckman's model of team development includes four steps: forming, storming, norming, and performing. Tuckman's model shows that teams can perform at their highest potential when they feel comfortable taking risks and providing feedback. Some teams never reach the performing stage, while others coast along in the norming stage. Psychological safety is a key ingredient.
- The great resignation is a term used to describe the wave of technology employees who are leaving their jobs in search of new opportunities. The leadership challenge posed by the great resignation is twofold: how to keep the talent you have and how to attract anyone new.

- Managing team conflicts is important. It involves being objective, listening to both sides and helping to find a resolution that works for everyone. Conflict provides an opportunity for team members to learn and grow, but it's important for the leader to remain calm and neutral in difficult conversations.
- A good leader knows how to ask questions that inspire people to think critically and come up with their own solutions. Coaching leadership style takes time and patience, but the benefits are well worth the investment.
- The GROW framework can be used to help individuals and organizations achieve more. It can also be beneficial for your own personal development. The steps of the GROW model include establishing a goal, assessing the current reality, exploring options, and deciding on a way forward.
- Team members can become disengaged, sometimes called "quiet quitting." This can be caused by a variety of things, such as a lack of communication, a lack of trust, or a lack of leadership.
- Being the calm in the storm is about leadership and being able to maintain your composure under pressure. It's about managing your emotions and providing support to others who might be struggling. Practice controlled breathing and mindfulness to stay calm under pressure and focus on the present moment. Remember that very few IT problems are life-or-death situations.
- Succession planning is a process of identifying and preparing potential successors for key roles in an organization. It can help improve retention and company culture and allows businesses to prepare for future changes.

REFERENCES AND FURTHER READING

Christensen, Clayton M. *The Innovator's Dilemma*. Harper Business, 2011.
Dyer, Wayne W. *The Power of Intention*. Hay House, 2004.
Lencioni, Patrick. *The Five Disfunctions of a Team*. Ediciones Urano, 2023.
Ries, Eric. *The Lean Startup: How Today's Entrepreneurs Use Continuous Innovation to Create Radically Successful Businesses*. Currency, 2017.
Surowiecki, James. *The Wisdom of Crowds: Why the Many Are Smarter than the Few*. Abacus, 2005.
Thorndike, William N. *The Outsiders: Eight Unconventional CEOS and Their Radically Rational Blueprint for Success*. Harvard Business Review Press, 2012.

Chapter 8

Execution and getting things done

Complexity is the enemy of execution.

Tony Robbins

WHY EXECUTION MATTERS

They say that action speaks louder than words, and this is especially true in the business world. Ideas are worthless unless they are put into action. Execution is the process of turning a plan or an idea into a reality. It involves putting people, process, and technology together and making sure that everything works together smoothly. Even when businesses have a great plan, many fail because they are unable to execute on that plan.

You can't do everything yourself and you shouldn't try to. Delegation is critical for good execution. Delegation doesn't mean abdicating responsibility; it means giving others the authority to act on your behalf. When you delegate tasks, you're still responsible for the overall outcome, but you're also freed up to focus on more important things. Delegation is just a way to make sure that someone is accountable for important projects and goals. When you have someone accountable and they know that they're accountable, you're more likely to get good results. Many projects fail because of collective or unclear ownership and accountability.

Building an execution-focused team begins with you. You can have the best strategy in the world but if you can't execute it, it's worthless. In fact, execution is so important that it has been called the "new differentiator" in businesses. In a world where products are becoming commoditized and competition is fierce, execution is what separates successful companies from unsuccessful ones. Failing to capitalize on a good idea also means falling behind the competition. When you fall far enough behind, you become the next Blackberry, Kodak, or Blockbuster Video.

This chapter looks at getting things done. If you and your team are getting things done, you will stand out from your peers and will also be positioned to take on bigger challenges in the future. But good execution isn't only about getting everything done, it's also about getting the right things done

DOI: 10.1201/9781003314707-10

and getting them done efficiently. This doesn't mean outworking everyone, it means saying no to other good ideas and focusing on what matters most. Steve Jobs said it best: "Innovation is saying no to 1,000 things."

Some people think that execution is about having a plan and then following it to the letter. But execution is more than just having a plan; execution requires being flexible and adapting to changes and overcoming obstacles. The best-laid plans often go off the rails and it's up to the execution-focused leader to be able to make course corrections and keep everyone moving in the right direction.

Action: what are your top work priorities? What are your boss's top priorities? If you don't know the answer, make sure to figure this out.

DEVELOP AN EXECUTION MINDSET

Most technology projects involve elements of people, process, and technology. To execute a plan effectively, you need to have the right people in place who are willing and able to do the work. You also need to have processes in place that are efficient and effective. If a process can't be automated, then people need to understand what to do and how to do it. Finally, you need to have the right technology. The right technology must consider how you interact with customers, employees, and partners. The right technology isn't always what works best, it's what works best at your company and for your specific circumstances. The same can be said for people. People are not just bodies that show up to work; they have mindsets, attitudes, and behaviors. Collectively, the way people behave in your company has themes and these themes form your corporate culture (see Image 8.1).

An execution-focused culture means that people are driven to get things done. They don't wait for someone else to tell them what to do; they take initiative and make things happen. An execution-focused culture also means that people are held accountable for results. Execution-oriented cultures share some common traits:

- **A bias for action**: it may seem obvious, but in an execution-focused culture, there is a strong bias toward getting started. This means that people take initiative and don't wait for permission or approval. Cultures like Silicon Valley and Wall Street use action-oriented cultures to help them keep up with competitors and enter new markets faster. A bias toward action doesn't mean creating a false sense of urgency for everything, just the important things. Urgency for every task regardless of importance is simply a culture of burnout.
- **Focus on results**: execution-focused cultures value results. This means that people are more likely to be measured by what they accomplish rather than by how they do it. In addition to the military and most sports teams, industries that offer employee bonuses generally base those rewards on results.

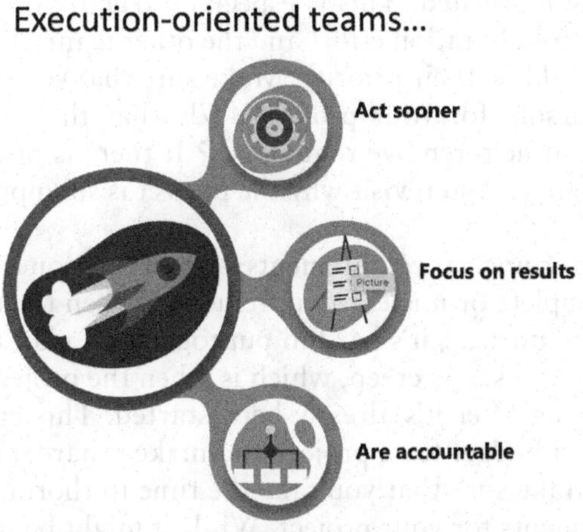

Execution-oriented teams...

Act sooner

Focus on results

Are accountable

Image 8.1 Execution-oriented teams prioritize feedback and iteration over endless planning, allowing them to achieve results faster and with greater agility.

- **A culture of accountability**: in an execution-focused culture, people are held accountable for their actions. This means there is a clear understanding of who is responsible for what and that individuals are held accountable for results. Professional services firms have a long history of accountability baked into their culture with named account executives assigned to each account.

Of course, having an execution mindset doesn't mean that you can't have fun getting work done. In fact, execution-focused cultures often have more fun because they're focused on results and not busy work. There's a sense of accomplishment. Having an execution mindset also doesn't entail sacrificing quality for quantity. Getting more things done poorly is not useful for anyone. Of course if execution seems so simple, it would be worth looking at why so many information technology (IT) projects fail.

THE TOP REASONS IT PROJECTS FAIL

Sometimes, IT projects fail even when the overall strategy is sound. In this section, we'll examine common causes for IT project failures and explore how to avoid these problems. IT projects go wrong for many reasons, but you can overcome challenges if you recognize them early. Let's look at common reasons that IT projects fail and how to address the issues earlier.

- **Lack of executive sponsorship**: one of the most common reasons for big IT project to fail is lack of executive sponsorship from the top. When there's no senior support for a project, it can be difficult to keep people motivated. This is especially true if you're working on a cross-team collaboration effort and the other teams don't see that your priority should be their priority. Make sure that you have clear executive sponsorship for your projects. Who has the authority to make decisions and help remove roadblocks? If there is no senior executive sponsor, go back and revisit why the project is so important in the first place.

- **Incomplete or unclear requirements**: another reason for IT project failure is incomplete or unclear requirements. When the requirements for a project are unclear, it's hard to put together a plan that works. This can also lead to scope creep, which is when the project's requirements keep changing after it's already been started. This can throw off the schedule and budget for a project and make it harder to complete successfully. Make sure that you take the time to thoroughly understand the requirements for your project. While it might be tempting to move directly into execution, make sure that you understand the objectives and what "done" looks like first.

- **Unrealistic expectations**: IT projects often have unrealistic expectations, which can lead to disappointment and frustration when the project doesn't deliver on those expectations. Unrealistic expectations may take the form of insufficient timelines, lack of budget, or clarity of scope. Make sure that you set realistic expectations for your project right from the outset and capture those requirements in a formal document that can serve as a project charter. Avoid scope creep by keeping a tight handle on changes that happen during the project. This doesn't mean saying no to changes, but it does mean being thoughtful about how changes will impact the overall health of a project and which changes are important to make regardless of their impact.

- **Lack of communication**: communication issues derail many projects. This can take the form of failing to keep stakeholders informed about progress, not sharing important information with the project team, or not having a clear process for issue escalation. Put together a simple communication plan for complex projects. Who needs to be kept in the loop and how often? What is the process for escalating issues? Make sure that all stakeholders are aware of how communications will work.

- **Lack of planning**: many IT projects fail simply because they are not properly planned. This can include failing to create a project schedule, not allocating enough resources to the project, or not having a clear plan for how the project will be executed. Make sure you take the time to develop a clear and concise plan for your project. Include milestones, roles and responsibilities, timelines, and budgets. Avoid overly complex plans. If you can't explain how you're approaching something in a few sentences, you might be making it overly complicated. If you don't understand a plan enough to explain it succinctly, no one else will either.

Bigger projects should have a formal project manager assigned. This shouldn't be a technical subject matter expert (SME); it should be a professional project manager. Many people think that a strong technical SME can also handle the mechanics of managing a project, but they're usually wrong.

- **Insufficient user involvement**: end-user feedback is critical to the success of most IT projects. Without user feedback, it's difficult to ensure that the final product meets needs and expectations. Many projects are considered failures only because end users don't accept the solution or understand how it works. Make sure that you build user feedback into your project plan from the beginning. Set up regular check-ins with key users to get their input and make sure that they are happy with the direction you are taking. Start with smaller pilot groups rather than deploying across many users all at once. Get a minimum viable product (MVP) out to a handful of users fast and then iterate based on their feedback.
- **Lack of talent**: the most skilled employees are usually in high demand across many projects. Sometimes a technology is new or there are only a handful of people at your company who understand it. Cloud, data science, and cybersecurity skills are in demand for many projects. Insufficient project resourcing creates bottlenecks and roadblocks if you can't get the right people in place. Make sure you have the right team assembled. This includes not only people with the right skills, but people with the right attitude. Consider hiring consultants to fill in gaps if this is an option.

Of course, there are many other reasons that technology projects fail. Make sure you're observing what approaches are working or not in your company and learn from those experiences. Most companies are not that big on new technology, regardless of what they claim. If a new tool isn't accepted by your users, clients, or customers, then all the efforts to get to the finish line have been wasted.

Action: do you have a planning process that accounts for things that can go wrong? Plans can often be too optimistic and not account for demands on key resources, competing projects and other variables that can throw off good execution efforts.

PRIORITIZE USING THE EISENHOWER MATRIX

Do you know what your top priorities are? Are you and your team overwhelmed with too much to do and too little time? If so, it might be time to start using the Eisenhower Matrix. The Eisenhower Matrix is a tool that can help you sort out priorities and figure out what's the most important thing to do next.

Simple Eisenhower Matrix

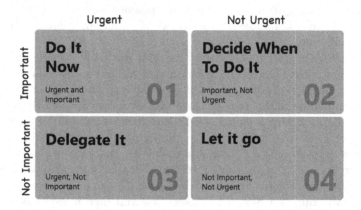

Image 8.2 The Eisenhower Matrix provides a simple and effective tool for technology leaders to prioritize their work, enabling them to focus on what's important and urgent and minimize busywork and distractions.

The Eisenhower Matrix (see Image 8.2) works its way into a lot of leadership books for good reason: it's a great way to prioritize both projects and tasks. It helps you to determine what's important, what can wait, what should be delegated, and what to ignore. The Eisenhower Matrix is named after US President Dwight D. Eisenhower, who was known for his effective time management techniques. The Eisenhower Matrix is a simple tool that helps you to prioritize. It is based on the premise that leaders should do things that are important or important and urgent, but not waste time on everything else.

The matrix consists of four simple quadrants:

1. **Urgent and important:** these are the tasks that you need to do now. They are important and if you don't do them, there could be consequences. For example, if your car is broken down and it's your only means of transportation, this is probably your top priority until it's resolved.
2. **Important, but not urgent:** these are tasks that are important, but they can wait. They are not as time-sensitive as the tasks in the first quadrant. Planning your long-term strategy and career development are important, but not urgent tasks.
3. **Urgent but not important:** these are tasks that seem like they need attention now, but they are not important to you or your team. These typically land on your desk in the form of other people's priorities and are great candidates for delegation. The sense of urgency sometimes causes leaders to jump in and handle it themselves, but this takes your efforts away from the first two quadrants which is where you should be spending most of your time.

4. **Not urgent and not important**: these are the tasks that you probably don't need to do at all. They just aren't that important. An example would be checking social media or attending some conferences. Tasks that fit into not urgent and not important should be delegated or eliminated.

The Eisenhower Matrix is a simple triage tool and can be very effective helping you prioritize work. When you are feeling overwhelmed with all the things that you need to do, take a step back and evaluate each task or project using the Eisenhower Matrix. Leaders should focus on the things that are important and not waste time on unimportant issues. Lately, I'm using this idea when I can't seem to finish my workday. I ask if what I'm doing right now is urgent and important? If it's not, it can probably wait for tomorrow and shouldn't take away from family time.

No matter how you prioritize your work and your team's work, it's important to use some system to distinguish one task from another. I once witnessed a security leader put close to 100 top priorities for his team on a whiteboard with ten number two priorities. As Jim Collins, author of *Good to Great: Why Some Companies Make the Leap and Others Don't*, said: "If you have more than three priorities, you don't have any." In comparison, I also remember a Chief Information Officer (CIO) who listed their top ten priorities for a huge area of a global financial services firm. He then narrowed that list down to the top three. Then he declared that if we failed on our number one priority, succeeding with the other two wouldn't make up for it. This was crystal clear direction that cut to the chase. This doesn't mean the other work never gets done, but it does mean that the focus stays on the most important things.

Action: where are you or your team being unproductive? Where could you start pushing back or saying no to unimportant tasks? Ask yourself throughout the day: "What the most important thing I could be doing right now?"

DISTRACTIONS AND LESSER GOALS

Robert Brault once said, "we are kept from our goal, not by obstacles, but by a clear path to a lesser goal." In other words, sometimes it's the little things, not the big things that get in the way of our execution. It's the everyday distractions and decisions that take us off course. Keeping the main thing the main thing is critical to make sure that the important things get done. This means saying "no" to distractions and lesser goals, whether they come from inside or outside your organization.

Distractions and competing priorities are execution killers and they are everywhere. Distractions show up in the form of emails demanding your attention, chat messages and notifications from your phone, colleagues dropping by your office for a quick chat, and so on. These distractions happen to you, your team, your boss, and probably just about everyone in your company. You can't control when or where distractions arise, but you can reduce the impact they'll have on important goals by constantly refocusing your team's efforts on the most important things. Common challenges to good execution include:

- **Lack of focus**: trying to achieve too many things simultaneously never ends well. Earlier in the book, we looked at the drawbacks of multitasking. The same principles apply to your team. If they don't understand prioritization and sequencing, they will end up working on things that don't matter or on projects that interest them instead of more important work. Limit your team's work in progress (WIP) by having no more than three to five top priorities at a time and even then, make sure everyone knows their individual top priority. Leaders often worry that everything needs to be done and that it's all equally important, but this is never the case. Put some projects on back burner and if you're not sure which ones, talk to your boss.

- **Indecision**: indecision is a form of procrastination. People put off making decisions in the hopes that answers will become clearer over time. But usually, indecision just leads to delay. Indecision builds stagnation, which is the opposite of momentum. Use the observe, orient, decide and act (OODA) loop to get started. It's better to iterate on "good enough" information and get started and start getting feedback from your results.

- **Not asking for help**: you need the right tools for the job. Many leaders don't ask for help, no matter if it's in the form of consultants or borrowing resources from other parts of the company. If your team doesn't have the necessary skills or technical knowledge, don't expect them to learn everything under the pressure of a tight deadline. While your people may be smart, no one is a fast learner when there is intense time pressure.

- **Perfectionism**: the belief that everything needs to be perfect before you can move forward keeps some teams from ever getting started. Progress is more important than perfection. Perfectionism kills good execution. Embrace the concept of "good enough" plans and minimal viable products.

- **Work environment**: are you working in an office? Remote work is covered in Chapter 9, but if your team works even part time in the office, their work environment can have a big impact on their ability to get things done. A noisy, disorganized, and chaotic work environment makes it hard to focus. Open seating arrangements, excessive noise, and constant interruptions all contribute to execution problems and high cognitive load for your employees. A research study at the University of California at Irvine found that, on average, it takes around 23 minutes for most workers to get back on task after an interruption. If you want your team to be execution-focused, you need to create an environment that supports focus and flow. Flow is a mental state of intense focus and concentration where we are completely absorbed in the task at hand, and we shut out all other distractions. In a flow state, it's possible to make big progress quickly. Bruce Lee once said that "The successful warrior is the average man, with laser-like focus." Better focus gets better and faster results. Creating a work environment that supports execution and flow means having a well-organized and comfortable workspace with enough privacy for people to concentrate on their work and separate areas for collaboration.

Thankless tasks and distractions need to be managed. A thankless task is something that isn't appreciated by your management. Thankless tasks include things like meeting with vendors you have no interest in using and other time wasters. You may be asked to do thankless tasks because your company has not yet established clear priorities or because you're the new person and no one else wants to do it. That's OK, just don't let the calendar get filled with nothing but lesser goals and thankless tasks.

Action: are you and your team getting enough time to work on important projects? Don't just be busy, look for opportunities to back out of unnecessary meetings and block off calendar time for more important work.

LEADING WHEN YOU'RE NOT IN CHARGE

There will be times when you need to get things done through people who don't report to you. In these cases, you may need to guide or persuade a diverse group of stakeholders, peers, and business managers that your projects are important and convince them why they should help you. Many bigger projects involve multiple teams now and getting results in a matrix environment can be challenging. Many of today's organizations have flatter management structures, increased outsourcing, and extensive use of ad-hoc teams. This means that managers need to work through people outside of their team to get things done.

Lateral leadership skills are critical to function in a matrix environment. Lateral leadership means leadership without authority, disciplinary capabilities, and without being the boss. In other words, it's how to lead when you're not in charge. As you can imagine, matrix environments are especially difficult for autocratic leaders who are used to having everyone follow their orders. The most effective leadership tactics rely on influence instead of command-and-control tactics in a matrix environment.

The next time you need cooperation from other teams, consider using these strategies in your messaging:

- **What's in it for them?** What are the benefits for someone working with you on this? How will your project help the other person meet their own objectives? If you can show them that there's something in it for them, they'll be more likely to help you. Make sure they understand why your request is important in the broader context of the company.

- **Communicate clearly.** No one wants to figure out what you want from them. Be clear on what you need and why you need it. Don't beat around the bush with your messaging. The more you can simplify your request, the more likely they will be to help you.
- **Make it easy for people to help you.** If someone agrees to help you, make it as easy as possible for them to assist. Give them all the information they need and be available to answer questions. The easier you can make it for someone to help you, the more likely they will be to follow through. I've seen a lot of requests that start by forwarding multiple email attachments with hundreds of pages of reading for project background. Why not offer to simply take a few moments and bring them up to speed on what they need to know and then articulate exactly what you need from them?
- **Honor your commitments.** Failing to keep commitments or over-promising is dangerous for relationships and erodes trust. When you commit to something, follow through on it. If something happens and you can't follow through, let the other person know as soon as possible and help them figure out an alternate solution that doesn't leave them hanging.
- **Show your gratitude.** Never forget to thank someone for their help. Show your appreciation by sending a thank you email and cc their boss when they've gone above and beyond. A simple "thank you" goes a long way.

Lateral leadership is a skill that's becoming increasingly important in today's business world. By understanding how to lead when you're not in charge, you can be more effective getting things done. Relationship building, clear communication, and showing appreciation are all key elements of good lateral leadership.

REPORTING PROGRESS AND FINISHING WHAT YOU STARTED

Good project execution deserves to be recognized. Make sure to schedule regular progress check-ins with your boss and relevant project stakeholders. Creating a scorecard, project plan, or other document that provides a visual representation of your progress can help tell the story of all the great work your team is doing and keep everyone informed (see Image 8.3). Be honest about progress and don't try to hide setbacks or gloss over problems. Celebrate success. Execution is hard work and it's important to take time to celebrate the wins, even if it's only a milestone on a bigger project that won't finish for a while.

A progress report is a powerful tool that keeps people around a project well-informed and ensures that every team member is operating efficiently

Reporting progress

There is no business
value from projects
that don't finish.

Image 8.3 Completing large projects demonstrates your ability to deliver results, meet deadlines and effectively manage resources.

with their goals being met on time. Whether to submit a progress report daily, weekly, monthly, etc., will heavily depend on the project's scope and complexity. Progress reports help keep track of different projects, provide insights on how to finish projects more effectively, and identify key issues affecting the team's productivity.

Finally, be careful about initiating new projects without completing the ones you've already started. It's easy to get caught up in the excitement of a new idea, which itself can become a form of distraction. There is no business value from projects that don't finish. It takes some discipline to finish what you've started and requires that you know what "done" looks like. Sometimes projects simply become an ongoing part of operations. In either case, know when something is no longer a top priority and make sure that you're re-orienting yourself and your team to the next priority. The busy IT leader may find it liberating to know when to let go of something and say: "close enough." This allows them to shoot for excellence, but also frees us up bandwidth to face the next challenge. Knowing when to stop working on something and when it's time to move on is the mark of a great leader.

Action: discuss project execution with your team. What's working well and what needs to be improved? Make a list of priorities and assign responsibility for each one. For each priority project, make sure that you have:

- Defined what "done" looks like
- Set up a regular status report tracking progress
- Limited your team's WIP by putting less important things into time-boxed efforts or into a project backlog

SUMMARY

Good execution doesn't happen by accident. Good execution usually requires a clear vision and a plan that everyone understands. It also requires a sense of urgency, a focus on results, and clarity about who's accountable for what. Just like not having a plan is wishful thinking, a brilliant plan falls short without good leadership and a team that can execute on that plan. This chapter also covered:

- To achieve execution in a technology leadership role, it is important to set priorities and sequence tasks, limit WIP, make decisions, and have the necessary skills and resources. Leaders often struggle with indecision and lack of resources. Perfectionism can be paralyzing. Work environment also have an impact on execution, with noise and chaos hindering focus and productivity. Create an environment that supports good execution and balances the need to collaborate.
- The Eisenhower Matrix is a simple time management tool that helps to prioritize tasks. The matrix is based on the premise that leaders should do things that are important or important and urgent, but not waste time on everything else. The matrix has four simple quadrants: urgent and important, important but not urgent, urgent but not important, and not urgent and not important. Tasks that fit into the last two quadrants should be delegated or even eliminated.
- Lateral leadership is the ability to lead without authority and it is critical for functioning in a matrix environment. To be successful in a matrix environment, it is important to build relationships with others, communicate clearly, and show appreciation.
- Knowing what "done" looks like is an important part of project execution. Establishing a clear vision and setting expectations up front can help.
- Communicating progress helps the people doing the work see their own progress, builds momentum, and keeps everyone on track. Celebrating successes is also key to maintaining focus and motivation. It is important to remember that execution is hard work, so take time to celebrate the wins.
- Limit the number of projects you have going at any given time. This allows you to give each project the attention it deserves and increase your chances of seeing things through to completion. Celebrate successes along the way.

REFERENCES AND FURTHER READING

Bossidy, Larry, and Ram Charan. *Execution: The Discipline of Getting Things Done.* Random House Business Books, 2011.

Burkeman, Oliver. *Four Thousand Weeks: Time Management for Mortals.* Picador, 2022.

Eyal, Nir. *Indistractable: How to Control Your Attention and Choose Your Life.* Benbella Books, 2021.

Funt, Juliet. *A Minute to Think: Reclaim Creativity, Conquer Busyness, and Do Your Best Work.* Harper Collins, 2021.

Gorman, Tom. *Execution: Create the Vision. Implement the Plan. Get the Job Done.* F+W Media, 2010.

Lepsinger, Richard. *Closing the Execution Gap How Great Leaders and Their Companies Get Results.* Jossey-Bass Publishers, 2010.

Perell, Kim. *The Execution Factor: The One Skill That Drives Success.* McGraw-Hill Education, 2019.

Stack, Laura. *Execution Is the Strategy: How Leaders Achieve Maximum Results in Minimum Time.* Berrett-Koehler Publishers, 2014.

Chapter 9

Leading from anywhere

A guide to the hybrid office

> When leadership is not predefined by proximity and walking around, the best communicators get the seats because they are the most proactive. Really engaged folks are figuring out a way to overcommunicate regardless of the distance.
>
> Adolfo Velasquez
> *SVP, JumpCrew*

Leadership material rarely covers leading in a remote or hybrid office and yet this is where more of us are finding ourselves these days. Like it or not, the pandemic forced many of us to work from home for years and there is no going back to "normal" from here. The pandemic enforced what technology workers already knew: that their job can be done from anywhere.

As the pandemic winds down, many companies will continue to use hybrid or even fully remote workforce models. Smart companies are embracing remote work as a competitive advantage. 3M launched "Work Your Way," a program that allows employees to choose whether they want to work remote, come to the office, or a mix of the two that works best for them. Coinbase adopted a "remote first" model back in 2020, where a remote location is the preference for all new hires. Sites like FlexJobs (https://www.flexjobs.com/) have been pushing the benefits and opportunities of working remotely for years. Many hiring managers I spoke to have reported that interviews are now ending abruptly when the candidate's expectations for remote work aren't met.

While we already covered managing high-performance teams in Chapter 7, there are enough managers struggling with the topic of remote work that it warrants its own treatment. Advances in technology have made it possible for us to connect with each other no matter where we are located geographically. Remote work gives employees increased flexibility and freedom, as well as improved productivity and creativity. However, there are also challenges that come with remote work arrangements, such as employee trust, communication, establishing a clear structure, and dealing with difficult situations without being in person. But with the right tools and strategies in place, remote work can be an incredibly rewarding experience for both employees and employers.

DOI: 10.1201/9781003314707-11

TRUST IS THE FOUNDATION OF REMOTE WORK

As I write this, CEOs like Elon Musk are ordering employees back to the office for a "minimum of 40 hours" a week or recommending they find another job. Many business leaders feel that employees are "pretending to work" at home. Companies are pulling badge records and trying to figure out how to measure productivity (not only attendance), because they don't trust their people. Companies continue to struggle with the concept of hybrid work, with some going so far as to say no to it outright. Employees are responding. Some have resigned, some have taken early retirement, and many are just complaining like crazy.

Leading a remote team begins with trusting them to get their job done (see Image 9.1). Micromanagement and autocratic styles simply don't scale well with remote workers, although I think they are also ineffective in office settings. This is especially true managing technical employees who may want to use their own approach for problem-solving. I'm also willing to bet that if someone isn't performing up to standards at home, they will do an equally bad job in the office.

As a boss, if you have a negative view of remote work or are waiting for things to go back to the way they were, you're going to need to start by adjusting your mindset. Negative attitudes toward remote work will come out in subtle ways. If you think your employees are slacking off because they're not in the office, chances are you will find examples everywhere you look. This lack of trust is obvious now in Wall Street and Silicon Valley companies who suggest that working remotely will hurt employee career progression. Yet studies show that remote workers are often more productive than their office-based counterparts.

A lack of trust is understandable. It is true that some workers have taken two full-time jobs and are doing both simultaneously, some even waiting to get fired from an extra job while the paychecks keep coming. Some members

There is no playbook for the hybrid workplace.

But successful strategies start with trust and focus on objectives and results.

Image 9.1 Remote and hybrid work is here to stay, but there's no playbook or one-size-fits all solution to make this work in every organization.

of the r/overemployed Subreddit claim to be working up to five full-time roles. These people believe that by acting in their own best interests, they are finally following the same rulebook that corporate businesses have followed for years.

There are also employees who have side hustles and are doing well at everything including their day job. These motivated self-starters may very well go on to start their own company. The point is that you can't see or control what people are doing in their home, nor should you try to. The gig economy has taken on a strange new twist by allowing people to work more than one job without their manager's knowledge. But the tactics that work best in the office also apply for remote work: set goals and measure performance. Everything else is just noise.

If you're struggling to trust your team in a remote work setting, the first step is to take a step back and ask yourself if you might be part of the problem. If you are, that's ok. You can still build trust with some effort and an open mind. But ask yourself why you don't trust the same employee in a different location. We are in a new world now, if you are going to try to be the one manager in your company who doesn't adapt, don't expect to attract and retain the best people. Trust issues can spiral out of control quickly and distrust almost always leads to micromanagement which leads to a big drop in employee motivation and morale. Expecting workers to be constantly available or to respond to electronic/phone messages immediately creates a high level of stress. If you have trust issues with your team, you either need a new team or they need a new manager. Just be sure which one is the real problem.

When I started as Chief Information Security Officer (CISO) for the State of Connecticut, most employees had never worked outside an office setting in their entire career. Interactions were almost all done face-to-face in an office. I had come from global companies, some with offices in 100 countries. You're not going to meet everyone face-to-face in an organization that large and employees working in a branch office aren't dramatically different than employees working from a home office. Leaders in larger companies also tend to travel quite a bit and may rarely be in the office themselves. If you are on the road more than you are in the office, your team is already essentially working remotely no matter where they are working from.

Some old school managers can't seem to get used to the concept of remote work. They are suspicious the moment an employee doesn't immediately answer an instant message or if they have an "away" status on their messaging system for too long. Bizarre productivity measures are being employed to put a metric on what it means to be productive. My remote employees don't sit at their desk all day long and neither do I. I get up and take breaks and expect my team to do the same. Just because someone's not responding to chats in real-time, doesn't mean they're off watching Netflix or cutting the lawn. Open your mind and trust that your employees can do their job regardless of their location and that they want to do a good job.

Set objectives and measure results, just like you should be doing if everyone was in an office.

Action: if you're experiencing trust issues with your team working remotely, ask yourself why. Is the work getting done? Are you setting clear expectations and managing performance? How could you let go a little and give your employees more autonomy to work in a way that suits them best?

COMMUNICATION

The biggest hurdle to effective remote work is communication. It turns out that this is also the biggest hurdle in the office, but it is magnified in a remote setting. If you already think you're a good communicator, you're probably still going to need to up your game and do some things differently in a remote setting. More often than you expect, you'll have to communicate the same messages repeatedly until everyone gets it. You may also need to use different channels of communication. Email is great for some communications, but it's not a substitute for an interactive conversation.

I wrote *The Security Leader's Communication Playbook* because CISOs need to communicate up and down an organization to businesspeople and technologists alike. Communication remains one of the biggest hurdles in information technology (IT) and remote work has introduced further complexity to making sure that everyone understands what needs to be done. Communication is a big topic and is harder to get right than most people think. Here are a few tips to help you improve communication with your remote team.

- **Adopt a tailored approach to communication:** good communication doesn't happen by accident. Think about what you're trying to convey. How long the message should be and how much detail should you provide? What do you expect the other person to do with the information? Don't assume that communication is easy just because everyone can do it. Good communicators are much more rare.
- **Use active listening:** most people think that the message itself is the most important part of a communication, but being a good listener is also important. You need to be able to understand what your team is telling you, especially when you're not in the same room. Active listening techniques such as paraphrasing what you heard can help increase everyone's understanding of an issue. But active listening isn't easy and takes practice. We are often distracted by thinking about what we will say as soon as the other person stops talking. Active listening is really just engaged listening. When we fully engage in a conversation, we don't need to think about the techniques that we're using. Being present and attentive is all you need.
- **Use the proper communication channel:** there is no one right way to communicate, but you should use the right medium for the message.

A chat message might be too impersonal for some topics. Complex communications are sometimes best written in email that can be referenced in the future. Other communications really need to be a conversation. Make sure your medium is appropriate for the message and make sure you're not just selecting what's easiest for you. Getting fired is a traumatic experience. Firing someone over chat is not the way to be compassionate.

- **Ask questions**: if you are unsure of what someone is saying, take the time and ask them to explain it. It's hard to gage someone's intent using email and text or chat messages. There's no body language or tone of voice to help you understand if a person is kidding, angry, upset, or confused. But even in a verbal exchange, words can have different meanings. If I say I need a little more time, do I mean days, weeks, or months? If I say I need something as soon as possible (ASAP), does that really mean dropping everything else? You'll never know without asking.
- **Repeat yourself**: just like you may not be the world's best listener, most other people aren't great listeners either. Less than 2% of corporate professionals receive any training in listening skills, yet we know that 60% of people in a group setting are tuned out due to distractions or being lost in thought. This means you are going to need to repeat yourself before your message gets through. How many times? Some people say three times. Others use the "rule of seven." Obviously, you don't want to repeat yourself 20 times in the same conversation, but you also shouldn't expect everyone to absorb the information the first time they hear it. Don't get frustrated with this, it's human nature.
- **Be present**: remote work makes it so easy to read email while you're blankly staring into the camera hoping that no one notices. Give everyone the gift of your presence and engage yourself fully with the meeting or conversation. You'll be happier, communication will be clearer, and your team will appreciate being heard and having your full attention.

According to Erica Dhawan, best-selling author of *Digital Body Language: How to Build Trust and Connection, No Matter the Distance*, people have cues and signals that make up the subtext of our messages. She breaks this concept down into four key principles: valuing visibility, communicating carefully, collaborating competently, and trusting totally.

Remote communication is more difficult because we can't see the other person's reactions to the level of detail that we can in person. However, by following these principles, we can make sure that our message is clear and that we are building trust. Let's examine each principle in a little more detail.

1. **Valuing visibility**: keep your meetings as concise as possible to respect people's time and schedules. This may involve using clear verbal cues such as "let's move on" or "we can discuss this later," so that attendees

know when it is appropriate to bring up new topics or questions. By prioritizing these key elements of effective meeting management, you can ensure that every meeting you host is both productive and engaging for all participants.

2. **Communicating carefully**: take the time to craft your messages and think about how your message will be received. This helps you avoid hasty or careless errors that cause misunderstandings or damage relationships. This also helps ensure your message is heard and understood the first time.

3. **Collaborating competently**: proximity bias can lead to a lack of diversity and inclusion in the decision-making processes, undermining the effectiveness of the team. To counteract this bias, leaders must actively seek ideas from underrepresented groups within the team and try to get everyone's perspective. Additionally, managers can help foster a culture of collaboration by promoting regular communication between team members and establishing clear guidelines for group problem-solving that allows everyone's input to be heard. By building trust and fostering open dialog among team members, organizations can better leverage digital collaboration tools to get better outcomes.

4. **Trusting totally**: trust, vulnerability, and honesty are all important in digital communication. Establishing a healthy connection with people requires trusting that they will be open and honest with you, even when mistakes or misunderstandings happen. This means taking responsibility for our own actions, as well as acknowledging when we have hurt others or made them feel uncomfortable. Additionally, it means being able to bounce back quickly when things don't go as planned and being resilient in the face of adversity.

Ultimately, by understanding and embracing digital body language, we can build strong relationships and communicate more effectively with the people around us regardless of location. Remote work doesn't have to mean worse communication, but it does mean we need better planned communications to make sure that our messages are heard and understood.

SET CLEAR EXPECTATIONS

Hopefully, you already have a recurring team meeting, even if it's just a daily scrum. If not, you need to start having one right away. I'm surprised how many managers fail to put this basic process in place. Team meetings are a great way to keep everyone on the same page and identify issues that need to be addressed together. On a big team, you should meet separately with your direct reports and then less frequently with the larger team.

To get the most out of remote work arrangements, you need to make sure your expectations are communicated and understood by your whole team.

As you begin to adjust your own approach to the new world of remote work, remember the following:

- **Trust is everything**: it bears repeating that remote work requires trust. Companies are pulling virtual private network (VPN) logs and counting keystrokes as ways of measuring how active their employees are at home. These same companies are now pulling badge access to make sure people are really coming into the office as much as they're supposed to in a hybrid work arrangement. The message is loud and clear: "we don't trust you." I don't go near fake productivity measures and neither should you. Being "active" online and getting results are two different things.
- **Encourage team bonding**: the feelings of isolation is a big problem cited by many remote workers. Even if your team is fully remote, it's important to encourage some form of team bonding. This can be done through social media, chat programs, or video conferencing tools like Zoom or Skype. I've grown to hate virtual happy hours, but if you can find a way to make them fun, they can still be a great way to bond with your team. Better yet, try to schedule a real team lunch or real happy hour even if it involves some travel. Bonding is still best done in person.
- **Make tools work for you, not against you**: especially in a large meeting, many people are more inclined to leave feedback or ask a question in the chat window than they would by speaking up. Use this to your advantage and make sure you're monitoring the chat window during meetings and encourage people to use it. Drop links to relevant documents if it's appropriate. My team created something called the Security Hallway to keep each other from feeling isolated at home and to keep communication channels open. The Security Hallway is just a Microsoft Teams open chat channel that includes everyone. It was created in the same spirit as sticking your head out into the hallway to ask someone a question. The ability to casually ask your entire team a question simultaneously is a powerful concept. We keep the Security Hallway lighthearted. It's not all business, we also make jokes, talk about the weather, and let everyone know when you're kicking off early on a Friday afternoon. Learn to leverage the new world of remote work for your advantage.
- **Cameras on or off?** I don't recommend forcing everyone to have cameras on all the time. But none of the time is probably also the wrong answer. Zoom fatigue is a real thing and everyone deserves a break. Strike a balance between asking people to have cameras on and letting them just listen sometimes. Most people will follow your lead if you turn your camera on but remember that everyone's still getting used to people being able to peek into their personal living space and don't always force the issue.
- **Don't ignore performance issues**: performance issues can happen in the office or in a remote setting. If an employee isn't meeting your

expectations, have a conversation with them about it. If the problem persists, take the appropriate action. Being remote isn't an excuse for keeping a badly performing employee or tolerating inappropriate behavior. Handle the tough conversations either in person or in a 1-1 meeting with cameras on so you can read body language.

- **Unplug and let your team unplug**: watch burnout with yourself and with your team. Everyone needs to be able to unplug at the end of the day to come back fresh the next day. This is especially important when working from home because the line between work and home is blurred. Respect your team's evening hours and weekends and encourage them to unplug at the end of the day. This is another great opportunity to lead by example by not sending unnecessary messages after hours.

Whether remote work is right for your company culture depends on a lot of factors. Remote work is best when your team members are self-motivated, disciplined, and good communicators. Remote work also requires strong, supportive leaders who can set clear goals, provide feedback, and resolve conflicts. If the senior leadership in your organization is not supportive of the concept of remote work, remote employees won't thrive.

A survey performed by Stanford professor Nicholas Bloom found that at-home employees were more productive, happier, and less likely to quit. Even agile and DevOps meetings, traditionally held in-person, have translated just fine to the remote world. But the key to successful remote work is clear and effective communication, leading by example and taking advantage of opportunities for team bonding. With the right tools and processes in place, your team can be just as successful working remotely as they are in person.

Remote work also works best with self-aware leaders who use a supportive or coaching leadership style. Autocratic leaders don't do as well since they usually can't overcome trust issues or else the team simply stalls waiting for further direction. While autocratic leaders can sometimes bring clarity to chaotic situations, they leave little room for collaboration and connection. This problem is only multiplied in a remote work arrangement.

Some companies worry about losing their culture, believing that their "secret sauce" is only possible with people working together in the same location. But the way we work is changing, whether we like it or not. For some companies, this shift has been a long time coming. For others, it's a sudden and unexpected change. The pandemic forced us to confront the reality that technical work can be done from anywhere and employees have taken note. Embrace the unknown and see the opportunity. Make remote work a competitive advantage, by giving employees what they want most of all: autonomy.

Action: does your company support remote work? Are your employees working in a hybrid setup or are they fully remote? What are your personal beliefs about remote work? Do you trust your team to get the job done regardless of where they are working? If not, why not?

MAKING HYBRID WORK ... WORK

As the pandemic seems to be nearing an end, companies are scrambling to formalize a clear work location strategy going forward. The 2022 Work Trend Index shows that hybrid work is going to be a major challenge for recruiting employees and that leaders should approach it with a growth mindset or risk being left behind. A hybrid work model reduces costs for businesses by reducing the need for office supplies, building utilities, and real-estate expenses. Employees save money by commuting less and enjoying a greater work-life balance. Companies around the world are testing the hybrid work model and every organization's approach will be different. Some are leaning fully into it and others are issuing back to the office mandates. The most successful companies will balance employee needs, culture, and business needs. If they have an office at all, they will make it somewhere that people want to go.

The future of work is hybrid. The most in-demand employees will gravitate toward companies that offer the flexibility to work wherever they choose. Employees will come into the office for specific meetings and collaboration, but they will also have the option to work from home when they need to focus more deeply. I used to commute two hours one way to an office in New York City. It seems like such a dated concept now and I would never go back to it. Pre-pandemic national commute times average closer to 30 minutes each way, but that still turns an 8-hour day into a 9-hour-day and doesn't offer the same flexibility to choose a work schedule that works best for the employee.

Of course, there are still some struggles with remote work arrangements (see Image 9.2). Employees report not being able to unplug from work at night or draw clear boundaries. Some struggle with feelings of loneliness and isolation.

Hybrid work issues can include:

✓ Career advancement
✓ Office capacity
✓ Lost thought leadership and collaboration
✓ Feelings of isolation

Image 9.2 Hybrid work arrangements can lead to communication and collaboration challenges and unequal treatment between remote and in-person employees if not managed effectively.

Others simply don't have a good working space at home and are stuck in basements, kitchens, and other less-than-ideal settings.

Hybrid work is introducing additional complexity. While the fully onsite model is clear enough, the hybrid work model still faces some challenges and there's no playbook since this is all new territory. A hybrid model allows workers to split their time between the office and their home, giving them permanent control of where, when, and how they work. Moving to a hybrid model can pay dividends including the potential for lower running costs and greater productivity but it also introduces issues including:

- **Lost thought leadership**: technologists love to write on whiteboards to sketching out problems and solutions. If your hybrid and remote employees can't see what you're doing in the office, you could be missing out on half the brainpower that could help solve the problem. Moderate conversations and give everyone a chance to speak up to keep the engagement level high for everyone. Virtual whiteboards are available on many platforms including Teams. Companies are investing in technology like interactive smart whiteboards that can bring all the benefits of a real white board while also allowing everyone online to see what's on the screen in real time. At a minimum, think about camera positioning and how people at home might be experiencing a hybrid meeting. Be creative, many tools can make hybrid work arrangements smoother, including rotating cameras so you can see who's talking even in a crowded office.
- **Equitable policies**: many hybrid work policies require workers to spend up to three days per week in the office, but then they let some employees get away with something different. If you're setting the parameters around remote work for your team, make sure there aren't favorites who follow different rules. Everyone will find out about it sooner or later and it's not a good look for a leader.
- **Career advancement**: despite the advantages of working from home, employees do worry about not having opportunities for career advancement. Make sure you're not unconsciously biased against people who are in the office less. Support career growth for every member of your team that's based on results and ambition, not on location.
- **Hire wisely**: the qualifications that might make someone a perfect hire for a face-to-face role in an office are different from those that would make someone a great fit for remote work. The best remote employees are self-starters, results-driven, and collaborative. Employees who can communicate well are going to be more effective at building relationships virtually, so make sure to factor this in with new hires if your company is planning to stay hybrid. When it comes to knowledge, it really doesn't matter how much you know if you can't communicate it to other people.

- **Days in the office**: many employees want to avoid Mondays and Fridays in the office. Problems with the hybrid model have manifested in cafeterias being closed on some days, insufficient seating on busy days, and other issues. Encourage people to come in on less popular days by offering perks. Pizza Fridays would work just fine for me.

To make office work more appealing, companies are going to have to make the office a place that people want to go. Excessive noise levels and open seating models lead to distractions and make it difficult to focus. People won't want to come to the office if they don't think they can get their work done there. Make sure there are quiet areas for your team to do work that requires concentration. Balance collaborative space with quiet space. Most of all, be flexible and embrace whatever is working and celebrate that success. Double down on winning strategies. Hybrid work models are still very much a work in progress and it will take some time to figure out what works best for each company.

SUMMARY

In this chapter, we learned about some advantages and disadvantages of hybrid work models. We also discussed some ways to make the office more appealing so that people will want to come to the office. Remember for remote work to work, you need to trust your employees. If you don't trust your team, it will be difficult or impossible for you to lead them remotely. Also remember that:

- Remote work arrangements require good communication. Be a good listener, use the right communication channels, and ask questions to keep the engagement level high.
- Remote employees are more productive, happier, and less likely to quit. Lean toward influencing or coaching leadership styles to be the most effective.
- The office needs to be a place that people want to go. Make sure that you balance quiet and collaborative space and give people environments that facilitate getting the work done.
- Stay away from misleading attempts to measure "productivity" and focus on outcomes and results instead.

REFERENCES AND FURTHER READING

Burkus, David. *Leading from Anywhere: The Essential Guide to Managing Remote Teams*. Mariner Books, 2022.
Gerst, Alexis. *Leading Remote Teams: Embrace the Future of Remote Work Culture*. 2021.

Gratton, Lynda. *Redesigning Work: How to Transform Your Organization and Make Hybrid Work for Everyone*. The MIT Press, 2022.

Osman, Hassan. *Hybrid Work Management: How to Manage a Hybrid Team in the New Workplace (a Super-Short Book about How to Analyze, Plan, Manage, and Evaluate Your Team's Hybrid Work Arrangement)*. Hassan Osman, 2021.

"Work Trend Index: Microsoft's Latest Research on the Ways We Work," 2022, https://www.microsoft.com/en-us/worklab/work-trend-index/.

Chapter 10

Giving back

Industry leadership and the next generation of leaders

When you reach a certain point of success as an information technology (IT) leader, you should consider giving back to your industry. Whether it's mentoring the next generation of leaders or actively participating in industry initiatives and organizations, there are many ways for you to help shape and support the future of this dynamic industry. By giving back, you are also helping to ensure that the next generation of leaders has the skills and knowledge needed to thrive in today's fast-moving world. By investing your time, energy, and expertise in young up-and-coming professionals, you are setting them up for success and ensuring that they will continue to drive innovation for years to come.

MENTORING THE NEXT GENERATION OF TALENT

If learning how to be a better leader while helping others succeed sounds good to you, you should try mentoring someone. Mentoring is when someone experienced decides to share their knowledge and give guidance to someone less experienced to help them learn and grow. Every mentoring relationship has both a mentor and a mentee. In the context of leadership, mentoring can be extremely beneficial in helping to develop future leaders. Mentoring doesn't need to be contained within the four walls of your company either. There are mentoring opportunities available through many different channels, including online mentorships, professional organizations, and even informal relationships with friends and colleagues. Mentors often find that they learn new things from their mentees and the relationship can help to keep them energized and motivated in their own career (see Image 10.1).

Mentors are beneficial for the employee. You can grow your career by getting a coach, trainer, or career consultant but a mentor is a unique combination of all of these. Coaches and career consultants are generally paid and have a formal obligation with specific goals. A mentor is usually not paid, it's just an informal relationship where you may meet casually over lunch every now and then and discuss relevant issues. Being a mentor helps you build your own leadership skills. It can also teach you new perspectives and teach you

DOI: 10.1201/9781003314707-12

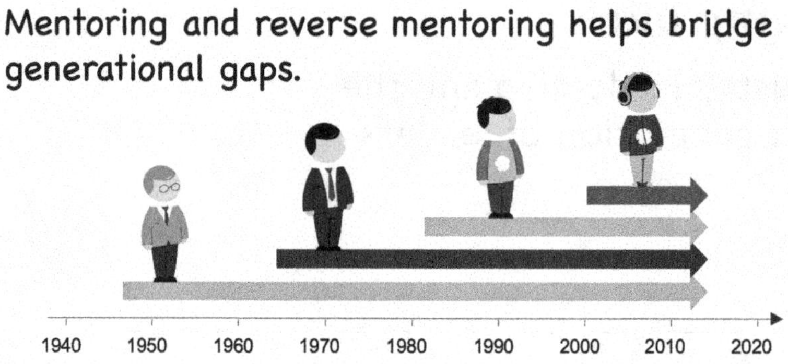

Mentoring and reverse mentoring helps bridge generational gaps.

1940   1950   1960   1970   1980   1990   2000   2010   2020

Image 10.1 Mentoring and reverse mentoring help develop and retain talent. Mentors help guide mentees and reverse mentoring fosters learning, innovation, and cross-generational communication.

ways of looking at things that you hadn't thought of before. Finally, mentoring can be satisfying on a personal level, knowing that you are helping others and doing your part to make the world a better place.

Mentors can guide people through corporate pitfalls, offer advice on promotions, and help think through difficult decisions or situations. As someone who's "been there, done that," they offer valuable advice and can help someone avoid making the same mistakes that they did. A mentor can also help guide you on your own learning path by suggesting the best way to prepare for certification or pursue other career development.

You're never too late in your career to be a mentor or to have a mentor of your own. Some of the most successful people in the world have had mentors at different points and most still have someone they call for career advice. If you don't have a mentor, seek one out. And if you're able to help someone else, consider being a mentor yourself. The best fit is usually when the mentor has a few years more experience, but that isn't always the case. Ultimately, it's personality match and trust that are the most effective elements of a successful relationship.

If you're interested in being a mentor, there are several things to keep in mind. First, it's important to find a mentee who you can really connect with and who is motivated to learn from you. It's also important to set realistic expectations for the relationship and make sure that both you and your mentee are clear on what you hope to accomplish. Finally, be prepared to invest some time and energy into the relationship – a successful mentorship takes work from both parties.

Some organizations have even implemented a program of "reverse mentoring" where senior executives are paired up with the younger generation to better understand their perspectives, their use of technology, and their general outlook on life. Today's workplaces are more diverse, with workers from several different generations contributing different perspectives and skills. However, this also creates challenges and generational divides. Reverse mentoring helps bridge this gap.

No matter if it's mentoring, reverse mentoring, or finding a mentor of your own, these relationships can have a very positive impact. For the mentor, it's an opportunity to share their knowledge and experience with someone who is looking to learn and grow in their career. The mentee gets the chance to learn from someone who has been there before and can offer guidance and support. These relationships help enrich your career journey, whether you're just getting started or if you are a seasoned professional.

If you want to implement a formal mentoring program at your company, here are five ways to get started.

1. **Create a vision for the program**. What is the purpose and goal? Who is involved? What outcomes do you hope to achieve? A mentoring program with a goal of building a more collaborative culture differs from one with a goal of developing future leaders.
2. **Get buy-in**. Let people know the importance of mentoring and what you hope to achieve through the program. Showcase the numerous benefits of sharing information, building relationships, and involving all employees.
3. **Pair people together carefully**. Consider the strengths, skills, and struggles of people in the program as you create partnerships that benefit both parties. For programs that aim to grow future leaders, think about gaps those future leaders may have that mentors could help fill, such as better communication.
4. **Provide training and guidelines**. What should happen during a mentoring session? How often will people meet? What topics will they discuss and is there anything off limits? By setting expectations, you can help the program run smoothly, just make sure to leave room for small talk and for issues that may have come up since the last meeting.
5. **Collect feedback and best practices**. Check in with the mentees and mentors to find out what is and isn't working and what can be improved. Your program should be agile enough to adjust based on input and as situations change. If something is working well, let others know so they can try it too.

Mentoring can take many different forms, but the goal is always the same – to help someone else grow and develop in their career. Whether you're looking for a mentor or want to be one, remember to keep an open mind, set realistic expectations, and be prepared to invest time and energy into the relationship.

INDUSTRY INITIATIVES AND ORGANIZATIONS

Another way to give back is by joining an industry organization. There are many groups geared toward helping members learn and grow. These groups offer educational resources, networking opportunities, and advocacy initiatives for their members. These groups also work to advance the industry through initiatives such as skills development and workforce training programs.

As an IT leader, you can get involved in associations and initiate to help shape the future of our industry. There are many ways to help, from simply joining an association and attending events to taking on a leadership role, joining a board, or volunteering your time and expertise. By getting involved, you can share your insights and knowledge with others, learn from your peers, and make a difference. Speaking at events or writing articles for publications are also great ways to share your expertise with a wider audience.

Giving back to your industry is not only good for the profession, but also for you. When you get involved in industry initiatives, you have an opportunity to learn new things, network with other professionals, and give back to the community. This can help you stay energized and motivated in your career and they can also help advance your career by offering opportunities to practice public speaking and writing.

The United States has the world's largest technology industry, with a wide variety of sub-industries. The sheer size and scope of the workforce means that there are many different industry associations and initiatives you can join. When you're looking for the right association to join, there are a few things to consider. First, think about what you want to get out of it. Do you want to learn new skills? Network with other professionals? Get involved in advocacy initiatives? Once you've narrowed down your options, do some research. Check the website and look for information on the association's mission and goals. Also, check out the member benefits, which will give you a better idea of what the association can offer you, including accelerated paths for certification, original research and white papers, exclusive events, and more.

The Association for Women in Computing (AWC) is one example of an industry association that offers educational resources, networking opportunities, and advocacy initiatives for its members. The AWC also works to advocate skills development and workforce training programs. The Project Management Institute (PMI) is another example of an industry association that offers educational resources, networking opportunities, and advocacy initiatives for its members. PMI also works to advance the industry through initiatives such as skills development and workforce training programs that offer accelerated paths to project management certification including the Project Management Professional (PMP) credential. By getting involved in these initiatives, you can keep your skills sharp, network with other professionals, and give back to the community.

Action: consider getting involved in an industry initiative or organization. A few common associations are included in the appendix of this book.

ROLL YOUR OWN LEADERSHIP
DEVELOPMENT PROGRAM

Many companies look to bring in high-paid consultants or leadership development experts to help grow their leaders, but this isn't always necessary or possible. At the State of Connecticut, we saw the need to develop our future technology talent and begin uplifting our managers into leaders. These programs can be low-cost and can be done without much outside help. This approach also leverages our own leaders who have experience, rather than relying on outside experts who may not understand your specific circumstances. Using your own leaders to teach others brings benefits including understanding of the organization's culture, mission, and values better. It also lets us to use real-life examples and apply them to different scenarios. Finally, it helps form deeper bonds among our own people by cross-pollinating talent.

If you're not growing leaders on your team, you're missing a real opportunity. After all, the future of leadership will be in their hands, not yours. But there are many advantages beyond that. Growing leaders comes with a high level of satisfaction. Watching someone develop and get better over time gives you a lot of perspective on your own journey. It also helps you build a stronger team. When everyone is focused on developing their skills and abilities, it creates a more cohesive unit.

Creating a pipeline of future leaders also helps build self-sustaining organizations. Surrounding everyone with excellence can even turn a company into a leadership factory. Firms like Amazon, Goldman Sachs, and General Electric seem to crank out a lot of leaders who move on to bigger roles as their career progresses, even if these roles are at other companies. That's because these companies invest a lot into their leadership programs. In its heyday, GE's corporate audit staff program, known internally as the Green Beret program, immersed entry-level GE workers in real-world audit, technology, and operations jobs. About 200–300 hopefuls enter the program each year with the hope of landing an executive-level position, but only 2% complete the process.

If you're looking to grow the leadership talent on your team, start with hiring the right people. Look for individuals who have leadership potential when you're hiring and make sure they are a good fit for your company culture. You might even have promising talent already on your team. Promoting from within is a positive signal to everyone, but make sure the person you promote is deserving and displays the behaviors you want to see from everyone else. Give these people the opportunity to lead by delegating larger tasks and projects and really letting them run with it. As they prove themselves, give them additional responsibilities and authority. These are the people you want to make sure you are giving coaching and feedback to help them continue to grow and develop their leadership skills.

Ultimately, growing leaders is an investment in your team and your company's future. It's also a way to give back to the industry by developing the next generation of leaders. One of the worst things we do as an industry is promoting ill-equipped leaders into situations they aren't prepared for and then waiting to see how it turns out. This is stressful for the leader and for the team as everyone fumbles their way through with little guidance or training. We need to invest in developing our future leaders and make sure they have the skills and the knowledge they need to be successful.

If you'd like to develop your own leadership development program, here are a few things to keep in mind. First, you need to identify the desired outcome of the program. What do you want your leaders to be able to do when they finish? Do you want them to be able to think more strategically? Be better communicators? Develop a deeper understanding of the business?

Once you know what you want the program to accomplish, you can start to develop a plan for how to get there. When you have clear objectives, it's easier to design a program that will help your leaders reach their potential and address real gaps in the organization, not just make "better leaders," which is too vague. Some of the most effective leadership development programs are experiential, meaning they provide opportunities for leaders to get out of the classroom and into the real world. This could involve shadowing senior leaders, working on special projects or taking on additional responsibilities outside of their normal scope. The key is to give leaders opportunities to stretch themselves and learn new things in a safe environment where they can make mistakes without consequences. This also provides opportunities for networking, better bonding, and a deeper understanding of how the company works.

Second, identify who should be involved in the program. A leadership development program is only as good as the people involved in it. People leading the program need to be experienced and knowledgeable about leadership. They need to be strong leaders in their own right, but they also need to have the time to devote to the program. You also need the right mix of people in the program. It should be a blend of up-and-coming leaders as well as more experienced ones. This mix creates a dynamic environment where everyone can learn from each other.

Third, what format will the program take? There are many ways to deliver a leadership development program. It could be a series of workshops, an intensive bootcamp, or even an online program. The key is to find a format that works for your team and that will allow the leaders to get the most out of it. A good leadership development program should also be flexible and adaptable to the needs of the team. It should be tailored to the specific needs of the organization and the leaders who are participating in it. The program should also be revisited on a regular basis to make sure it's still meeting the needs of the team. Leaders are and technology are constantly evolving and so should the development program.

Finally, don't forget to adjust the program based on what's working. Successful leadership development programs are not one-time events. Make sure you have a plan for how the leaders will continue to develop after the program is over. Follow up with them and see how they are doing. Make sure they are implementing what they've learned and that the program is being revised based on feedback. Don't be afraid to make changes. If something isn't working, drop it and if it is working, make sure to continue.

Leadership development is an important topic for any organization, but it's often something that gets neglected. Leadership development is an investment for the future of the company and in the employees' career path. It's a way to develop the next generation of leaders and to make sure your team has the skills they need to be successful. When done right, it can have a profound impact on the organization.

Action: are you growing leaders on your team or in your company? Hire individuals with leadership potential and give them opportunities and training.

BECOMING A THOUGHT LEADER WITHOUT MAKING IT ALL ABOUT YOU

There are a lot of self-declared "thought leaders" in technology. While some offer genuine insight, many are just trying to sell you something or they are busy selling themselves. They see being a thought leader as a way to get attention and build a personal brand. But true thought leaders don't make it all about themselves. They make it about everyone else. Thought leaders challenge the status quo, push boundaries, and think outside the box. They offer new perspectives and ideas.

If you're looking to give back by becoming a thought leader, start by thinking about how you can help others. What problems can you solve? What ideas can you share that will make a difference? It's not about self-promotion or selling your products or services. It's about providing value and helping others. When you're focused on helping others, the personal brand will take care of itself. People will start to recognize you as someone who is making a difference. And that's what true thought leadership is all about.

To be a thought leader, you need to constantly challenge yourself to come up with new and better ideas. This means doing a lot of deep thinking, reading, and research. But it also means being open to feedback and criticism and being willing to change your perspectives when you're presented with new information. In other words, you need to change your mind as the facts change by continuously re-orienting yourself.

Thought leaders are not afraid to put themselves out there or be controversial. They realize that to push their field forward, they need to take some risks and be bold. This means being OK with having your ideas challenged and receiving criticism. Not everyone is going to agree with you and that's OK. The important thing is that you're starting a conversation and getting people to think about things in a different way. Thought leaders create new ideas that didn't exist before. They connect the dots in ways that people hadn't thought of. They innovate.

If you want to become a thought leader, start by constantly learning and expanding your knowledge. Then contribute your ideas, whether through writing, speaking, or simply sharing them with others. Too many people want to become influencers, thought leaders, and Chief Information Officers (CIOs) without having enough experience. Just because you finished a book about business, it doesn't make you a CEO, and just because you have 10,000 followers on Instagram, it doesn't make you a thought leader. There's a big difference between someone who is an expert in their field and someone who likes to talk about themselves. Being a thought leader requires a deep level of knowledge and insight that can only be gained through years of experience. It's not something you can fake.

If you aspire to be a thought leader in your industry, start by focusing on becoming an expert first. Build up your knowledge and experience, then start sharing your ideas with the world. Here are five important considerations for aspiring thought leaders:

1. **Originality**: the most important trait of a thought leader is originality. If you're not offering something new, you're not going to be taken seriously. People follow thought leaders because they're looking for new ideas and perspectives. This means you need to have something new and different to say. This could be a new perspective on an old problem or a completely new idea. Original research offers you the chance to promote your expertise in your industry by providing concrete data and information. Think about the things you're passionate about and the problems you want to solve. What can you offer that no one else can offer? Your insights should be backed up by data and evidence. Find an original problem to work on and start by answering the questions that no one else is answering.

2. **Insightfulness**: your ideas need to be well thought out and based on a deep understanding of issues and challenges. Simply regurgitating what others have said is not enough. What are your own unique insights and observations?

3. **Relevance**: your insights don't matter if they are irrelevant to your audience and industry. Insights should be applicable, useful, and actionable. No one wants to hear someone pontificating about a topic no one cares about.

4. **Timeliness**: the Internet helps news travel in near real time. People are accustomed to receiving timely updates and news from around the world. Thought leadership requires you to be a bit ahead of the curve. This means sharing your ideas before they become mainstream. You

need to be early enough that people are interested, but not so early that no one knows or appreciates what you're talking about.

5. **Communication**: thought leaders obviously need to be able to communicate their ideas clearly and effectively. This means being able to write or speak well and using stories and examples to illustrate important points. People follow companies and thought leaders on a variety of different platforms, including blogs, social channels, YouTube, and other video channels. Thought leaders need to create content that impacts people across multiple different platforms.

Self-reflection is important across all areas of life, but especially for thought leadership. If you can't sit down and analyze your thoughts, you're going to have difficulty sharing big ideas with others. Take some time to self-reflect every day by journaling. This practice will help you become more self-aware and see the big picture when thinking more broadly. Journaling also helps you track your progress and identify patterns over time.

Finally, if you're going to be a thought leader, you're going to have to read a lot and take in a lot of new information. Reading helps you understand different perspectives and see things from different angles. It also helps you improve your communication skills by teaching you how to better express yourself. When you're constantly reading, you're exposing yourself to new ideas and concepts, which helps you come up with original insights of your own. There's no way to connect thoughts if you're not constantly learning new things across a broad range of subjects. Reading also helps improve your writing skills, which is essential for creating compelling content.

Don't rush the process and don't try to force it. If you're meant to be a thought leader, it will probably happen organically. The best way to become a thought leader is simply to start sharing your original ideas with the world. The more you do it, the better you'll become at it. Over time, your reputation will grow, and you'll reach the point where people see you as an authority in your field.

GIVING BACK THROUGH ENTREPRENEURSHIP

One of the most exciting ways to give back and show industry leadership is by becoming an entrepreneur. When you become an entrepreneur, you are taking a risk of starting something new and making it successful. This is a leadership role by itself, regardless of how many people are involved in your efforts. In many senses, this is the toughest leadership role. In his book *Zero to One: Notes on Startups, or How to Build the Future*, author Peter Theil suggests that incremental improvement is easy. Going from one version of a product to another is simpler than going from "zero to one" where you are creating something that never existed before.

Entrepreneurs enjoy:

✓ Giving back to their industry
✓ Solving problems
✓ Creating something new
✓ Independence

Image 10.2 Entrepreneurship provides technologists with the opportunity to create, impact, and gain personal and financial rewards including autonomy, independence and financial gains.

Being an entrepreneur isn't just about making money. It's about solving problems and making a difference in the world. When you're an entrepreneur, you can create something that didn't exist before and make an impact. You can also use your platform as an entrepreneur to raise awareness for important causes. For example, if you're starting a company that is focused on sustainability, you can use your platform to talk about the importance of environmental issues. This will help raise awareness and get people to think about these problems in a new light.

The challenges entrepreneurs face every day would overwhelm most managers. Entrepreneurs need to identify and assess opportunities, raise capital, hire talent, develop and execute business plans, deal with customers and channel partners, manage revenue and growth, and the list goes on. But many entrepreneurs relish the opportunity to build something new from the ground up and see it through to success.

Successful entrepreneurs often wear many hats and juggle many different responsibilities. They need to be a visionary who can see the big picture, but they also need to be able to focus on the details and get things done. They must be able to motivate and inspire others, but they also need to be able to roll up your sleeves and do hard work. In short, entrepreneurs must be leaders, managers, and a doers all rolled into one.

Almost anyone with the right mix of skills and motivation can become an entrepreneur. Technology already allows people to pursue entrepreneurship in the form of side hustles and work-from-home opportunities. For many people, the dream of entrepreneurship is born out of a desire to give back to their industry (see Image 10.2). They want to create something new, innovative, and valuable – something that didn't exist before. Entrepreneurs want to make a difference and solve problems. There's no better way to do this than by starting your own business.

Of course, starting a business is no easy feat. It takes a lot of hard work, dedication, and determination. But if you're up for the challenge, the rewards can also be great. Not only will you get to make a difference in your industry, but you'll also can create something truly special – something that you can be proud of for years to come.

If you're interested in exploring entrepreneurship as a way of giving back, there are a few things you should keep in mind. You need to have the right skillset or acquire the right skills. You need to be prepared to work hard, probably harder than you would work in a regular job. You need to be willing to take risks. You may also need to get by without a steady paycheck for a while, as it can take time to get a business off the ground. For this reason, many people start their company while they're still employed elsewhere. This way, they have a safety net in case things don't go as planned.

If you think you might want to become an entrepreneur, the first step is to do some research. Talk to people who have already started their own businesses and see what their experience has been like. Read books and articles about entrepreneurship. There is no one-size-fits-all formula for success but understanding the basics will give you a good foundation on which to build your own business. There are five things that stand out from successful entrepreneurs: they have a clear vision, they're passionate about their work, they're willing to take risks, they're adaptable, and they're excellent at networking.

Of course, the most important thing for entrepreneurs is to have a clear vision that solves a real market need. It's not enough to just have an idea, you need to be able to articulate what your business does and why it's necessary. This is what will help you get funding, attract customers, and rally employees around your cause. All this takes a lot of passion, which to me is the key difference between successful entrepreneurs and the ones who give up when the work gets too hard.

Action: if you're interested in pursuing this entrepreneurship, the first step is identifying a need or opportunity in the marketplace and then filling that need with a product or service that is superior to what is already available. Start with research and create a process to do a little bit each day. Remember that starting an entrepreneurial endeavor can be done in your spare time. I wouldn't start by quitting your day job.

OTHER WAYS TO GIVE BACK

Be creative, there are so many ways that you can give back including tutoring, teaching classes or workshops, and donating money, time, or equipment to a cause or organization you believe in. Look for opportunities in your community that align with your interests and consider how you can make a difference. You may be surprised at how easy it is to get involved and make a positive impact.

Advocate for technology education in your school system. If we want more diversity in technology, we need to start with the young people who are still in school. It's up to us to make sure they know that there are opportunities for them and that they have the skills and confidence to pursue those opportunities. Be an advocate for change in your community and help make technology education accessible and affordable to everyone. Even donating older but working computers or other electronics to a school, library, or community center can make a difference.

Other ways to give back include volunteering your time or expertise to help a non-profit organization with their technology needs or working with local organizations to help them get started with using technology. You can also donate money or equipment to a cause or organization you believe in. Technology is a powerful tool that can be used for good and there are many ways that you can use it to make a difference in your community.

I'm a big believer in education and leveling the playing field for everyone with skills-based learning. I'm currently giving back in the form of the Connecticut CyberHub, which is a program sponsored by the State of Connecticut, in partnership with iQ4 Corporation and SDG Corporation. This effort will help students develop cybersecurity skills through formal education and hands-on internship experience. It will reduce the cost of finding, developing, and retaining cybersecurity talent. It will also help the state mitigate security risks as students enter the workforce. Whatever you choose to do, know that even the smallest act of kindness can make a difference. Choose something that feels meaningful to you and get started today.

SUMMARY

Giving back can be a great way to make a difference in your community and there are many ways to do it. Choose something that feels meaningful to you and get started today. Remember that:

- Mentors can share their knowledge and experience with someone who is looking to learn and grow, while mentees get the opportunity to learn from someone who has been there before.
- Creating a successful mentoring program includes creating a vision for the program, getting buy-in from management and employees, pairing people together carefully, providing training and guidelines, and collecting feedback.
- Industry groups and associations offer educational resources, networking opportunities, and advocacy initiatives for their members. By getting involved, individuals can share their insights and knowledge with others, learn from their peers, and make a difference in the industry.
- You can design your own leadership development program using existing leaders at your company as a great way to both give back and help develop the next generation of leaders.

- Thought leaders are people who challenge the status quo, push boundaries, and think outside the box. They offer new perspectives and ideas that can help move the industry forward.
- Entrepreneurship can help make a difference in the world by solving problems and creating new things. It is a challenging but rewarding career path that allows people to make a real impact.

REFERENCES AND FURTHER READING

Demarco, M.J. *Millionaire Fastlane: Crack the Code to Wealth And Live Rich for a Lifetime.* Viperion Publishing, 2021.

Ferriss, Timothy. *The 4-Hour Workweek: Escape 9-5, Live Anywhere, and Join the New Rich.* Harmony Books, 2012.

Fried, Jason, and David Heinemeier Hansson. *Rework.* Vermilion, 2020.

Hoffman, Reid, and Ben Casnocha. *The Startup of You: Adapt, Take Risks, Grow Your Network, and Transform Your Career.* Currency, 2022.

Ries, Eric. *The Lean Startup: How Today's Entrepreneurs Use Continuous Innovation to Create Radically Successful Businesses.* Currency, 2017.

Sinek, Simon, and Hye-ri Yun. *Start with Why: How Great Leaders Inspire Everyone to Take Action.* Penguin Books, 2011.

Chapter 11

Leading from the edge
The future of work

Considering the pace of change in technology, you may be wondering what the future of work is going to bring. Factors shaping this future include technological advancements and changing societal norms. One trend that is already having a major impact on the workplace is the rise of artificial intelligence (AI). AI is changing the way we work by automating tasks and providing employees with new tools to be more productive. Chatbots can handle customer service inquiries, freeing up employees to focus on other tasks. As AI continues to evolve, it will likely have an even bigger impact on the workplace, potentially changing the very nature of work itself. There are also changing demographics of the workforce. In many developed countries, the population is aging and the number of young people entering the workforce is declining. This is having a major impact on industries trying to attract new talent including healthcare, manufacturing, and government.

The way we work is also changing, thanks to advances in technology. The rise of the gig economy and Web 3.0 are giving employees more flexibility in how they work. With the ability to work from anywhere, at any time, more and more people are choosing to freelance or work on a contract basis, essentially working for themselves instead of a company.

Technology is also changing the way we communicate and collaborate with each other. Social media, instant messaging, and video conferencing are making it easier for employees to connect with each other and share ideas at scales never imagined before. As these tools become more common, they will have a major impact on the way work gets done. The future of work is an exciting and dynamic landscape. Leaders who can stay ahead of the curve will be positioned to capitalize on the opportunities.

Work is a central part of human life, and as such it is important to our well-being. In today's world where technology can easily take over many tasks that were once done face-to-face, we need to offer more than just a salary as an incentive if we want our employees to be satisfied. While salary is an important factor in deciding on a job, generation Z values interesting work more than the paycheck and generation Z will soon surpass millennials as the most populous generation on Earth.

DOI: 10.1201/9781003314707-13

The speed of disruptive innovation will continue and the threat from new competitors who may be more agile will disrupt the old guard. Imagine what will disrupt Amazon in the future, it's bound to happen one day. This chapter features a very speculative look at the future of work, the implications of disruptive change and some light-hearted predictions about what the next decade might hold. You may disagree with some or all these picks and that's fine. Is AI just a term for a fancy computer algorithm or is it something that will destroy 90% of all jobs, as AI expert Kai-Fu Lee warned? You be the judge.

IT LEADERSHIP AND THE FUTURE OF WORK

The future is already here. It's just not evenly distributed.

William Gibson

From small businesses to Fortune 500 giants like Walmart or Amazon, everyone will need leaders who are prepared to handle disruptive change at paces faster than ever imagined before. This new world requires a very different type of leader who can embrace the fact that change is the norm and some of this change will probably seem scary at first. Technology will continue to change in unpredictable ways. The future of information technology (IT) leadership requires leaders who can focus on the organization's long-term business goals and help figure out how technology can help achieve those goals.

To begin to understand the future of technology leadership, you also need to have some idea of the future of technology. There are big innovations in play today that are not widespread right now including 5G, machine learning (ML), AI, wearable technology, virtual reality (VR), and that whole Metaverse thing. Machines are changing the way we think about productivity and decision-making. This will have a big impact on how we work with people, including our employees and customers.

Unimportant or repetitive work almost always gives way to automation or elimination sooner or later. The rise of computerization and robotics has resulted in the loss of many jobs in manufacturing and other traditional industries. Even further back in time, the development of irrigation systems and crop rotation made some farm jobs obsolete. Change is inevitable, but it's usually beneficial over the long haul.

Future IT leaders will need to consider what work can and should be automated. They will need to determine where chatbots, ML, and AI can be used to create a better 24/7 customer experience. They will also need to think about how to use technology to create new products and services that generate new revenue streams in markets that may not even exist yet. We can't predict the future, but we can be prepared for it. Here are four skills for the future IT leader:

- **Embracing change:** the successful future leaders of IT will be those who are able to adapt to change and use it to their advantage. Leaders who react faster will have a clear competitive advantage over those who don't or can't react.

- **Focusing on the long term**: technology changes quickly, but businesses have a much longer time horizon. Future IT leaders will need to focus on the long-term goals of the organization and figure out how technology can help achieve those goals. Future IT leaders aren't technologists, they are business leaders who understand technology.
- **Strong people and communication skills**: with remote work, the reliance on third party vendors, and the rise of automation, future IT leaders are going to need to be expert communicators. They are going to manage and motivate people who may not be in the same location, including employees, vendors, and contractors. They will also need to be able to explain complex technical concepts to non-technical people.
- **Creativity**: with the rise of automation, future IT leaders will need to be creative to find new ways to use technology to create value for their organizations. They will need to be able to think outside the box and come up with new ideas that can help their businesses grow.

Leaders who master these skills will be well positioned to take advantage of the opportunities that disruptive technologies present. Now, let's look at some of the trends influencing the future of work.

WEB 3.0: POWER TO THE PEOPLE

Web 3.0 and the rise of the creator economy is here and it may be one of the biggest threats to the traditional IT workforce ever. Web 3.0 is the third generation of the evolution of web technologies. Companies like Uber and Airbnb disrupted traditional businesses like hotels and taxis with innovative technologies that allow for peer-to-peer transactions. But the sharing economy is only one aspect of an even larger creator economy, which refers to the growing trend of people making a living by creating and selling content online. As Internet connectivity becomes more ubiquitous and affordable, people are starting their own businesses and selling their products and services online. This is particularly true in developing countries, where the barriers to entry are much lower. A Kenyan farmer can now sell his produce directly to customers in Europe through an online marketplace like Jumia. Technology will be the great equalizer.

Platforms including YouTube, TikTok, and Instagram are creating a new generation of Internet superstars with stratospheric pay. Some TikTok high earners make between $100,000 and $250,000 for a single-branded video, depending on their popularity and engagement rate. The rise of the influencer is here and the potential for unlimited income is attracting a lot of attention away from taking more traditional career paths. There has never been an easier time to make money online for motivated and talented people.

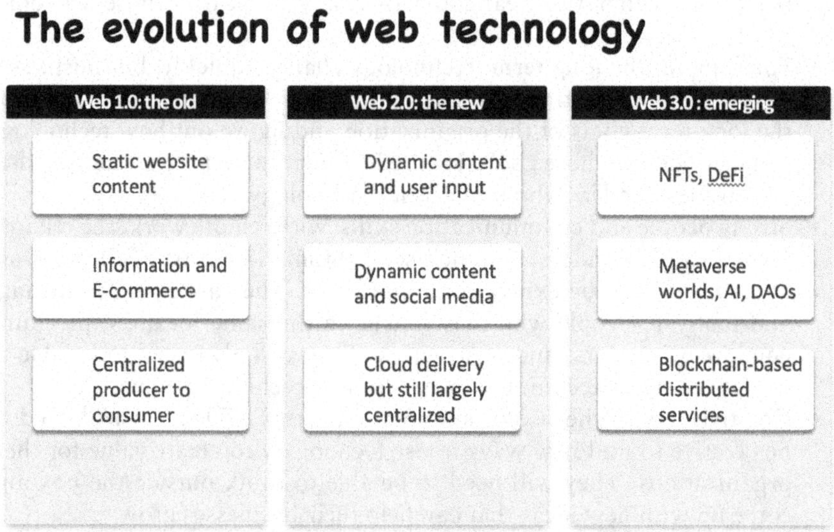

The evolution of web technology

Web 1.0: the old	Web 2.0: the new	Web 3.0 : emerging
Static website content	Dynamic content and user input	NFTs, DeFi
Information and E-commerce	Dynamic content and social media	Metaverse worlds, AI, DAOs
Centralized producer to consumer	Cloud delivery but still largely centralized	Blockchain-based distributed services

Image 11.1 The progression from Web 1.0 to Web 3.0 marks a significant shift in the Internet's evolution, where the focus has moved from static web pages and basic user interactivity to a more dynamic and personalized experience.

The arrival of Web 3.0 foreshadows a decentralized Internet where open standards and protocols will drive digital ownership rights that are better protected. Creators will have greater control over their data and new business models will flourish. Web 3.0 (see Image 11.1) has also introduced the concept of the DAO, or the Decentralized Autonomous Organization. A DAO is simply a governance structure that runs on blockchain and theoretically disposes of an organizational hierarchy or even the concept of a company altogether. In other words, DAOs are more reliant on code and common objectives than on employees and corporate leadership. Imagine a group of people coming together to work on a common project, then disbanding when the project completes. Skilled technical workers could go from one DAO to another and support themselves while also doing the most interesting or most lucrative work available. It's the gig economy taken to a whole new level. Savvy DAOs could theoretically morph into a company with very few employees, yet still run globally significant operations by pulling in expertise on demand. The complications of hiring, retaining, and onboarding employees go away completely.

I won't go into the mechanics of a typical DAO, including smart contracts. The concept isn't significantly different from a company hiring freelance labor. But what the DAO model does is to provide an easy-to-set up, easy-to-dissolve corporate structure. This enables a sort of "employee as a service" model that allows companies to pay for only the work they need only when they need it.

DAOs are exciting for employees because they provide variety and autonomy over where, when, and how to work. DAOs could also provide the freedom to do more fulfilling work than would be possible as an employee working for a single company. Imagine working for different employers every day on projects that require your specific expertise. You might wake up and work on a project revolutionizing healthcare, then on another one for the financial services industry in the afternoon. People complete for tasks (bounties) such as building a software component or moderating an online community and the buyer gets to pick the most talented, cost-effective bidder. The use of cryptocurrency ensures that all this happens with a global talent pool.

Web 3.0 enables the "Creator Economy" which features vloggers, bloggers, and podcasters who make money across multiple platforms including YouTube, SubStack, Medium, and others. While we've all heard the stories of the video blogger making six figures a month, these are usually extreme scenarios. But supporting yourself at more modest income levels is easier to accomplish than ever and some people will opt for working for themselves rather than working for a company.

With Web 3.0 still in its infancy, the DAO movement still needs to tackle some tough questions when it comes to governance, trust, and legal liability. However, the benefits of the model are strong for both employers and employees. There's no need to work through talent agencies or recruiters who take a cut of the profits. Similar models like this are already succeeding in the cybersecurity world, where "bug bounty" professionals find holes in applications, earn credibility and dollars, and move from project to project. They make a lot of money, they work for themselves, and they provide a valuable service across many companies rather than just one.

There are other promising technologies related to Web 3.0 including nonfungible tokens (NFTs). While NFTs became an overheated market, they didn't go away. The global NFT market is still expected to grow at a rate of 23.9% during 2022–2028, reaching a whopping market size of USD 19.57 billion. NFTs could be used in many ways benefiting the individual worker or artist including publications, selling tickets, and authoring original content. NFT royalties are automatic payouts to the author that come from resales. Royalties are added to the overall cost when purchasing the NFT, excluding gas fees, in the form of a percentage markup. NFTs allow creators and artists to track subsequent transactions with their work and they can benefit from secondary sales no matter how long those sales take. NFT royalties give artists and creators a never-before-seen opportunity to increase their earning potential.

The bottom line is that there are going to be more options than ever for talented technical employees to skip the company altogether and work for themselves. Their income will be limited only by their talent, drive, and the demand for their skills. This creates the potential for a more decentralized and fairer global economy based on skills, and this is something we should all get behind.

How technology leaders can prepare for Web 3.0 starting today:

1. Educate yourself and your team on the potential of Web 3.0 and how it could impact your industry.

2. Keep an open mind toward new models of employment and be prepared to embrace this change.
3. Consider how you could utilize NFTs or other Web 3.0 technologies for your business.

ARTIFICIAL INTELLIGENCE (AI) AND MACHINE LEARNING (ML) REPLACES SOME JOBS BUT CREATES OTHERS

> Humanity is essentially creating an alternative species that has enormous capacity to see past patterns and process many different ideas very quickly, has little or no common sense, has trouble understanding the logic behind relationships, and doesn't have emotions. This species is simultaneously smart and stupid, helpful, and dangerous. It offers great potential and needs to be well-controlled but not blindly followed.
>
> Ray Dalio

A painting that was generated with AI won first place in the digital art category at the 2022 Colorado State Fair Fine Art Show, sparking an online debate and attracting international attention. Jason Allen created the winning submission using a popular AI image-generation program called Midjourney. The judges of the Colorado Department of Agriculture's fine art competition said they did not know Allen used AI for his entry but stated that it wouldn't have changed their opinion. Some art communities have already moved to ban AI artwork including Newgrounds, Inkblot Art, and Fur Affinity. Artists are wondering how they can adapt to software that can potentially produce a seemingly unlimited number of works of art on demand.

AI is a powerful tool that has the possibility of improving human life, but it's also threatening to potentially put millions of people out of work. As AI continues to improve and spread, concerns about job displacement and larger social divides continue to be magnified. AI can now perform tasks that once belonged to skilled knowledge workers including writing, art, and technical analysis. But not all jobs will be displaced and AI is likely to produce a host of new jobs as well as making our existing jobs easier. The rapid advance of AI is transforming our world in ways we are only beginning to understand. One of the most profound changes will be the impact on jobs and the way we work.

AI is a broad term that refers to a range of technologies that enable machines to perform tasks that traditionally required human brainpower. ML is a subset of AI that involves teaching machines to learn from data sets and adapt to new information. This is accomplished using neural networks inspired by the way the brain works. ML helps find patterns in large data sets to make better predictions or decisions in the future.

It used to be that when a new technology emerged, there was a period of adjustment as workers learned new skills and found new jobs to replace the ones that were gradually fading away (see Image 11.2). However, it is

Artificial Intelligence (AI)

• Will it replace jobs?
• Make jobs easier and better?
• Fizzle out?
• Replace humankind?

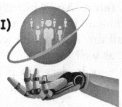

Image 11.2 AI brings benefits but may cause job displacement and skill gaps. Upskilling and reskilling programs can help workers adapt to AI-driven economy.

becoming increasingly clear that AI poses a much more interesting threat. AI doesn't just automate tasks, it's now encroaching on things that have previously been considered the exclusive domain of human beings including understanding natural language, recognizing objects and faces, and making complex decisions. AI tools already create artwork and write articles, but they can also create computer code based only on input from natural human language. Tools like ChatGPT, OpenAI Codex, and Polycoder use AI to write code generated in multiple programming languages. Are developers, writers, lawyers, and artists all going to be out of work?

As AI continues to advance, an ever-increasing number of jobs will be at risk of being automated which is leading some governments and world leaders to investigate the concept of a universal income. But I don't think that all jobs will be in danger. Creative jobs and jobs that require heavy human interaction, such as social workers, are still not ideal for computer automation. But IT jobs including lower-level data scientists, cybersecurity analysts, and data engineers could be at risk as AI proliferates. This could eliminate the need for many entry-level jobs, which would have a downstream effect on an already aging workforce.

AI is still in its early stages, but it is exploding in popularity. ChatGPT had 100 million active users in January 2022 only two months after its release. It attracted one million users in just one week and has become the fastest growing application ever as of the time of this writing.

As AI continues to advance, many jobs that are safe now may be at risk as the technology continues to improve. AI is also becoming increasingly cheaper and more easily accessible. Companies like NVIDIA and Graphcore continue to push the envelope for AI computing performance. This means that small businesses will soon be able to use AI-powered automation in ways that were previously only available for much larger companies.

A game-changing event is on the horizon, one that will revolutionize both our personal and professional lives in ways we can't fathom yet. I think that AI will continue to drive massive innovation that will fuel many industries and will likely lead to more jobs overall, not fewer. I still think we're at a safe distance from robots doing everything for us and getting it right. But the definition of what a skilled entry-level employee looks like may be dramatically different in the future. And AI working together with the human mind may just make us superhuman if we learn to master these tools to augment our mind.

Of course, all this automation will no doubt create a new set of cybersecurity headaches as well.

How technology leaders can prepare for AI starting today: leaders need to start thinking about how AI is going to impact their industry and begin planning for it.

- Think about what jobs could be replaced or automated at your company. Does your company support upskilling or reskilling workers?
- What business opportunities do you see using AI?
- Be aware of the ethical implications of using AI. As AI gets better at making decisions, it will become increasingly important to ensure that these decisions are ethically sound and unbiased.

MIDDLE MANAGERS GO EXTINCT

The pandemic magnified the increasingly debatable need for middle managers and the overall number of managers needed to run a company. Top executives often feel entitled to distance themselves from frontline workers and this sense of entitlement has trickled down to many middle managers who now act as more of a supervisor. This situation (see Image 11.3) is starting to heat up as frontline employees who have been working independently from home believe they can do their job without a manager who is becoming increasingly irrelevant.

Middle managers make up over 17% of the US workforce, but as more employees shift to working from home, the need for their oversight has massively decreased. Some forward-thinking companies had already been experimenting with a less hierarchical workplace structure before the pandemic. In the remote world, middle managers are currently being paid large salaries to act as a sort of "workplace hall monitor." But the need for this oversight has massively decreased.

Middle management:

- More necessary than ever?
- About to be replaced by automation?
- About to be re-imagined?

Image 11.3 Flat organizational structures and the growing emphasis on agile methodologies have led to an increasingly marginalized role for middle managers, who are often replaced by cross-functional teams and self-organizing groups.

At the same time, a new generation of workers are entering the workforce who are not as inclined to pursue traditional managerial roles. Technical advances have made it easier for workers of all levels to communicate and collaborate, blurring the distinction between front-line and back-office workers. As a result, many organizations are considering whether middle managers are necessary at all.

Organizations often promote people to manager positions and hope for the best. The promotion is a reward for hard work, delivering results, or technical excellence. But it also creates a layer of middle managers who don't want to manage people and can't do it well anyway. Some firms have taken steps to address this problem with the IT technical fellow career path. Technical fellow roles require you to hold a high level of technical skills, knowledge, and expertise. When a company can reward both career paths, they can retain top technical talent and provide a better path for career progression without forcing people into management jobs they don't want and that the company no longer needs.

Managerial roles are best left to people with strong communication and interpersonal skills. Managers need to excel at decision-making, problem-solving, planning, strategy, mentoring, and coaching. They should also have a sense of commercial awareness and be a bit more business savvy. The technical fellow (or equivalent) rewards technical expertise for people who can help set the company's strategic technology direction. These technical leaders help achieve operational excellence, minimize technology risk, and are generally highly respected by both business and IT leaders. Technical fellowship positions help companies retain their best talent rather than forcing them into increasingly unnecessary middle-manager roles.

How technology leaders can prepare starting today:

- Leaders of large technology teams should evaluate the roles and responsibilities of your middle managers. Are they truly necessary and adding value? Could you better leverage some of them working more deeply on hands-on technical work and technology strategy?
- If you are a new manager or are looking to move into a management position, be honest with yourself about whether you have the skills and temperament to lead people. If you don't, look for a leadership role where you could continue to hone your technical skills and add more value to the organization.

5G AND 6G BRINGS HIGH-SPEED INTERNET EVERYWHERE

As if remote work was going away, 5G is going to add even more fuel to the fire. 5G stands for "fifth-generation" wireless and is the latest generation of mobile technology offering advanced speed and reliability for Internet

5G and 6G:

- Internet of Things (IoT) explodes?
- Nothing special?
- Changes the world with fast Internet access for everyone, everywhere?

Image 11.4 5G and 6G will enable faster data speeds, lower latency, and increased connectivity, unlocking new possibilities for applications like IoT, artificial intelligence (AI) and virtual reality.

connections. 5G is much faster than current 4G networks, with speeds of up to 10 gigabits per second. It's also more reliable, with less latency and better connections in crowded areas.

5G will have a big impact on the workforce (see Image 11.4) and continue to push the demand for remote work. A fast and stable Internet connection is all the average technology professional needs to be productive, whether it's at home, in a coffee shop, or on the road. 5G also enables new types of remote work, including augmented reality (AR) and VR which need wider bandwidths for network connectivity. 5G will make it possible for businesses to operate in completely new ways.

To really understand the impact of 5G on the future of work, you need to think beyond the average work-from-home employee who may already have a fast Internet connection. 5G will certainly make your video streaming faster, but it will also impact the entire digital economy. It will dramatically accelerate the Internet of things (IOT) as all kinds of devices will now be able to add Internet connectivity. Businesses will have new ways of collecting and analyzing data, making decisions and interacting with customers by providing more reliable connectivity. 5G isn't just faster, it also comes with a much lower latency. Latency is the time it takes for network traffic to travel from its source to its destination. Even as strong 4G connection that has high latency will make video conference calls slow down or even fail.

Qualcomm summarizes the future potential of 5G as:

> That kind of speed changes everything. Latency would disappear. Engineers could build networks of connected vehicles that would relay relevant traffic information and automatically maintain safe driving distances. Telemedicine would become viable. Imagine a world where doctors in Boston use cutting-edge robotics to perform delicate surgeries in Mumbai. Drones and self-driving cars would be able to build real-time 3D maps to operate more efficiently.

5G speed will unlock a host of opportunities that were never possible before. It will have a big impact on the way we live and interact with the world around us. It will enable new types of connected devices, such as self-driving cars and smart homes. 5G will change the way we live and work in profound ways, and it's only just beginning.

When combined with extended reality (XR) technology, remote workers may be able to have an entire virtual avatar appear in meetings from anywhere on the globe. While this may not seem that interesting at first, imagine the possibilities of a virtual avatar master surgeon standing over the shoulder of another doctor as they advise how to treat a patient. I think we're still years away from the benefits that 5G networking will bring to the workforce, but when it arrives in enough density, expect to see dramatic shifts in how and where we work. Employees will use avatars and have real-time language translation services for any country in the world enabling a whole new world of human collaboration.

Of course, 6G is not far behind. 6th-generation wireless communication technology will deliver even higher data rates, lower latency, and more reliable network connectivity than 5G. It will also focus on optimizing the network experience for machines rather than just human subscribers. The bottom line is that the wireless futures is much faster from here and new technology will emerge to take advantage of all this new connectivity and bandwidth.

How technology leaders can prepare starting today: 5G will continue to drive the ability to work from anywhere. Technology leaders should:

- Continue to invest in collaborative tools and technologies that enable their teams to work together regardless of location.
- Begin to think about how they could use 5G to improve customer experience by improving in-the-moment, personalized interactions from anywhere.

THE SKILLS-BASED ECONOMY ELIMINATES THE NEED FOR A COLLEGE DEGREE

Colleges are in big trouble. Enrollment is down, costs are up, and frustration with the whole concept is at an all-time high. Colleges are being seen as boring, behind the times, and expensive. The college degree can also be out of reach for people with lower incomes, single parents, veterans, and others returning to the workforce. And the college degree is becoming increasingly irrelevant in the technology field, where everything changes at the speed of light while universities have struggled to not only keep up but also attract the right teachers (see Image 11.5).

A college degree has long been seen as the ticket to a good job and a comfortable middle-class lifestyle. But in recent years, this ticket has become much less valuable. Technology companies and others are now recruiting workers with specific skills, but no college degree. Jobs that once required a college education can now be done just as well by someone with some basic skill with the rest handled through on-the-job training.

College degrees are increasingly unnecessary for many jobs and the cost of college tuition continues to soar. The return on investment (ROI) for most

Skills-based economy:

- Is the college degree dead?
- Will higher education prevail?

Image 11.5 The rise of the skills-based economy is being driven by rapid technology advancement and increasing employer demands across all industries. Employers increasingly value skills, experience and demonstrated abilities over formal education or degrees.

advanced degrees also falls apart quickly. Although master's students only account for 12% of all college students, the higher price tag on their degree means that they're burdened with 26% of all the student debt. Master's students owe an average of $65,000 in debt compared with $32,000 owed for most bachelor's degrees.

In 2020, Google announced a "degree killer" that promises to disrupt the education industry. Google Career Certificates is a collection of courses designed to help people get qualifications for high-paying, high-growth jobs without attending a university. The response has been overwhelmingly positive, though not without controversy. The program can be completed in less time than a traditional degree and can better equip graduates for job searching since employers can tap directly into graduates of the program. These employers include Walmart, Intel, and Bank of America among other prestigious firms.

The program takes three to six months to complete and Google considers it to be the equivalent of a 4-year bachelor's degree for their own hiring needs. It's also 100% remote with very little cost to the student. The concept of an IT degree from a four-year university may be an endangered species. Future hiring is going to be based on your applicable skills. Programs with highly targeted curriculums that get people into the workforce faster will thrive.

Google is not the only one. iQ4 has been beating the skills-based economy for a long time. CEO, Frank Cicio, worked with Wall Street giants to identify the need and solution for the shortage of cybersecurity professionals in the 1990s. Now, they are partnering with private industry, federal and state governments to target a more diverse and inclusive workforce focusing on skills instead of degrees that may be out of reach for some.

The "skills-based" economy is already thriving. If college degrees are going to remain relevant, they need to adapt to this new reality by offering programs that enable jobs of the future and find ways to make college tuition more affordable and accessible to everyone. Otherwise, the college degree will become increasingly irrelevant, and especially for technology.

It also turns out that many with a four-year technology degree are having trouble finding that first job as even entry-level positions are becoming more specialized. It seems that a general computer science degree is just too broad to be valued by some employers. Meanwhile, specializations like cybersecurity and cloud computing are faring better, but are still not keeping pace with market needs and the changing technology landscape. Skills-based learners are pivoting into $60,000 a year jobs and up while the unfortunate computer science major owes the same in education debt and yet can't find a job.

Many will still pursue college because it's what their parents did, but times have changed. Will degrees go away entirely? That's a tougher question to answer. The traditional four-year college degree is becoming an albatross around the necks of millennials and generation Z, and it is being replaced by new, cheaper, more specialized credentials that are more closely aligned with the labor market. Certifications like CISSP, CompTIA, and others are beginning to look more relevant and important than a degree.

Skills-based learning represents an agile approach to education. You are immediately productive with a minimum viable education and then you expand as circumstances and business needs change. What's missing is the coming-of-age experience that many young people crave. Going from high school straight into the workforce with no transition may not be appealing for some. Colleges are working to stay relevant by offering shorter duration programs, but it's not clear that this will be enough since they're missing the corporate relationships and job opportunities that come with the other skills-based models.

A survey on Indeed.com, one of the biggest job posting sites on the Internet, lists 10 High-Paying IT Jobs You Can Get Without a Degree. The list even includes IT managers and lists a national average salary of $88,959 a year. The playing field is level now and the trend will only continue. In the past, a college degree was seen as a key to the job market, but this is no longer true. Employers are looking for people with specific skills, not an institutional pedigree. This shift has been especially apparent in IT, although I don't think any industry is immune. Hiring managers and human resource (HR) departments will need to show some flexibility and keep an open mind when recruiting new talent or they may find themselves without very much to pick from.

How leaders can prepare for the skills-based economy starting today: leaders should rethink the role of learning and education in their hiring process.

- Do you really need a four-year degree for every position?
- Is there a way to get the same results with shorter, cheaper programs or tap into skills-based candidate pools?
- Strengthen your internal career development programs to support on-the-job training for both technical and business skills.
- Can you create an apprenticeship program or work-study arrangement in your company that could give someone the real-world experience they need while still earning a salary?

THE METAVERSE MAKES WORK EVEN WEIRDER

If you believe the hype, then it will soon be possible to meet with colleagues and customers in virtual spaces that make it seem like we're physically in the same room. Experts predict that the Metaverse will fundamentally change the way many people do their jobs and create new jobs in virtual offices (see Image 11.6).

The term "metaverse" was first coined by science fiction novelist Neal Stephenson in 1992. Now that Facebook has changed its name to Meta, the term has gone mainstream. The metaverse is not a single place, but really several VR spaces, typically accessed through VR headsets. The metaverse is an immersive three-dimensional (3D) digital world based on VR gaming experiences that allow you to buy and sell digital inventory using crypto currency and tokens. While Meta is trying to take the lead with this technology, immersive-reality technologies from Apple, Google, IBM, and others are also poised to try and dominate this new space.

The metaverse provides value by bringing people together in shared collaboration spaces with real-time feedback between teams. The metaverse is a place where our 3D avatars interact with others in a way that gives the experience of being there. The metaverse is not a new technology, but rather a way of combining many technologies, including VR and AI.

The metaverse isn't just for technology companies either. Walmart, Nike, and Gucci are all investigating this technology for virtual office space, immersive training centers, and other corporate needs in addition to leveraging it as a potential sales channel for customers. There is a lot of promise with this technology. Think of possibilities like creating safe virtual environments for training employees how to use dangerous equipment or practice surgery. The three obvious benefits for corporate offices include the virtual space for meetings, virtual training centers, and the equivalent of the virtual water cooler employee lounge.

The metaverse will be built on sensors, cameras, and headsets. Laws and regulations are sure to follow. The metaverse will require a lot of thought and creativity to build entire digital worlds where all aspects of it are visible. This requires technologies including computer vision, neural rendering, scene reconstruction, and computational imaging. In other words, it's a lot of work

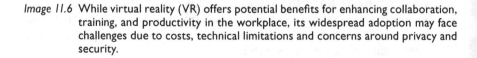

The Metaverse:

- Work is getting weird?
- Amazing new jobs?
- Fizzles out completely?
- Changes the concept of "being there"?

Image 11.6 While virtual reality (VR) offers potential benefits for enhancing collaboration, training, and productivity in the workplace, its widespread adoption may face challenges due to costs, technical limitations and concerns around privacy and security.

and takes a lot of technology and will cost a lot of money. At the time of this writing, Meta's $15 billion investment in Reality Labs, the business segment responsible for the metaverse, has been questioned in light of poor user retention, feature glitches, and the high cost of access.

New jobs are already emerging to support this space. Virtual stores and online places need to be created and will also need technical support. Developers, NFT experts, and other social media and customer interaction positions are being created today. The metaverse requires creators, communities, and participants to succeed. It will also require some serious computing power. Intel predicts that virtual worlds will demand 1000x more computing power as companies leverage NFTs and build their communities in virtual space. Of course, the metaverse will also prove to be a juicy target for cyberattacks, stalkers, and scammers and there have already been complaints of virtual harassment against individuals.

Skeptics say that immersive environments will never be more anything more than a fringe interest for gamers. Others think we will be spending most of our time working and shopping in virtual space in three to five years. Either way, the success of the metaverse is far from guaranteed. Internal Meta documents obtained by the Wall Street Journal reveal that most Horizon Worlds users fail to return to the company's flagship metaverse space after just one month of use. If users reject the metaverse, it will be dead on arrival.

When Pokémon GO was created, it seemed like we might have been on the cusp of an AR revolution, but it never materialized. The hardware needed to create a fully digital world is expensive and complex. If the business value isn't realized, many think this technology will be relegated to games and a handful of specialized training simulations including flight simulators. Meta is also designing their version of the metaverse to be a walled garden, like the Apple App Store. They will no doubt profit from personal data generated over the platform, which will also have privacy advocates rightly concerned. The metaverse requires a sustainable business model for it to be anything more than a curiosity.

If it succeeds, the metaverse will encourage collaboration in new and different ways. Even if it's only moderately successful, you could still imagine scenarios where this technology would be more effective than most training videos are today. It also promises the ability to work anywhere and collaborate in a more natural way, but the technology needs to deliver on that promise.

How leaders can prepare for the metaverse starting today: Apple, Meta, or some other tech company will eventually get some form of a metaverse concept right. Until then, there are costs and usability factors that will slow the propagation or make it nothing more than a niche technology for simulators. Technology leaders should consider:

- Are there uses for virtual shopping, workplaces, or other ideas that would provide business value for your company? Where do you see the opportunities?

- Without obvious business applications or the need to be a trailblazer, IT leaders should adopt a "wait and see" approach.

CREATIVITY BECOMES THE NEW DIFFERENTIATOR

> Imagination is more important than knowledge. Knowledge is limited. Imagination encircles the world.
>
> Albert Einstein

The most important skill for the future may well be creativity and the ability to see old things in new ways, invent new things that don't exist, and connect the dots across multiple disciplines. For example, when Uber first launched, many people assumed that the company would never be able to compete with established taxi companies. But Uber's founders saw the problem from a different perspective. They realized that people wanted a more convenient and affordable way to get around and they were able to create a solution that met those needs.

Creativity is problem-solving. This means that if you solve problems, you're already creative. It doesn't matter if you are a designer, a writer, an entrepreneur, an engineer, or a plumber. You can be creative in any field by solving problems. Creativity is essential to start a new business, but it also helps big companies sustain their market share and create new products. Creativity helps leaders come up with new and innovative solutions to problems, which can be the difference between success and failure in a business.

But creativity is not just about coming up with new ideas – it's also about being able to see the world in different ways. And while AI can probably brainstorm better than most humans, it can't imagine new technologies, business plans, or corporate strategies (see Image 11.7). Many companies offer some form of creativity training, but it rarely seems to hit the mark. Lone visionaries don't work either and can leave the company stranded when that person quits or starts their own competing firm.

Here are a few ideas to begin fostering more creativity at your company:

- **Offer support and encouragement for creativity**: innovative companies have a culture that values creativity. Leaders should provide opportunities for employees to work together and reward those who

Creativity:

- The last thing that makes us special?
- About to be replaced by computers?
- Ready to help us become superhuman?

Image 11.7 In a world where artificial intelligence (AI) is increasingly pervasive, creativity will become a vital skill for professionals across a range of industries, as it is uniquely human and isn't easily replicated by computers.

come up with ideas or products, even if they're not always successful. Remember that failure is a necessary step when something has never been done before.

- **Don't be the only ideas person**: too many leaders think of themselves as the source of all ideas that employees will then go execute. Instead, try to be the filter for ideas. If you're constantly coming up with all the ideas, your team will never have a chance to share their own. Step back and encourage creativity from others by being open to new ideas and willing to take some risks.

- **Encourage collaboration and cross-pollination**: the best ideas come from diverse teams working together. Encourage employees to share their ideas with each other and work on projects together. You can also bring in people from other departments or even other companies to help with brainstorming sessions.

- **Make time for creativity**: many people say they don't have time to be creative, but that's just an excuse. If you want your team to be creative, you need to make time for it. Set aside some time each week or each month for employees to work on creative projects. It doesn't have to be a lot of time, but it should be enough to allow them to explore new ideas. The best ideas often come when people are allowed to take a break from their work and just think. Encourage your team to take walks, meditate, or just spend some time alone to allow their minds to wander. Stress, pressure, and burnout destroy creativity, so make sure your team has some time to relax.

The best way to improve creativity is to practice it regularly. The more you try to be creative, the better you'll become at it. And as you get better at it, you'll start to see the world in new and different ways. Create an environment that supports creativity by making it a priority. Tomorrow's workplaces will demand new ways of thinking and human creativity will be critical to moving us forward faster. Machines are getting more creative too. With the rise of AI, we're seeing creativity become more democratized. AI is being used to create art, write novels, and compose music. While AI still has a long way to go before it can match human creativity, it's becoming an increasingly important tool for facilitating human creativity and innovation.

Action: what are you doing to encourage creativity in your organization? Is your team open to new ideas and approaches to solving problems? If not, how can you help people become more curious and creative?

Action: creativity isn't a natural gift; anyone can train for creativity. In his book *Become An Idea Machine: Because Ideas Are The Currency Of The 21st Century*, Author James Altucher recommends creating lists of ten ideas every day to answer creative questions like "what are ten things I could do this week to get out of my comfort zone?" Doing this every day will help you work out your creative muscles and get more creative over time.

BECOME A TECHNOLOGY FUTURIST

The future is already here – it's just not evenly distributed.

William Gibson

"Technology futurist" isn't a job title you see often, but is something that many technology leaders are expected to be. IT leaders are expected to create order from chaos, simplicity from complexity, and make future-focused decisions. While it may seem like a daunting task to predict the future, it's important for technology leaders to have a good understanding of where the industry is heading. This allows them to make better decisions about investments, partnerships, and strategies.

So how do you keep up with all the changing trends in technology? We spend so much time trying to look ahead, trying to predict what's coming next and then the future comes and surprises us anyway. As technology leaders, we try to stay one step ahead of the curve and anticipate future trends. I'm always skeptical of self-proclaimed technology futurists but that issue aside, what is the best way to keep up with the pace of change?

Predicting the future of technology begins by paying attention to trends and recognizing patterns before they unfold. Industry trends help you anticipate where markets are heading so you can position your company to stay ahead of the curve. But it's not enough to simply be aware of trends; you need to understand their implications. In other words, you need to think like a futurist. Futurists examine existing trends and extrapolate from them. To think like a futurist, you need to be open-minded, creative, and willing to try new ideas before they go mainstream. Futurists are not just aware of the latest technology; they anticipate how technology will be applied. This requires some imagination. For example, when the Internet first emerged, it was primarily used for email and web browsing. But then someone had a simple idea to use it for online shopping. This single idea changed the way we used the Internet forever.

As technology leaders, we need to learn to see around corners if we want to stay ahead. Future-minded leaders scan the horizon for things that could be major disruptions. They get their information from online reports, podcasts, and conferences. But there isn't just one way the future will work out, so futurists look at different possibilities and are open to new ideas. They follow each path to its fullest potential instead of stopping short and dismissing crazy ideas. By doing this, you'll be exposed to a variety of different perspectives and ideas, which will ultimately help you think more creatively about the future of technology.

I'm old enough to remember when computers weren't networked and the Internet was still accessed through a dial-up modem. Technology changes at a speed that doesn't compare to any other industry. Now the speed of change seems to be compounding and the future will be a very different place than where we are right now. And that's exciting.

There are many so subjects I didn't touch on in this chapter. Low and no-code software, edge computing, and many other game-changing technologies are on the horizon. But really understanding how technology will be applied also requires a good sense of people. If you'd like to have a better eye on the future, you should study both people and technology. VR may seem promising, but if people don't accept it then it won't be the next big thing. The Wall Street Journal reports that Meta is struggling to keep users engaged for more than a month with glitchy features and empty worlds. Even employees don't appear to enjoy the platform. People ultimately decide the fate of any technology, no matter how promising it may seem on paper.

Change brings opportunity and you need to think like a futurist to spot the opportunities. When you think like a futurist, you need to pay attention to what's going on around you, construct scenarios, and see the possibilities. Only then can you begin to forecast what will happen next. IT leaders who want to be futurists should adopt an entrepreneurial attitude to identify new revenue opportunities everywhere you look. But you need to respond to change and see things as they are. In the early days of the Internet, many people including myself saw the possibilities of web development as the "next big thing," but if you didn't adapt as that market changed, you were left behind as the world shifted to mobile apps and web development became commoditized.

Action: what are you doing to prepare for the future of technology? Podcasts and books are a great way to keep up with future trends. Make sure you're getting your information from reliable sources. O'reilly's Safari Books (https://www.oreilly.com/) is a great source of technology information including podcasts, audiobooks, and ebooks.

SUMMARY

This chapter took a lighthearted look into technology and the future of work. It explored the idea that technology will continue to change the way we work and live. We also looked at how technology is already changing the workforce. While it's impossible to say exactly what the future holds, it's clear that technology will continue to play a major role in our lives. Other topics we covered include:

- The future of work is being shaped by technological advancements, changing societal norms, and the rise of AI. AI is already changing the way we work, and it will likely have an even bigger impact in the future.
- Web 3.0 will help create new solo job opportunities and the DAO will help make working from anywhere even easier. The "Creator Economy" will enable people to make money from their own projects.
- The pandemic has magnified the debate over middle managers and the overall number of managers needed to run an enterprise. As more

employees shift to working from home, the need for middle managers has massively decreased and many are being replaced by computer programs.

- Some firms are creating IT technical fellow career tracks to reward people for their technical expertise and help them progress without forcing them into middle management roles.
- 5G will have a big impact on the workforce, enabling new types of remote work such as AR and VR.
- The success of the metaverse is far from guaranteed. The hardware to create a fully digital world is going to be expensive and complex, and the business value will probably be limited to games and training simulations.
- Creativity is important for businesses because it can lead to new and innovative solutions to problems. Leaders should provide opportunities for employees to work together and reward those who come up with ideas or products, even if they're not always successful. Employees need time to relax and think creatively to come up with new ideas.
- Futurists don't predict the future, but they make sure their organizations are prepared for what the future may bring. They look at multiple different possibilities and are open to new ideas.

REFERENCES AND FURTHER READING

Diamond, Peter. *The Future Is Faster than You Think How Converging Technologies Are Transforming Business, Industries, and Our Lives.* Simon and Schuster, 2020.

Gates, Bill. *The Road Ahead.* Viking Penguin, 1995.

Murphy, James S. "Millennials and Gen Zers Are Getting Swindled by the Biggest Scam in Higher Education." *Business Insider*, 2022, https://www.businessinsider.com/masters-degree-scam-higher-education-millennials-genz-student-loan-debt-2022-5.

Perez, Josue. "Colorado State Fair Staff to Review Digital Art Requirements Following AI Controversy." *The Pueblo Chieftain*, 12 Sept. 2022, https://www.chieftain.com/story/news/2022/09/12/colorado-state-fair-to-review-rules-following-ai-art-controversy/66849123007/.

Reese, Byron. *The Fourth Age: Smart Robots, Conscious Computers and the Future of Humanity.* Atria Paperback, 2020.

Tegmark, Max. *Life 3.0: Being Human in the Age of Artificial Intelligence.* Penguin Books, 2018.

Weinersmith, Kelly. *Soonish: Ten Emerging Technologies That'll Improve and/or Ruin Everything.* Penguin Books, 2019.

Conclusion
Time is the ultimate disruptor

> Indeed, the final test of leadership is: do you leave things better than you found them?
>
> James C. Hunter
> *The Servant*

Wherever you are in your leadership journey, the only thing that is certain is that things are going to be different in the future. The business world is changing and technology plays a big role in the pace of that change. Meanwhile, technology itself is also changing. New products and services are being developed at a rapid pace and companies need to adapt to stay competitive.

Leaders should never feel comfortable that they've "made it" and can somehow sit back and stop growing when they hit a certain level. This is why it's so important to set aside formal time for your own personal growth and development and let your team do the same. No matter how stable your company seems to be, one day change will catch up and be the ultimate disruptor. Lehman Brothers and Bear Stearns are now names from the past. Now, "sure thing" technology giants like Meta and Google are facing their own day of reckoning. Who knows what the future holds other than more change?

The best way to prepare for this future is to embrace it and change yourself along with it. Your view of reality, your skills, and your knowledge needs to change as everything around us continues to change. As a leader, you need to be constantly learning and evolving and you need to create an environment where your team can do the same. Be open to new ideas, encourage creativity and risk-taking, and provide opportunities for growth and development. Be comfortable with change and demonstrate that behavior to your team.

James Hunter, author of *The Servant: A Simple Story About the True Essence of Leadership*, says that the final test of leadership is whether you left things better than they were when you found them. This is ultimately how all leaders will be judged. Did the team get better under your watch? Did projects complete? Did your people thrive or just get by? How many of your employees went on to leadership roles of their own? This is the mark of great leadership.

DOI: 10.1201/9781003314707-14

While it may seem far off right now, one day you will be at the end of your own journey. What do you want your legacy to be? Remember that leadership casts a long shadow. How do you want to be remembered? When it comes time to hand over the reins to a younger generation, you want to be confident that you've done everything you can to prepare your team for the future. Technology has provided life-changing wealth and opportunity in a relatively short period of time, so also consider giving back by volunteering, mentoring, and sharing your knowledge.

They say that books, like paintings, don't finish but only end in interesting places. There's so many more topics to cover, especially on a subject as big and broad as leadership. I hope you found this book thought-provoking. But I also hope that you found something to take away and practice and refine, no matter how small that something is. The only way that changes happen is when we act, and the only way things get better is when we try to improve them.

If you found the material in this book useful, be sure to check http://www.digital-leadership.com/ for more information on becoming a digital leader and on technology leadership in general. There are checklists and other content available to help you on your leadership journey.

Action: the final action I leave you with is this: are you doing everything you can to leave your team better off than when you started? Are you preparing them for the future? If not, right now is the best time to start. There will never be any other time.

Appendix

FURTHER READING FOR IT LEADERS

Books are a source of inspiration, knowledge, and power. In the business world, they can be especially helpful for leaders looking to gain new perspectives and insights into their field. If you're interested in learning more about information technology (IT) leadership, the following list is a good starting point for further reading.

1. *Zero to One* by Peter Thiel. It's easy to improve something that already exists but starting something brand new is much harder. The book *Zero to One* presents an optimistic approach to innovative thinking. When somebody introduces a new concept, they go from zero to one. This book shares philosophies and strategies for startup success. The lessons in the book are shared by Peter Thiel, who is the co-founder of PayPal and Palantir Technologies.
2. *Five Dysfunctions of a Team* by Patrick Lencioni. The book *Five Dysfunctions of a Team* focuses on how to overcome team dysfunctions to create a more effective team. The five dysfunctions include the absence of trust, fear of conflict, lack of commitment, avoidance of accountability, and inattention to results. The book provides leaders with lessons on how to manage a team and eliminate these dysfunctions.
3. *The Innovator's Dilemma* by Clayton Christensen. Businesses can lose their market leadership, even if they do everything right. The main reason for this is that they are unable to stand against the innovation and disruption presented by new businesses. The book *The Innovator' Dilemma* provides tips on how incumbents can secure their market leadership, despite these challenges.
4. *The Lean Startup* by Eric Ries. This book is about a methodology that uses a combination of business-hypothesis-driven experimentation, validated learning, and iterative product releases to discover if a proposed business model is viable. It also helps entrepreneurs and wantrepreneurs to learn what customers want, how the development cycle can be shortened, how to measure business growth without vanity metrics, and more.

5. *Managing the Unmanageable: Rules, Tools, and Insights for Managing Software People and Teams* by Mickey W. Mantle, Ron Lichty Mantle. The book provides a guide on how to hire, motivate, and mentor a software development team that functions at the highest level. It draws on the authors' combined seventy years of experience and highlights the insights and wisdom of other successful managers. The book is useful for new and experienced software engineering managers alike.

6. *Start With Why: How Great Leaders Inspire Everyone to Take Action* by Simon Sinek. The book *Start With Why* by Simon Sinek discusses how great leaders are able to inspire others to take action. These leaders are able to do this by starting with why they do what they do instead of what they do. The book provides a framework for organizations, movements, and people to be inspired by this way of thinking.

7. *The CTO ¦ CIO Bible: The Mission Objectives Strategies and Tactics Needed To Be A Super Successful CTO ¦ CIO* by Rorie Devine. This book covers everything needed to be a successful CTO ¦ CIO. It includes mission objectives, strategies, and tactics that are needed to be successful. The book is filled with insight and humor, making it an enjoyable read. Rorie is the only person to have been featured on the cover of *CIO* magazine twice, has held more than 20 interim and permanent CTO ¦ CIO roles, and was awarded IT Leader of The Year by *Computing* magazine.

8. *The Manager's Path: A Guide for Tech Leaders Navigating Growth and Change* by Camille Fournier. The journey from engineer to technical manager can be difficult, but with this practical guide by Camille Fournier, you can learn the skills you need to navigate growth and change in your organization. This book is ideal whether you're a new manager, a mentor, or a more experienced leader looking for fresh advice. With this book, you'll learn how to become a better manager and leader in your organization.

9. *Everyday Chaos: Technology, Complexity, and How We're Thriving in a New World of Possibility* by David Weinberger. The book explores how artificial intelligence, big data, and the Internet are changing our understanding of the world and how we can take advantage of that. It's a good read for IT professionals who are looking for inspiration to create possibilities for their field.

10. *Women in Tech: Take Your Career to the Next Level with Practical Advice and Inspiring Stories* by Tarah Wheeler. This book is a guide for women looking to pursue a career in technology or those already working in the field who want to advance their career. The book includes stories from successful female tech professionals, offering advice and tips on how to achieve success in the industry.

11. *Remote Leadership: How to Accelerate Achievement and Create a Community in a Work-from-Home World* by David Pachter. The book

tells the story of a business that realized it needed to embrace a geographically diversified workforce to move forward. The book examines how to build an organization into a more vital and influential group, as well as what it means to be a leader when this traditional role is being questioned.

JOURNAL PROMPTS

If you could spend just five minutes a day centering yourself, planning your day, and setting yourself up for success, would you do it? What if that same exercise improved your mindset and helped you become a better writer at the same time? One of the most powerful practices a leader can do is journaling. It is a way to document and process your thoughts and emotions related to your work. It can help you make sense of what is happening, identify patterns, and develop insights about yourself and about your leadership style. Journaling can also help you manage stress, build resilience, and maintain good well-being.

There are many ways to journal, so find a way that works for you. You can use a traditional paper journal or an electronic journal. You can write in long hand or use shorthand. You can write every day or once a week. The important thing is to be consistent and to commit to journaling on a regular basis.

I do both morning and evening journaling. In the morning, I write down my goals for the day and what I need to do to achieve them. This helps me to focus on what is important and to stay on track. In the evening, I reflect on my day – what went well and what didn't. I also use this time to process any emotions that I am feeling. This practice has been invaluable in helping me to stay sane and balanced as a leader.

If you're not sure how to get started, here are some journal prompts that I have used over the years. Keep things fresh, I like to swap out my prompts every few months, so I don't start tuning out to the questions or start filling in the same answers every day.

Morning

- What are my top three goals for the day/week/month? How can I achieve these goals?
- What challenges am I facing in achieving my goals?
- What am I grateful for today?
- What decisions do I need to make?
- What challenges am I facing today?
- What am I curious about?
- Where could I use some help?
- Where am I overly distracted?
- What am I looking forward to? (personal or professional)
- If I only got one thing done today, it would be...

Evening

- What's the most important thing I accomplished today?
- How did I handle a difficult situation today?
- What did I learn today?
- What made me smile or laugh today?
- What were my successes today (big or small)?
- What am I still thinking about that I need to process?
- Where could I do better tomorrow?

LEADERSHIP SUPERPOWERS

You can train in almost anything from building a muscle to increasing your creativity to becoming a calmer person. Leadership is not a one-time event. It's a continuous journey that requires flexibility, creativity, and resilience. It also requires the ability to learn and adapt to new situations. That's why it's important to be constantly evolving your leadership style and developing new skills. Here are ten skills that will help you become an even better leader in the years ahead if you do the work. You get what you train for.

1. The ability to articulate a clear and inspiring vision.
2. The ability to listen to also understand multiple perspectives.
3. The ability to communicate effectively, both verbally and written.
4. The ability to engage and motivate people to achieve common goals.
5. The ability to build strong relationships and networks both inside and outside of your company.
6. The ability to think strategically and make decisions from a business perspective.
7. The ability to navigate change and lead others through it.
8. The ability to develop and implement creative solutions to problems.
9. The ability to motivate and inspire individuals to do their best work and to grow.
10. The ability to continue learning and adapting to an ever-changing world.

BREATH AWARENESS MEDITATION

If you recall from Chapter 4, establishing a meditation practice is one of the most beneficial things you can do for your mind and body. It will not only help you show up more present as a leader, but also in your day-to-day life. The benefits of meditation are vast and include improved mental clarity and decreased anxiety and stress.

When you first start to meditate, you may find it difficult to silence your thoughts and focus on your breath. However, with regular practice, you will be able to clear your mind faster and learn to be more present. I can't promise you a guaranteed path to inner peace. But hey … you never know.

Breath awareness is great form of meditation for beginners because everybody breathes and your breath is always with you. With breath awareness meditation, you focus your attention on your breath without trying to control it. When your attention wanders, you gently return your focus back to your breathing. It's really that simple. Your mind will invariably drift and you'll start thinking about something else. When you recognize that you have drifted, simply note it as thinking and return your attention to the breath. Don't be overly judgmental if this is hard for you. It's hard for everyone. Try to simply sit still and follow your breathing. Setting a timer will help you relax and not worry about the time. Start with a 5- or 10-minute timer and gradually increase the time as you become more comfortable with your practice.

Over time, meditation can help you act calmer and with more rationale if you can detach yourself from your problems. Start small but start. Many people report long-term effects including:

- Staying calmer in a crisis.
- Understanding yourself better by realizing that you are not your thoughts.
- Better focus and the ability to lower cognitive load on demand.
- Developing an increased presence and awareness which makes you feel alive and connected with the world around you.

By focusing your attention on your breath without trying to control it, you can begin to understand how your mind works and learn to act with more calm in difficult situations. Over time, many people report an increased presence and awareness. In my personal experience, consistency is important. Even if you can only do a few minutes a day, try to do it every day.

IT ORGANIZATIONS

There are many IT organizations that leaders can look to for guidance and support. Some of these organizations are listed below:

- American Society for Information Science and Technology (ASIS&T) (https://www.asisonline.org/)

   The Society for Technical Communication is an interdisciplinary organization of 4,000 members from such fields as computer science, linguistics, management, librarianship, engineering, law, medicine, chemistry, and education. It focuses on techniques and technologies in the fields of library and information science, communications, networking, and computer science.

- Association for Women in Computing (https://www.awc-hq.org/home.html)

  A non-profit professional organization dedicated to the advancement of women in technology. Events calendar and articles on a variety of topics.

- Association of Information Technology Professionals (https://www.comptia.org/)

  CompTIA provides quality IT-related education, information on relevant IT issues, and forums for networking.

- Institute of Electrical and Electronics Engineers (IEEE) (https://www.ieee.org/)

  IEEE is a professional organization that provides authoritative guidance in computer engineering, telecommunications, electric power, aerospace, and other technological fields.

- Project Management Institute (PMI) https://www.pmi.org/

  PMI is an organization focusing on the needs of project management professionals worldwide and is responsible for the Project Management Professional (PMP) and other related certifications.

Index

Printed in the United States
by Baker & Taylor Publisher Services

Printed in the United States
by Baker & Taylor Publisher Services